OECD Public Governance Reviews

Slovak Republic: Better Co-ordination for Better Policies, Services and Results

OECD
BETTER POLICIES FOR BETTER LIVES

Please cite this publication as:
OECD (2015), *Slovak Republic: Better Co-ordination for Better Policies, Services and Results*, OECD Publishing, Paris.
http://dx.doi.org/10.1787/9789264247628-en

ISBN 978-92-64-24762-8 (print)
ISBN 978-92-64-24763-5 (PDF)

Foreword

The Slovak Republic is pursuing a comprehensive reform of its public administration to enhance the efficiency, effectiveness and quality of government decision making to support growth and development. The Slovak Republic is entering a new phase in its pursuit of more effective governance. This represents a unique opportunity to design and adopt public administration reforms in a way that addresses the government's institutional fragmentation and strong ministerial silos.

The public administration reform programme launched by the Ministry of the Interior in 2012, known as the ESO Programme, recognises the importance of stronger collaboration across institutional boundaries and seeks to rationalise the structure of the deconcentrated state administration. The design and implementation of a public administration reform agenda that promotes more robust whole-of-government co-ordination led by the centre of government, along with more systematic use of evidence-based policy making tools such as regulatory impact assessment and e-government can strengthen decision making capacity to improve results, reduce costs, facilitate the daily work of the public administration and enhance the quality of services provided to citizens and businesses. In addition, a comprehensive human resources management reform agenda provides opportunities to strengthen the quality and the performance of the central civil service in designing and delivering services effectively and efficiently to citizens and businesses.

In this context, the government of the Slovak Republic asked the OECD to analyse the comprehensive public administration reform strategy that the Slovak Republic plans to implement over 2014-20 and to advise on how to build capacity to carry it out. The resulting OECD Public Governance Review looks at the following aspects of the Slovak public administration, which the reform seeks to improve:

- the capacity of the centre-of-government to steer and lead policy development and implementation
- the analytical and evaluation capacity for better policy making
- the ability of the state civil service to steer and lead policy
- the digitisation of the public administration
- transparency and integrity across the public administration.

This Review deepens the OECD analysis undertaken in 2013 and presented in the 2014 review entitled: *Slovak Republic: Developing a Sustainable Strategic Framework for Public Administration Reform*. It also follows up on the 2014 *OECD Economic Survey of the Slovak Republic* and its recommendations on reforming the public sector. In carrying out the Review, the OECD focused on the state administration, comprised of both the central state administration and the deconcentrated state administration at the sub-national level.

This Review is part of a series of OECD Public Governance Reviews. It was conducted under the auspices of the OECD Public Governance Committee on the basis of its long-standing expertise in public governance reforms and engagement on open government issues in member and non-member countries.

Public Governance Reviews contribute to the work on public administration and management reform of the OECD Public Governance Committee with the support of the Governance Reviews and Partnerships Division of the OECD Public Governance and Territorial Development Directorate. The Public Governance and Territorial Development Directorate's mission is to help government at all levels design and implement strategic, evidence-based and innovative policies to strengthen public governance, respond effectively to diverse and disruptive economic, social and environmental challenges and deliver on government's commitments to citizens. The goal is to support countries in building better government systems to design and implement policies at both the national and regional levels that can lead to sustainable, inclusive economic and social development.

Acknowledgements

OECD Public Governance Reviews are co-ordinated by the Governance Reviews and Partnerships Division, headed by Martin Forst, in the Directorate for Public Governance and Territorial Development, headed by Rolf Alter, Director. This Review was co-managed by Adam Ostry and Daniel Trnka. Chapter 1 was drafted by Helge Schröder, Deputy Project Manager for this Review, under the guidance of Adam Ostry. Chapter 2 was drafted by Daniel Trnka. Chapter 3 was drafted by Laura Skoratko with substantive input from Maria Maguire under the guidance of Daniel Gerson. Chapter 4 was drafted by Ryan Androsoff. Chapter 5 was drafted by Yukihiko Hamada.

The Review team would like to thank the following peer reviewers who participated in the fact-finding mission and the series of capacity-building workshops held in support of this Review:

- Michael Kell, Chief Economist and Director of Analysis, National Audit Office, United Kingdom
- Märt Loite, Deputy Strategy Director, Government Office, Estonia
- Gregor Virant, former Minister of Public Administration, Slovenia
- Margus Sarapuu, Strategy Director, Government Office, Estonia
- Olivia Neal, Head of the Digital Service Standard, Government Digital Service, United Kingdom
- Peter Parycek, Head of Centre for E-Governance, Danube University Krems, Austria
- Siim Sikkut, Senior Advisor for ICT, Government Office, Estonia
- Ari Holopainen, Financial Counsellor, Office for the Government as Employer, Ministry of Finance, Finland
- Krzysztof Banaś, Counsellor to the Prime Minister, Unit for Communication and International Co-operation, Department of the Civil Service, Poland
- Kaido Paabusk, Director of Praxis Academy and former Head of Public Administration and Public Service Department, Ministry of Finance, Estonia
- Hannah Glatz, Expert on budget law reform (*Fachexpertin Haushaltsrechtsreform*), Ministry of Finance, Austria
- Terry Lamboo, Senior Advisor, Ministry of the Interior and Kingdom Relations, the Netherlands
- Katarzyna Dudzik, Counsellor to the Head of the Chancellery of the Prime Minister, Chancellery of the Prime Minister, Poland

- Kristien Verbraeken, Integrity Officer, Flemish Government Authorities, Belgium.

This Review reflects significant contributions from a number of participants from across the government of the Slovak Republic to whom the team expresses their appreciation. Special thanks go to Denisa Saková, Adrián Jenčo, Rut Erdélyiová, Samuel Arbe, Matúš Šesták, Markéta Golhová and Ivana Michalcová from the Ministry of the Interior, as well as to the Government Office's Tatiana Janečková.

Editorial work and quality control were provided by Ciara Muller and Jennifer Allain, who prepared the manuscript for publication. Administrative assistance to the Review team was provided by Alpha Zambou.

Table of contents

Tables

Figures

Boxes

Executive summary

The Slovak Republic's centre of government (CoG) is currently focusing on ways to strengthen its capacity to co-ordinate government strategy more effectively, starting with the Political Manifesto drafted at the beginning of the government's mandate, while improving its ability to develop whole-of-government plans and monitor policy implementation. In support of these efforts, the Review recommends:

- Defining the Slovak CoG as polycentric, as a means to highlight the need to strengthen co-ordination both among the CoG institutions – the Government Office, the Ministry of Finance, the Ministry of Foreign and European Affairs and the Ministry of the Interior – and between these CoG institutions and line ministries and agencies across the public administration.
- Strengthening policy making and monitoring capacity in the Government Office so that the CoG can improve the development, implementation and monitoring of the Government Manifesto and its associated work programmes.
- Strengthening the Government Office's role in leading whole-of-government co-ordination by explicitly confirming its mandate in this area, allowing it to steer whole-of-government strategy, policy-setting and steering exercises effectively.
- Reinforcing co-operation and co-ordination among the CoG institutions and between the CoG institutions and the public administration as a whole to overcome the existing silo-based approach to government while ensuring that policy and spending are better linked, thus improving the government's capacity to assess spending performance against the achievement of strategic policy outcomes.
- Developing a communication strategy to ensure that the CoG as a polycentric driver of whole-of-government strategy is well understood in line ministries and agencies across the system, and to explain the co-ordination role of the CoG institutions so as to ensure that line ministries understand that they are exercising their sector-specific mandates as part of a coherent, integrated government-wide strategy while confirming to line ministries that their competencies as set down in legislation are not being affected in this process.

The Review argues that decision making by the Slovak administration on policies, legislation or spending could be based more systemically on objective, fact-based evidence and sound analysis. While the government of the Slovak Republic is attempting to improve the situation, progress remains slow, notably due to a lack of systematic demand for such evidence and analysis on the part of decision makers. While the obligation to evaluate the impacts of newly developed regulations is in place, it appears to be rarely enforced. The quality of regulatory impact assessments is rarely satisfactory. Procedures for stakeholder engagement in policy and regulation-making in the Slovak Republic are also well-established; however, many consultations take place solely on an informal basis or too late in the process. This Review provides the following recommendations:

- Strengthening analytical capacity in key ministries, and increasing the demand for analysis and evidence by establishing formal procedures for *ex ante* and *ex post* assessment of government policies, programmes and regulations.
- Increasing the use of performance indicators when adopting policies, programmes or regulations; adopting a government-wide policy on *ex post* evaluation of these policies/programmes/regulations; and using the analytical units to provide strategic foresight to the government.

Capacity in the state civil service can be strengthened with the adoption of strategic human resource management (HRM) practices that build on the government's current and planned legal and institutional reforms. The Review supports the findings and proposals contained in the government's HRM Strategy to 2020, underlining the need for HRM practices that ensure merit, professionalism, continuity and the development of human capital in staffing and managing the workforce in the civil service. The consistent application of basic HRM procedures and standards can be strengthened through the planned establishment of an impartial and independent Council of the Civil Service. The Review recommends:

- Improving the quality of data collected on the public workforce and developing the skills and capacities needed to use such data for strategic workforce planning and management. This includes building tools such as competency-based management and job profiling, and eventually integrating a competency framework into planning, career management and skills development practices.
- Reinstating the principle of merit in recruitment and selection arrangements by ensuring common standards and oversight, and clarifying the compensation system and ensuring it is based on merit and transparency.

The Slovak Republic has been actively implementing a programme of digitisation over the past decade; however, in many respects it has yet to meet expectations. The government has made measurable progress in a number of areas, particularly with regard to Internet connectivity and usage, online delivery of public services and citizens' engagement in the Slovak Republic have lagged behind peer country performance. Digital government initiatives are hampered by a lack of strong whole-of-government co-ordination mechanisms led from the centre; this has fostered siloed approaches to ICT usage and digital service development in ministries. Nonetheless, the potential demand for digital services is strong, as relatively high uptake levels of Internet-based activities by the Slovakian population shows. The Review thus recommends:

- Broadening and deepening the whole-of-government vision for digital government and communicating it widely across the public administration, building on the Government's National Conception of Public Administration Systems.
- Establishing a Chief Information Officer (or equivalent) position to serve as a central focal point to act as co-ordinator and facilitator for implementing the Slovak Republic's vision for digital government.
- Strengthening the digital government co-ordination body's capacity to allow for regular exchange of information between officials responsible for digitisation

initiatives and the management of ICT, while strengthening capacity in line ministry digital government/IT departments to drive enhanced performance in digital service design and delivery.

In order to make government more cost-effective, improve accountability and prevent corruption, enhancing the integrity and transparency of public governance is a key element in the Slovak Republic's political reform agenda. While the level of perceived corruption in the Slovak Republic remains high, the government has made efforts to enhance integrity across the public administration. This Review contributes to the anti-corruption debate in the Slovak Republic by advising on how to improve integrity measures and their enforcement through strengthened co-ordination. It assesses existing integrity mechanisms in the Slovak public sector, especially in relation to the public administration's code of conduct, its management of conflict of interest and ethics training. It also underscores the importance of institutional arrangements in coordinating integrity policies and in monitoring their effectiveness. The Review recommends:

- Defining clear, easily understandable values and standards of conduct in a consultative and participative manner, and establishing a government-wide co-ordinated system for ensuring consistency throughout the public sector in understanding the values and standards of conduct promoted by the code of conduct.
- Monitoring and assessing the implementation of the code of conduct and its impact on promoting integrity in the public sector, while promoting the consistent application of sanctions for ethical misconduct by public officials and ensuring that sanctions are both proportionate and dissuasive.
- Establishing a central function within the public administration responsible for the development and maintenance of the conflict of interest polices and ensuring top-level buy-in for ethics training government-wide, and establishing a leading department/agency for central co-ordination of the planning, delivery and evaluation of ethics trainings.

Assessment and recommendations

This Review covers the following five key public governance themes identified as priorities by the government of the Slovak Republic:

- improving centre-of-government (CoG) capacity to steer and lead policy development and implementation
- strengthening analytical and evaluation capacity for better policy making
- strengthening the capability of the state civil service to steer and lead policy
- scaling up digital government
- enhancing transparency and integrity across the public administration.

Two overarching themes run through these five priority areas. The first is the need for more effective whole-of-government co-ordination of strategy-setting and implementation efforts, led by the centre of government. A key sub-theme is the need for greater collaboration and co-operation between the key components of the Slovak CoG: the Government Office, the Ministry of Finance, the Ministry of Foreign and European Affairs and the Ministry of the Interior.

- This requirement applies to basic efforts relating to advising the political leadership on the articulation of its Manifesto, to translating the Manifesto effectively into multi-year and annual outcomes-based government programmes focused on a small number of high-level, policy objectives to be implemented by line ministries in a way that encourages working across institutional silos to achieve integrated policy outcomes for people and businesses effectively and efficiently.
- This theme relates to the management of the Slovak Republic's interests at the EU level: it will be important to ensure that the mandate boundaries between the Government Office and the Ministry of Foreign and European Affairs with respect to managing relations with the EU are clearly defined. At a minimum, the Government Office's responsibility for managing the transposition of EU legislation into national law, and the Ministry of Foreign and European Affairs' mandate of advancing the Slovak Republic's national interests in Brussels before, during and after the EU decision-making process, implies that these two CoG institutions need to work closely together and co-ordinate their activities *vis-à-vis* line ministries effectively on an ongoing basis.
- This theme finds echo in the Review's argument that the management and governance of the generation of, demand for and effective integration of evidence into the policy-making and implementation process could be enhanced: CoG-led co-ordination of information generation across line ministries is needed to ensure that policy development in pursuit of the integrated outcomes identified in the Manifesto takes into full account all of the available evidence. This applies to

managing regulatory impact assessment (RIA) effectively both *ex ante* and *ex post* decision making, it applies to generating results from strategic foresight and horizon scanning from both private and public sector sources, to embed within the medium-term Manifesto and government programme the emerging risks and policy challenges that reflect a longer term planning horizon. It also applies to developing and implementing effectively a robust whole-of-government monitoring and evaluation framework complete with feedback loops which ensure that performance assessment results fully inform successive generations of policy development and decision making.

- This theme also reflects this Review's proposition that the governance of the Slovak Republic's approach to strategic human resources management, its transparency and integrity frameworks and its strategies for digital governance and open data could be strengthened. Greater CoG-led whole-of-government co-ordination is required to ensure common standards in strategic human resources management and the uniform implementation of the new Civil Service Act to ensure the uniform adoption of common codes of conduct and robust conflict of interest guidelines, and the effective training of civil servants in this area, and to lead a vision-based implementation of digital governance and open data strategies uniformly across the Slovak public administration.

The second theme relates to the use of evidence itself. All five of the public administration reform areas assessed highlight the need to engage in more effective generation of evidence on which to take decisions, whether in strategy setting, monitoring the performance of policy implementation, measuring spending results against policy outcomes, strategic human resources management, digital governance strategies or in fighting corruption. While certain key government actors appear to generate strategically useful information for policy development purposes, especially the Ministry of Finance's Institute for Financial Policy, disparities in evidence-generation capacity across the government are pronounced. Demand for policy relevant evidence appears low, which affects the quality of policy design and strategic decision making in all five of the areas under review.

These issues need to be addressed if the government of the Slovak Republic is to enhance the strategic agility of the state over the medium term. Many good practices already exist in these areas, which augurs well for the pursuit of the government's public administration reform agenda over the period through 2020.

Improving centre-of-government capacity to steer and lead policy development and implementation

Strengthen centre-of-government institutions and government co-ordination

The Slovak Republic applies a narrow definition to its centre of government (CoG), listing only the Government Office as its CoG institution in its responses to the questionnaire carried out for this review. In practice, however, its Ministry of Finance, Ministry of the Interior and Ministry of Foreign and European Affairs fulfil important transversal, whole-of-government functions and could therefore also be regarded as CoG institutions. This state of affairs is, in fact, similar to the institutional arrangements that characterise the CoG across most, if not all, OECD countries. Thus, in any CoG consisting of more than one institution, it becomes crucial to ensure effective communication and co-ordination between these institutions and collectively with line ministries.

Recognition by the government of the Slovak Republic that its CoG is polycentric could have significant implications for the way in which the Government Office interacts with the other CoG institutions, as a more robust, integrated working relationship between CoG components can improve coherence between national strategy development, national budget setting and strategic workforce planning for the government as a whole. This, in turn, helps the government to monitor and evaluate its strategic policy performance effectively, so that it can assess its performance against the achievement of results and the improvement of outcomes. Reporting to the public regularly on this performance can help enhance government transparency and accountability while reducing overlap and duplication in roles and responsibilities among CoG institutions and between the CoG and line ministries, and ultimately improve public trust in the government and its institutions.

While good working relations between the four Slovak CoG institutions appear to be the norm, their interaction seems to lack institutionalisation and a strategic dimension. It appears there is no common understanding or willingness to engage collectively in steering the design and implementation of the government's strategic policy agenda. The Government Office – and overall government co-ordination – could benefit from involving the other institutions more closely. It would be particularly relevant to have the Ministry of Finance actively contribute to whole-of-government steering, as it not only controls the fiscal framework but also appears to be leading at this juncture improvements to the government's analytical capacity.

Given the importance of sustaining productive working relations between the various components of the Slovak CoG to design, implement and monitor the performance of a national strategy that is properly resourced and based on evidence generated by properly qualified and trained civil servants, the government could consider the following recommendations.

Intra-governmental co-ordination and co-operation could be heightened in the Slovak public administration. The CoG institutions need to work more closely together on an ongoing basis in order to set and steer strategy effectively, co-ordinate the contribution of line ministries to developing and implementing this strategy, and achieve a whole-of-government approach to policy making and implementation. Most crucially, the Government Office and the Ministry of Finance could be better aligned to sustain coherence between the national strategy and the national fiscal framework, and the Ministry of Finance integrated more deliberately into whole-of-government decision making as a key institutional component of the centre of government.

Strengthening the analytical capacity in the Government Office could enhance its ability to engage effectively with the other CoG institutions and line ministries in setting, implementing and evaluating the performance of national strategy. Enabling line ministries to contribute effectively to whole-of-government strategy setting and implementation by breaking down institutional barriers to cross-sector collaboration could significantly enhance the government's ability to achieve multi-dimensional outcomes for citizens and businesses. There are good examples of co-ordination in the Slovak Republic which could be replicated, such as the Ministry of Foreign and European Affairs' co-ordination on EU matters or the Government Office's own co-ordination of EU funds. Yet here as well the mandate boundaries between the Government Offices' responsibilities for transposing EU legislation into national law and the Ministry of

Foreign and European Affairs' responsibility for advancing the Slovak Republic's interests in Brussels could be clarified so as to eliminate the potential for overlap and duplication and be communicated throughout the public administration; co-ordination between these two CoG institutions on EU matters as they work with line ministries could be strengthened.

Strengthening the capacity in the Government Office so that it can take a more systematic and active approach to co-ordinating whole-of-government policy making, does not imply that the Government Office should evolve into some sort of overbearing, centralised "task-master" bent on concentrating power whose mandate would be to "dictate" policy and actions to the rest of the government. This also does not imply that line ministry competencies or line ministry enabling legislation be modified in any way. On the contrary, increasing the competencies and capabilities of the Government Office will result in better government co-ordination if the Government Office manages to become a valued partner and interlocutor for the other CoG institutions as well as for line ministries. To achieve this, it will be crucial to communicate the necessity for reform and to invest in building and sustaining a government-wide culture of co-operation and collaboration both within the government's CoG institutions – starting with the Government Office – and in line ministries.

Recommendations

- Define the Slovak Republic's centre of government as polycentric, in recognition of the fact that in addition to the Government Office, the Ministry of Finance, the Ministry of Foreign and European Affairs and the Ministry of the Interior also fulfil important transversal functions. This definition could be communicated broadly across the public administration to ensure that the CoG as a polycentric driver of whole-of-government strategy is well understood in line ministries and agencies across the system – and more generally by citizens and business.
- Strengthen and reinforce co-operation and co-ordination among the CoG institutions and between the CoG institutions and the public administration as a whole. Crucially, this could contribute to overcoming the existing silo-based approach to government while ensuring that policy and spending are better linked and potential overlap and duplication reduced, thus improving the government's capacity to assess spending performance against the achievement of strategic policy outcomes. This could also ensure that a strengthened Government Office is not perceived by other government bodies as an adversary but as a true partner.
- Ensure that the mandate boundaries between the Government Office and the Ministry of Foreign and European Affairs with respect to managing relations with the EU are clear so as to eliminate the potential for overlap and duplication and are well communicated across the public administration; at a minimum, the Government Office's responsibility for managing the transposition of EU legislation into national law, and the Ministry of Foreign and European Affairs' mandate of advancing the Slovak Republic's national interests in Brussels before, during and after the EU decision-making process, implies that these two CoG institutions need to work closely together and co-ordinate their activities *vis-à-vis* line ministries effectively on an ongoing basis.
- Strengthen the Government Office's co-ordination capacity by explicitly confirming its mandate and leadership role in this area, allowing it to lead whole-of-government strategy and priority policy-setting and steering exercises effectively. Enabling the

Recommendations *(continued)*

Government Office, in co-operation with the other CoG institutions, to lead the co-ordination function of defining and steering of government-wide policy priorities could contribute to improving overall government coherence and implementation capacity.

- Develop a communication strategy to explain the co-ordination role of the CoG institutions and the need for CoG reform so as to ensure that line ministries understand that they are exercising their sector-specific mandates as part of a coherent, integrated government-specific strategy. At the same time, confirm to line ministries that their competencies as set down in legislation are not being affected in this process. Mandate the Government Office to lead this exercise. It would be important to target this strategy at both citizens and the public administration, particularly the senior civil service. This could raise awareness of the CoG's institutional make-up and mandate, and stimulate understanding and buy-in for greater cross-silo co-operation on important multi-sector national strategic initiatives, including the design and implementation of the Manifesto itself.

Strengthen strategic planning processes and governance

Clearly, the Slovak Republic's Government Office constitutes the main CoG institution. As defined by the Statute of the Government Office of the Slovak Republic, the Government Office's main responsibilities include checking the performance of tasks in the performance of the state administration and of those resulting from government resolutions, checking action taken on petitions and complaints, co-ordinating the performance of tasks for the development of the information society, and co-ordinating the implementation of policies of the European Communities and the European Union.[1]

The Government Office fulfils a number of key CoG functions:

- It works with line ministries to prepare the Government Manifesto. It co-ordinates activities relating to the development of state policy. It develops analytical, strategic and operational documents in all areas of the Slovak Republic's development and participates in the development and implementation of concept and strategic documents stemming from the Government Manifesto. It co-ordinates with ministries and other agencies in meeting the goals of the Manifesto. In so doing, it monitors the development of the government's draft work plans that aim to implement the Manifesto, providing expert and administrative services in strategy planning and steering, in economic and social policy and in matters relating to legislation.
- The Government Office acts as the government's main co-ordinating body on the transposition of EU legislation (while the Ministry of Foreign and European Affairs acts to advance the Slovak Republic's interests in Brussels and internationally), providing expert consultation and co-ordination relating mostly to the process of developing the Slovak Republic's positions in various stages of the decision-making process; it evaluates draft EU legislation and the EU's strategic, conceptual and programme documents. It leads the process of transposing EU directives into national law and functions as a national co-ordinator for the EU 2020 strategy.

- It has the primary responsibility for preparing Cabinet meetings, for communicating government messages to the public and to other parts of the public administration, and for monitoring the implementation of government policy.
- It is responsible for the government's human resources management strategy in the civil service and for designing and implementing civil service reform.

The Review finds, however, that the Government Office as the lead CoG institution could improve its capacity to pursue a more strategic and proactive approach to implementing the Government Manifesto and to monitoring its performance. In addition, the centre of government could work more effectively to prepare the annual work programmes to implement the Manifesto in co-operation with line ministries. Ensuring that this leadership responsibility is effectively shared between line ministries and the CoG by enhancing the partnership between the two could not only foster a whole-of-government approach but also allow for the definition and adjudication of clearer whole-of-government strategic priorities. Line ministries obviously need to be closely involved in this process so that the government's work plan reflects sector-based issues and priorities, and so that line ministries can effectively translate the government's work programme into individual institutional work plans.

Both the government-wide work programme as well as the individual work plans need to be based on more robust, outcomes-based performance information and informed by the results of strategic foresight. These could be tasks for the emerging analytical centres, potentially also for an analytical centre of the Government Office, which could also engage in co-ordinating the strategic foresight efforts of line ministry analytical centres and integrating the results of this activity coherently into medium-term, whole-of-government strategy (see below and Chapter 2).

It will be important to align budgetary allocations more strategically with government priorities. In line with the 2015 OECD *Recommendation of the Council on Budgetary Governance*, the Slovak government could task the Government Office and the Ministry of Finance to ensure that strategic priorities are sufficiently financed in the national budget.

Recommendations

- Strengthen the Government Office's role with regard to strategic planning and the work programme. While the Government Office is in charge of planning and the work programme, many tasks are *de facto* being carried out by the line ministries. A more proactive Government Office could continue to gather inputs from line ministries but could set the work programme according to whole-of-government priorities.
- Consider framing the Government Manifesto around a small number of key, overarching strategic priorities under which the "tasks" could be organised. Such a narrative can be both a powerful communication tool and a way to evaluate progress at the end of a political term.
- Develop the annual work programmes with a clear, strategic hierarchy of goals in mind. Not all tasks in a government work programme are of equal importance. Stating the priorities creates clarity about the intentions of the government and contributes to focusing efforts on, and allocating human and financial resources to, the most important priority tasks.

Recommendations (*continued*)

- Make explicit how a specific measure in the work programme is supposed to achieve the strategic priorities identified in the Government Manifesto. The Government Manifesto could thus play an important role after its adoption. Furthermore, policy makers would need to convince the centre of government that the proposed measure indeed contributes to the implementation of the whole-of-government strategy.
- Create linkages between strategic planning and budgeting, thus strengthening the means by which the government can achieve its policy agenda through the judicious allocation of human and financial resources. This can only be achieved through close co-operation between the Government Office and the Ministry of Finance.
- Use strategic foresight and horizon-scanning to inform government strategies and work programmes. Capacity could be vested in an analytical centre at the Government Office (see immediately below), working in close co-operation with the other analytical centres (see Chapter 2).
- Consider establishing an analytical unit in the Government Office, focusing on whole-of-government strategy as well as the work programme. Such a unit could be staffed partly by Government Office and Ministry of Finance experts. It is important to stress that such an analytical unit would need to be built up slowly and carefully. It could first manage the translation of the Government Manifesto into the annual work programmes. At a later stage, it could look at strategic foresight.

Enhance implementation, evaluation and reporting

The principal planning document of the Slovak Republic, the Government Manifesto, is currently not being closely monitored against the achievement of strategic outcomes as it is being implemented by the government. The Government Office could therefore be tasked to monitor and report on progress toward achieving specific strategic policy outcomes on a regular basis to the political leadership, parliament and the general public. This could enable the government to adjust policies and measures in the case of unsatisfactory performance. A similar monitoring system, on a more detailed basis, could be established for the annual work programmes, building on the work the Ministry of Finance's Institute for Financial Policy (IFP, see below) has been pursuing in developing sets of indicators to monitor progress in different areas.[2] For example, to monitor and evaluate progress in the education system, the IFP has proposed a detailed set of indicators as a supporting mechanism to measure the impact of budgetary expenditures in education.[3] It would appear, however, that these indicators are not yet used extensively by policy makers (hence the recommendation on this matter below). Lessons learnt could be communicated and feed into the development of future Government Manifestos and annual work programmes.

In order to strengthen the Government Office's monitoring capacities, it could be beneficial to establish a dedicated monitoring unit. This unit would build on and support the existing practice of implementation days by measuring progress on a continuous basis. It would be important not to overload such a unit but rather to have it focus on a limited number of key cross-governmental priorities. The unit's scope could be expanded at a later stage, if needed.

Recommendations

- Strengthen whole-of-government performance monitoring and assessment capacity. For the centre of government, in particular the Government Office and the Ministry of Finance, to exercise its mandate in strategy setting and implementation, it needs reliable outcomes-based performance information to be able to determine whether policies are working, and if they are not, change course so that they do end up achieving the results they were designed and adopted to achieve. High-quality, comparable indicators could be developed to monitor progress and evaluate the impact of government policies and measures against expected results for citizens and businesses. The Government Office could thus reinforce its existing monitoring unit (or create a new one within the analytical unit, see above), mandating it to track policy implementation against the achievement of strategic outcomes for citizens and businesses, in addition to assessing implementation against annual outputs, as it does now. This unit could be mandated to act as the government's central co-ordination and communications hub; in so doing, it could monitor on an ongoing basis progress being made on the small number of key government-wide priorities identified in the Manifesto using the performance monitoring evidence it generates, while drawing upon performance data provided by the analytical centres. The data generated by such a monitoring unit could provide the political leadership with real-time information on the government's performance and enable it to address potential difficulties earlier and more effectively.
- Mandate the Government Office to provide parliament and the general public with annual reports on the implementation of the Government Manifesto. These reports could embed analytical units' quantitative and qualitative outcomes-based performance analysis within a whole-of-government policy narrative. Debates on these reports, in turn, could increase citizens' engagement with the Government Manifesto and would represent a means to hold the government publicly accountable.

Strengthening analytical and evaluation capacity for better policy making

The use of robust evidence and sound evidence-based analysis in government decision making with respect to policies, legislation and spending appears to be limited when compared to other OECD countries. In the Slovak Republic, decisions tend to be based on political priorities and the relative strength of individual ministers rather than on rational analysis of costs and benefits and potential outcomes. There are attempts to improve the situation; however, the progress remains slow especially due to the lack of demand on the side of the decision makers. The procedures for stakeholder engagement in policy- and regulation-making in the Slovak Republic are well-established; however, many consultations take place solely on an informal basis or too late in the processes when it is rather difficult to change the policy or regulation substantively.

Use analytical capacity more deliberately in the Slovak administration

Relatively unusual among OECD countries is the lack of demand on the part of the Slovak Republic's CoG for evidence and analysis from line ministries. This is also connected to the issue of insufficient policy co-ordination from the CoG where performance of government policies and/or spending programmes does not appear to be measured and evaluated, be it *ex ante* or *ex post* decisions. Senior decision makers do not seems to be aware of the ways in which analytical support could help them in their daily work and there is a tendency to consider formal obligations to support government decisions with evidence and analysis as additional administrative burden.

The Slovak Republic needs to strengthen analytical capacities in line ministries. Conditions could be created to attract skilled personnel with the necessary analytical skills. At the same time, clear procedures could be established at each line ministry on how to use these analytical capacities to improve the decision-making process. Line ministry units could benefit from more co-ordination, and sharing of recruitment, training, etc. Co-ordination from the centre of government could be strengthened for using the evidence and sharing it across the administration.

Probably the most visible example of good practice is the Institute for Financial Policy (IFP), which operates within the portfolio of the Ministry of Finance. Similar analytical units exist or are being set up as part of several other ministries, namely the Ministry of the Interior, the Ministry of Economy, the Ministry of Education, the Ministry of Labour and Social Affairs, the Ministry of Environment and the Ministry of Transport, Communications and Public Works. However, these analytical units are much smaller in scale and in many cases, their influence on the decision-making process of their ministry is rather limited. The Government Office does not yet have any formally established analytical unit.

Recommendations

- Consider strengthening analytical capacity in key ministries. Create conditions to attract and keep personnel with the necessary analytical skills. Use the current EU-funded project to raise awareness in line ministries on the need to strengthen analytical capacities.
- Increase the demand for analysis and evidence to support government decisions by establishing formal procedures for *ex ante* and *ex post* assessment of government policies, programmes and regulations. Clear procedures could be established government-wide and at each line ministry on how to use the analytical capacities to improve the decision-making process.

Use performance information and strategic foresight more systematically

Quantitative information on the performance of policies, programmes and regulations appears to be used sporadically. Such performance indicators are rarely established up front – at the stage when a policy, spending programme or law are being adopted by the government. This makes it impossible to assess whether these policies, programmes or regulations are achieving their goals. *Ex post* evaluation could be conducted more often to find out whether there is a need to change, abolish and/or replace them with more effective ones.

The results of strategic foresight and long-term horizon scanning tend not to be used to inform the preparation of the Government Manifesto, with the exception of macroeconomic short- and medium-term forecasts prepared by the IFP. No other foresight activities are conducted by other institutions. In the future, analytical units could provide the government with results from strategic foresight activity, conducted both in-house and by the private sector. This work could be co-ordinated by an analytical unit within the centre of government – preferably within the Government Office (see the recommendation to this effect above). This co-ordination could help build both horizontal and vertical coherence in the development and implementation of the government's agenda.

Recommendations

- Make the use of performance indicators more widespread when adopting policies, programmes or regulations. Adopt a government-wide policy on *ex post* evaluation of these policies/programmes/regulations. When drafting new regulations, make it obligatory to set the goals the given regulation should achieve in quantitative terms, wherever possible. The drafting institution should also set a timeframe during which the regulation's performance has to be reviewed (mandatory reviews policy).
- Use the analytical units to provide strategic foresight to the government. While ministerial analytical units could conduct horizon scanning as well as take into account results of private sector-led foresight activity in their sector, this activity could be co-ordinated from the CoG to provide a synthesis of these sector-specific scans and to maximise the impacts of foresight activities on whole-of-government strategy setting and implementation, notably with respect to designing and implementing the political Manifesto and its corresponding government-wide and ministry-specific programmes of work.

Improve regulatory impact assessment and consultation processes

While the obligation to conduct regulatory impact assessment (RIA) has been in place since 2008 in the Slovak Republic, it does not seem to be complied with as a general rule. Recent changes aimed at improving the RIA system are an important step forward. The creation of a semi-independent advisory body overseeing the quality of impact assessments would put more pressure on line ministries to take RIA more seriously. At the same time, draft legislation should be the subject of consultations with external stakeholders, especially business and also civil society organisations, where relevant, early in the process. On the other hand, the fact that budgetary, economic, social and environmental impacts are assessed in an isolated manner and that the quality of such analyses are evaluated by four different institutions (though members of the same commission) might not contribute to an integrated view on the assessment of the potential impacts of draft regulation.

As in the case of RIA, the necessary formal obligations to engage stakeholders are partially in place and should be strengthened by implementing the new RIA methodology. The Ministry of the Interior is responsible for the overall co-ordination of the RIA process. What lacks is enforcement, quality oversight and sufficient demand from the government for engaging stakeholders in the decision-making process. Therefore, stakeholders are insufficiently consulted, especially in the early stages of the process of developing policies and/or regulations. The government's online consultation portal is not used to the optimal extent by external stakeholders due to low user-friendliness and lack of awareness of its existence on the part of the public.

Recommendations

- Implement the approved changes in the RIA process without further delay. Ensure full compliance, including the obligation to always assess several alternatives (including the "do nothing" option and non-regulatory alternatives, where appropriate). Evaluate the system after two years to assess whether it is working in an efficient manner and adopt changes if necessary.
- Adopt a methodology for early-stage consultations. Enforce the obligation to consult all legislative proposals with all relevant stakeholders as part of RIA. Train civil servants in

Recommendations *(continued)*

consultation techniques.

- Make the new consultation portal more user-friendly and inform the general public better on the functionalities of the portal as well as on the possibilities to engage in the government's decision-making process.

Strengthening the capability of the state civil service to steer and lead policy

Strengthening the capability of the state civil service in the Slovak Republic is a crucial factor in ensuring an efficient and effective public sector that can promote strong, sustainable and inclusive growth. The performance of the public service depends on the capacity of its civil servants, as well as stability and continuity in public service staffing. Good human resources management (HRM) contributes significantly to the efficiency of government, its capacity to deliver public services effectively and the agility required to implement reforms in all areas of government.

The Slovak government has recently committed to assessing and improving HRM in the civil service. Work already in progress to support these aims includes the draft of a new Civil Service Act and inter-ministry collaboration to develop and finalise an HRM strategy for 2015-20. These efforts are positive first steps along the path to HRM reform in the Slovak civil service. It is important to recognise that developing and implementing reforms to HRM is a long-term project which requires ample time and continued commitment. OECD experience demonstrates that developing and embedding strategic HRM requires an incremental approach to reform while maintaining impetus and political commitment. These recent efforts set a solid foundation and pave the way for future implementation and improvements to HRM in the Slovak civil service.

Strengthen strategic workforce planning and management

The Slovak government has made positive first steps toward improving the quality of data on the public workforce, which in turn will ensure that there is accurate information on the level, allocation and trends in public employment. The analysis carried out by the Government Office in the context of the HRM strategy has started to build a basic overview of the structure and quantification of civil servants and efforts to establish civil service registers will contribute to better planning of the workforce. These efforts will in time facilitate improved control of public employment costs and provide more reliable data for decision makers to determine how best to manage the workforce to deliver public services. A more standardised approach to defining civil service positions across ministries, as proposed in the HRM Strategy to 2020, would facilitate the collection of workforce data. The fact that a number of ministries have their own human resource information systems (HRIS) is likely to complicate the establishment of a centralised workforce information system to the extent that data may not be in a standard format. Investing in ministry-specific HRIS does not represent the most effective use of resources and a more co-ordinated approach is desirable.

The capacity and skills of service offices could be strengthened to enable them to develop workforce planning. An important contribution that the Government Office could make to support the development of workforce planning capabilities would be to develop tools and frameworks which organisations could use and to organise training in workforce planning. It would also be important to communicate, incentivise and demonstrate the benefits of strategic workforce planning and management to staff in service offices. Pilot projects to highlight benefits could be a useful starting point, particularly by demonstrating how this can enable capacity-building in areas such as analysis and digital government. In addition, ministries and the Government Office could consider co-operating when building the analytical capacities necessary for existing analytical units, or for new units being developed in some ministries.

Competency management and the use of common job profiles are tools which could help the Slovak government to advance the strategic orientation and integration of key HRM areas, including workforce planning, recruitment and selection, mobility, and training and development. Moving away from the current practice of traditional job descriptions and adopting a competency-based management framework could help the Slovak central government reinstate the principle of merit in recruitment and selection arrangements while also standardising the structure of job descriptions across ministries, making it easier to promote mobility. A competency-based management framework could also ensure a more strategic approach to career and skills development in the Slovak government, contributing to the development of human capital along the lines already highlighted in the HRM Strategy to 2020.

Recommendations

- Collect data on the public workforce to use as a foundation for strategic workforce planning and management. The Slovak government should consider prioritising the collection of quality data on the public workforce as a basis for strategic HR planning and management. A central database of workforce statistics would be a first essential step to improve workforce planning in order to better align the capacity of the public service with organisational and service demands.
- Start to develop strategic workforce planning and management. In parallel with building up the collection of workforce data, it is necessary to build skills and capacity in the ministries' service offices to use this data effectively. The necessary skills will need to be developed through targeted training programmes and it is likely that skilled HR personnel will also need to be recruited. Rather than trying to get all ministries at the same level simultaneously, a more promising approach may be to start with pilot projects in ministries that are better prepared to take this on.
- Build on competency-based management and job profiling. The Slovak government could move towards more strategic HRM by building tools such as competency management and job profiling. The roadmap for implementing competency management (see Box 3.6) would be a good starting point. Developing common job profiles for public service functions and incorporating a common competency framework could be the first step. This would help improve recruitment and selection methods and support a merit-based recruitment process. A common competency framework could eventually be integrated into planning, career management and skills development practices.

Focus on building a professional, educated and stable workforce through fair, rules-based and transparent management practices

The Slovak government's focus on reinstituting the principle of merit in recruitment and selection arrangements is a welcome step. The key requirements for merit-based recruitment are that the selection criteria are objective and relevant to the work the person is being recruited to do; that the selection process is transparent, adequately documented and open to audit; and that the recruitment process is open to competition. Recruitment and promotion decisions could be adopted collectively through a collegial body, not entrusted to a person individually, regardless of his/her rank in the hierarchy. A strategic oversight body in relation to recruitment and merit protection, as envisaged in reform plans, could be an important contribution to upholding merit.

The compensation system in the Slovak civil service is not functioning in a transparent, merit-based or logical manner. The Slovak government needs to strengthen the merit principle by ensuring that employees' compensation is based on the nature of their work and the competencies they bring to it and not so strongly on seniority or length of service factors. The most important factors for determining base salary in OECD countries are job content, experience and qualifications. Performance-related pay is also common among OECD countries (tied to performance appraisals); however, it often constitutes a smaller portion of an employee's annual basic salary than in the current case of the Slovak public administration, and is sometimes only applied to certain groups of employees, generally senior staff.

Establishing a predictable career path within the Slovak civil service and making promotion and tenure less dependent on discretionary managerial decisions could increase the attractiveness of the civil service and thereby contribute to improving the overall quality of staff. Ensuring recruitment processes are not overly cumbersome for applicants could also increase the attractiveness of the civil service for suitable candidates. High turnover, whether for political reasons or due to better salary and career prospects in the private sector, creates instability in staffing that discourages ministries from trying to plan their workforce and undermines attempts to develop a training strategy and build up core skills. Stability at management level and ensuring a certain level of tenure and employment guarantees for civil servants is essential for the overall effective functioning of government, and for the successful implementation of the PAR agenda, as recognised in the HRM Strategy to 2020.

Recommendations

- Reinstate the principle of merit in recruitment and selection arrangements by ensuring common standards and oversight. The government could work to achieve standard methods and procedures for recruitment and selection across the administration, and ensure employment decisions are based on merit. This could be done by allowing the proposed Civil Service Council to play a strategic oversight role, to monitor and ensure merit in the staffing of the public service (similar to a public service commission in many OECD countries). The council could focus on setting principles and guidelines, carrying out audits of recruitment and investigating suspected breaches of merit.
- Clarify the compensation system and ensure it is based on merit and transparency. The Slovak government could consider active approaches to clarifying the political-administrative interface, and to managing and developing the competencies of senior leaders in the civil service. It is recommended to make a clear distinction between political appointees and professional senior civil servants, and to start managing and training senior managers in order to build competencies specific to this group.
- Professionalise the civil service through ensuring appropriate tenure arrangements. Reasonable tenure arrangements for civil servants are essential to stability, continuity and ensuring a professional civil service. The Slovak central government could consider stabilising the civil service by managing civil servants' careers through fair, rule-based

Recommendations *(continued)*

and transparent practices, and by ensuring a reasonable degree of tenure and employment guarantees for them. The Slovak government could consider widely communicating the benefits of a stable and professional workforce. This could be done, for example, by highlighting the successful management practices of the Institute for Financial Policy in this regard.

Press on with improvements to institutional arrangements for human resources management

Central frameworks can guide strategic HRM and enable a whole-of-government approach to managing the workforce, while delegated HRM responsibilities for ministries need to be underpinned by appropriate accountability mechanisms. The Slovak government could adopt an incremental approach to strengthening central HRM responsibilities as the Government Office builds its capacity to take on such functions. The current activities and collaboration in the joint development of the new draft Civil Service Act and the HRM strategy show co-operation with regard to HRM is possible, and that the Government Office can lead these efforts. Ensuring institutional capacity and adequate resourcing in the Government Office to co-ordinate and oversee the implementation of the reforms, are key factors that will need to be balanced against the current model of strongly independent line ministries.

The government's HRM reform agenda will require strong leadership at the political and senior management levels if it is to be successful. It may be necessary to consider building shared responsibility for HRM reforms across CoG institutions, namely between the Government Office, the Ministry of Finance and the Ministry of the Interior – each operating in their appropriate domain, but fully co-ordinated to achieve the common purpose of designing, implementing and monitoring the performance of a strategic HRM strategy. The Government Office is an appropriate location for central HRM responsibility; however, the Ministry of Finance could also play a role in driving HRM reforms and the efficient and effective use of the public workforce.

Recommendations

- Ensure adequate capacity, knowledge and resources in the Government Office to support ministries' service offices and make government-wide HRM reform happen. This will be essential to support the proposed reform initiatives and help ministries' service offices implement new working methods. As the proposed HRM reform envisions that the Government Office will play a strategic and co-ordinating role, set frameworks and standards, and lead the implementation of reforms, the Slovak government could consider building adequate human and financial resources, and a solid knowledge base, to enable the Government Office to execute these new competencies.
- Build professional networks across ministries' service offices and with the Government Office to share best practices and support new working methods. Ensuring two-way communication between the Government Office and service office staff – through information sharing and genuine consultation – will be important for the implementation of the proposed HRM reforms. It will also be important to develop a network of support among HRM professionals across government, as a forum for ministries to discuss and

Recommendations *(continued)*

share experience and best practice with each other.

- Integrate change management strategies into the design of HRM reforms. Integrating change management strategies into the reform at an early stage will help to identify the concerns of key stakeholders and develop ways of addressing the issues and tensions that inevitably arise in the course of a reform. This includes communicating with and involving stakeholders, as well as anticipating possible difficulties and devising ways of building support for changes.

Increase performance management, accountability and leadership capacity

The Slovak government could benefit from enhancing its performance orientation and developing a foundation for performance management by linking the management of people with organisational goals and strategies and, ultimately, with the government's programme and objectives. The reimplementation of performance measures at the individual level provides a good opportunity to start linking these to organisational objectives and strategies. Linking employee effort to organisational output requires that each organisation clearly articulate its strategic objectives, which each sub-unit clearly articulates its own objectives in a way that contributes to the overall objectives of the organisation, and that each employee's work objectives contribute to the goals of his/her work unit. Overall, human resource management needs to be understood as supporting organisational performance.

While managers in the Slovak government enjoy a high degree of managerial flexibility, this could be counterbalanced by accountability for management practices and results so that managers will perceive a clear link between strategic HRM and the results they are expected to produce. This may warrant a reform strategy linked to using performance indicators and organisational performance management frameworks to drive and incentivise HRM. Finding the right balance between flexibility and control is particularly important in a public service which is still developing its core values and essential administrative foundations. The Slovak government could consider building monitoring mechanisms to determine where additional support may be needed. This should, however, be done in a way that is sensitive to the limited capacities of small HRM offices.

Management of the administrative-political interface is a critical part of the development of a professional civil service, yet the Slovak central government has yet to develop a common framework to manage the senior civil service. The government could make a clear distinction between political appointees and professional senior civil servants, and start managing and training senior managers in order to build competencies specific to this group along with a common value set that upholds its members' duty to serve a "single" government and pursue the "common purpose" of meeting the needs of citizens and businesses regardless of which portfolio or ministry employs them. Over time, this could lead to more effective collaboration across institutional silos by the senior ranks of the civil service in pursuit of common, whole-of-government strategic objectives, notably those identified in the Government Manifesto at the beginning of the government's mandate, and could thus contribute over time to breaking down barriers to cross-ministry collaboration at all levels of the civil service.

Recommendations

- Develop performance and accountability mechanisms to drive and ensure results. The Slovak government could consider developing an integrated performance management framework to drive public organisations to deliver on government-wide objectives. The government could consider developing performance appraisals based on objective setting, and tying individual objectives to organisational and whole-of-government priority goals. Furthermore, the Slovak government could develop management accountability structures to ensure delegation of HRM is met with capacity and accountability at the ministry level.
- Clarify the political-administrative interface and manage senior civil servants as a group serving a "single" government. The absence of a cohort of permanent, professional civil servants at senior or middle management levels undermines continuity in public service management and is bound to weaken impartiality as the boundary between political appointments and professional managers is unclear. The Slovak government could consider active approaches to clarifying the political-administrative interface, and to managing and developing the competencies of senior leaders in the civil service.

Scaling up digital government

Although the Slovak Republic has had in place an active programme of digitisation over the past decade, it has not met expectations. In some areas there has been measurable progress, particularly with regard to Internet connectivity and usage. However, when it comes to the online delivery of public services and citizen engagement, the Slovak Republic has lagged behind peer countries both within the EU and the OECD. And while there are initial indications that some of the Slovak Republic's investments from the last EU programming period are beginning to reach fruition, it is clear that this progress is not happening as quickly or robustly as would be desired, and in most cases the development of these new online services lack a user-centric approach.

Enhance digital governance and national strategies

Robust government-wide co-ordination of the digital government agenda framed by a strategic vision of the purpose and use of ICT in government can go far in reducing barriers to progress in realising fully the benefits of implementing digital government that can accrue to the government itself, to citizens and to businesses. The current approach appears to be characterised by ministries operating with a focus almost exclusively on meeting accountability requirements for accessing EU funds as opposed to driving towards a shared whole-of-government vision on why and how digital government ought to be implemented. Having had almost all strategic activity in this area explicitly tied to funding sources has led to muddled priorities where obtaining funding for digitisation has gone from being a means to an end to, in many cases, being the end itself. This short-term approach to digital government has led to challenges in being able to absorb these funds and neglect in building internal capacity in favour of outsourcing procurement to large private sector vendors. Lack of internal capacity has also manifested itself in a relatively weak focus on the data assets of the Slovakian government, both from the perspective of internal interoperability as well as the provision of open data as an economic and public asset to citizens, businesses and academia.

There is thus a clear need to build on the current steering mechanism for digital government initiatives in the Slovak Republic located in the Ministry of Finance. At issue is not so much "who is in charge" but the need to provide mechanisms for those involved in the digital agenda, both at an operational level within line ministries and from a direction-setting level within the centre of government, to learn from each other's experiences and build a common sense of ownership based on a government-wide consensus on the strategic results that government stakeholders should be achieving as they pursue their digital government implementation agenda.

Recommendations

- Broaden and deepen the Slovak Republic's whole-of-government vision for digital government and communicate it widely across the public administration. A good starting point could be the government's new National Conception of Public Administration Systems, a document outlining a strategy for digital government that aims to bring a new systematic and co-ordinated approach to addressing e-government. The Ministry of Finance could use this concept document as the basis for engaging key digital government stakeholders from across the government in a substantive dialogue on this vision, its desired outcomes, how to achieve them and how to measure success. Given the fragmented nature of the current digitisation initiatives underway in the Slovak government, there is a need to broaden and deepen the government's overarching vision for priorities in this area. As virtually all national strategies have been explicitly tied to funding sources, this has prevented a wider and more strategic discussion on the role that digital technology could and should play in helping to modernise and reform the Slovak government in the long term and on what is needed to achieve those changes using digital government tools.

- Establish a Chief Information Officer (CIO) or equivalent position and associated information-sharing mechanisms. This review points to the need to have a strong central focal point that can act as co-ordinator and facilitator for implementing a vision for digital government and its various components government wide. The position of CIO could build on the existing mandate and functions of the Director General of Information Society in the Ministry of Finance, strengthening it to cover all aspects of public sector digitisation. Given the current split of responsibilities, the CIO position, while located in the Ministry of Finance, could be structured to report jointly to the Government Office, the Ministry of Finance and the Ministry of the Interior. This would not necessarily require transferring any responsibilities from the existing ministries responsible for digital government activities; as is the case with the responsibilities of CIOs in other OECD countries, this "hub" role could focus on exercising levers related to leading and co-ordinating digital government strategy-setting and implementation across the government, and information-sharing both within the Slovak administration and with international partners.

- Strengthen the digital government co-ordination body's capacity to allow for regular exchange of information between officials responsible for digitisation initiatives and the management of ICT. The Ministry of Finance leads a committee through its Architectural Office of Public Administration that looks at ICT-enabled projects, focused on funding and project oversight government-wide related *inter alia* to the Operational Programme Integrated Infrastructure. This co-ordination body could be led by the CIO and could more fully act as a forum to bring together those leading ICT-related work across the government on a regular basis to share lessons learnt both within the government and from other jurisdictions.

Recommendations *(continued)*

- Strengthen capacity in line ministry digital government/IT departments to drive enhanced performance in digital service design and delivery. Limited capacity and weak performance in the IT departments of individual institutions in the Slovak public administration have been defined as a major challenge to the successful development and implementation of government-wide digital government strategies and to successfully delivering digital services to people and businesses. The structure and size of these units tend not to correspond to the requirements of rolling out state-of-the-art IT strategies and could put at risk the ability to reach government-wide performance targets in this area.

Develop further online service delivery

There is strong demand-side potential for digital services, evidenced by the relatively high uptake levels of Internet-based activities by the Slovakian population as a whole. Moreover, while there have been challenges around connectivity, it appears that this is becoming less of a concern with increasing mobile penetration and the hopefully successful completion of major broadband projects in progress during the coming EU programming period.

The launch of a number of new online services by ministries during 2015 and 2016 – in part as a result of Act No. 305/2013 on e-government, which laid out a largely non-mandatory three-year time period from 2013-16 for the digitisation of public services – means that many citizens will soon have tangible incentives to start interacting more regularly with government through online channels. This represents a singular opportunity to build a sense of momentum in the government's digitisation agenda.

Recommendations

- Reinforce the application of mandatory standards for digital services across the public administration. Standards for online services are part of a set of standards for information systems of public administration, which are published by order of the Ministry of Finance and are legally binding. Indeed, the Ministry of Finance's Architectural Office manages customised open architecture standards – TOGAF® and ArchiMate®. That said, the Slovak Republic has consistently ranked poorly in the quality of its digital services, and this should be a key area of focus going forward. Building on the experience of countries such as Estonia, the United Kingdom and the United States in building user-centric digital services, the application of mandatory standards for all new online services could be reinforced, including through robust communications government-wide. Emphasis could be placed on interoperability and interconnectivity between new digital services so as to start breaking down the barriers between the systems and databases that exist in various ministries. To ensure compliance, these standards could be linked to access to funding sources such as through the project evaluation process in the Operational Programme Effective Public Administration.
- Put in place performance measures to ensure ongoing improvement of new digital services. While it is a positive development that a number of new online services are being launched in 2015, experience in other OECD countries has shown that it is important to put in place continual improvement processes to ensure ongoing enhancements and optimisation. This can include having active feedback mechanisms for those using the services as well as tracking and publishing metrics on the use of

Recommendations *(continued)*

these services. For example, the Ministry of Finance currently conducts an annual survey on e-government user satisfaction. The government could expand this practice and use the survey results along with other input factors to inform decision making in the design and delivery of online services to citizens and businesses.

- Increase the uptake of the e-ID card. As a fundamental enabler of digital services, seeing a greater uptake of e-ID cards is an important priority. To date only 5% of the approximately 1 million e-ID cards issued have had their digital signature activated. There is a need to increase public awareness of the services that can be accessed through the use of an e-ID card, particularly as new services come online in 2015/16. Finally, being able to provide incentives to encourage the use of e-ID enabled services over traditional in-person or paper-based formats could be explored.

Prioritise open government data to unlock value for government, citizens and businesses

The Slovak Republic is poised to make rapid gains in the area of the strategic use of data. Investments from the previous EU programming period are now bearing fruit with the launch of the first set of online services and the corresponding databases that power them. Initial efforts via the Open Government Partnership have led to some initial work moving forward in the realm of open government data. However, these have yet to be mainstreamed within the civil service and the use of data for other analytics or public release is still largely viewed as a side project as opposed to a key enabler. A greater focus on interoperability and identifying areas of high value for the use of data both inside of government and with external partners could lead to a significant advancement in this area while supporting other key areas of the public reform agenda, such as improved analytical and evaluation capacity.

Recommendations

- Increase the number of datasets available on the open government data portal. The lack of high-value datasets on the open data portal is providing a barrier to the greater use of open data by government and non-governmental actors. Building on consultations that have been carried out through the Open Government Partnership and related initiatives, high-value datasets that have the greatest potential for reuse should be the primary focus. There is a need to also ensure uniform standards across similar datasets released from different ministries. As well, ensuring that the licencing regime for any datasets released allows for unrestricted reuse is also important to fostering a more dynamic open data ecosystem in the Slovak Republic.
- Foster greater capacity for the use of open data inside government. The creation of a network of open data champions across all ministries could be an important first step towards greater institutionalising the creation and use of open data in the administration. Moreover, there may also be a need to develop greater centralised capacity and expertise on open government data – particularly with regards to the technical skills related to the creation, formatting and reuse of open government data – which can work with ministries and their open data champions as needed to enhance their open government data initiatives. This centralised capacity could take the form of a dedicated team of open data experts that can work with departments as well as a central data repository to ensure that all ministries can access data across the administration and the ability to put in place interoperability between various databases.

Encourage the use of social media within the government

The use of social media by the government has not yet reached its full potential in the Slovak Republic. While some ministries have gone further in experimenting with its use, there remains a lack of central guidance or vision for how it could best be utilised as a part of the broader digital agenda for the modernisation of the Slovak Republic's public administration. When leveraged to its full potential, social media can provide a useful platform for not only communicating with citizens but also for incorporating feedback into the design and delivery of policies and services. It also provides an important mechanism for improving government transparency and responsiveness.

The current lack of centralised guidance on the use of social media is a barrier to its greater use across the government. Greater use of social media by the Slovak government is important to help promote new digital services and can serve as a cost-effective channel to gather feedback from citizens as digitisation initiatives are implemented. Use of social media can also provide an effective way to gather information on key policy issues and engage with citizens to build trust in government, particularly with the younger generation, which has a comparatively higher rate of social media usage.

Recommendation

- Develop and apply social media guidelines across the public administration. Building on the work done in other OECD countries, the Slovak Republic could put in place centralised guidance on both institutional use and civil servant use of social media which aims to promote the use of social media as a way to inform and engage citizens, while mitigating legitimate risks.

Improve public procurement for ICT projects

While outside of the scope of this review, throughout discussions with government and non-governmental experts, concerns were raised about the limitations of existing procurement rules for ICT-enabled projects. Future reviews by the OECD or other organisations on the topic of government procurement could make ICT-enabled projects a priority.

Recommendation

- Review procurement processes for ICT-enabled projects. Allowing mechanisms for smaller companies to get involved in ICT procurements and making procurement processes more agile with projects broken into smaller pieces would allow more competition and reduce the risk of project failure that has often been observed with high-value, long-duration contracts. The ability to use open source software could also be explored.

Enhancing transparency and integrity across the public administration

Though the level of perceived corruption in the Slovak Republic remains high, the government has undertaken steps to enhance transparency and integrity across the public administration: the fight against corruption is included in the programme of the government of the Slovak Republic for the years 2012-16. Furthermore, the government approved a Strategic Plan for Fighting Corruption in 2011 which included preventive measures such as publication of state contracts, reform of the judiciary to increase the transparency of court decisions, competitive selection of judges and presidents of courts, as well as stricter rules for judicial governance and clear provisions for public procurement.

Update, apply and enforce the government's code of conduct across the public sector

With the new Civil Service Act currently under discussion, the Slovak Republic has the opportunity to update and adopt a new code of ethics which has enough substance and powers of enforcement to address existing shortcomings. An inclusive, consultative approach towards designing codes of conduct is essential to ensuring take-up and implementation. The experience of OECD countries demonstrates that consulting or actively involving stakeholders in drafting the code helps build a common understanding of public service values and expected standards of public employee conduct. Stakeholder involvement would, in addition, improve the quality of the code so that it met both public employees' and citizens' expectations. The government would also be able to demonstrate commitment to greater transparency and accountability, thereby gaining public trust.

The inter-ministerial working group of experts preparing the code of ethics could define: *i)* the values of the public administration; *ii)* the standards of conduct expected of public officials; and *iii)* the scope of the code and to whom it shall apply. Similarly, surveys and other tools for collecting empirical data could help the Slovak Republic to identify the issues and concerns that are most relevant to its public service. It is essential that the content and issues covered by the code build on the Slovak Republic's existing sector-related codes of conduct so as to promote consistent values and standards of conduct throughout the public service.

A code of conduct must be part of a wider organisational strategy, with the institution in question committed to provide clear guidance and education on the behaviour expected of public officials in the workplace. At the moment, the Slovak Republic does not have a regular educational programme or government-wide manual on the code of conduct. It could consider tasking a specialised organisation with designing a single code of conduct to ensure that all public employees have the same understanding on the subject. Such an organisation could also offer guidance and counselling to public officials facing ethical dilemmas. Each public service body could then ensure that it takes into account the specific nature of its area of work.

A code of ethics being a flexible instrument, regularly monitoring its implementation will help determine whether it fits the bill of promoting high standards of conduct within the public service. If it does not, further guidelines may be drawn up to clarify the values and standards of conduct that the code lays down. A body which oversees and monitors the implementation of the code of conduct and compliance with standards of behaviour is also crucial.

Recommendations

- Define clear, easily understandable values and standards of conduct in a consultative and participative manner. The new Civil Serve Act currently in discussion will provide an opportunity to update and adopt a new code of ethics which has enough substance and powers of enforcement.

Recommendations *(continued)*

- Establish a government-wide co-ordinated system for ensuring consistency throughout the public sector in understanding the values and standards of conduct promoted by the code. This could be tasked to an independent Civil Service Committee currently under discussion.
- Ensure that all public officials have the same understanding on the code of conduct through guidance and training on how to apply the code in daily work. In particular, guidance and training on how public officials should apply their codes of conduct in sensitive situations must be provided.
- Monitor and assess the implementation of the code of conduct and its impact on promoting integrity in the public sector. Surveys could provide useful information to help determine whether the code serves its purpose.
- Incorporate ethical dimensions into management frameworks to achieve compliance with the values of the public service. The Slovak Republic should establish a clear mechanism to ensure compliance with the code of ethics.
- Promote the consistent application of sanctions for ethical misconduct by public officials while ensuring that sanctions are both proportionate and dissuasive.

Improve the management of conflict of interest

The management of conflict of interest does not appear to be strictly enforced in the Slovak Republic. Adequate enforcement of the rules on asset disclosure and conflict of interest requires strengthening the mandate of the Committee of the National Council of the Slovak Republic on Conflicts of Interest. As for management of conflict of interest among civil servants, their annual asset declaration is not subject to the internal audit and staff members are not educated on the content of conflict of interest policy. Establishing clear procedures for identifying, managing and resolving conflict of interest situations is crucial. The Slovak Republic could also consider tasking a specialised organisation with designing and providing procedures for establishing a conflict of interest offence and proportional consequences for non-compliance with conflict of interest policy, including disciplinary sanctions. The Slovak Republic also needs to adopt diagnostic tools in assessing the implementation of conflict of interest policies.

The Slovak Republic could also consider designing and providing central national programmes to raise awareness for managing conflict of interest in the public sector. While most OECD countries adopt various awareness-raising policies such as initial dissemination of rules/guidelines to public officials upon taking office and providing training, there is no systematic initiative to promote understanding of conflict of interest in the Slovak Republic. In order to ensure co-ordination across the government, the Government Office or the Ministry of the Interior could ensure that training, education and guidance on management of conflict of interest are available to all public officials. The government could also develop a national awareness programme which the heads of public entities could then apply and tailor to the organisational level.

Recommendations

- Establish a central function within the public administration responsible for the development and maintenance of the conflict of interest polices. Such function could be assigned to either the Government Office or the Ministry of the Interior.
- Develop clear procedures for identifying, managing and resolving conflict of interest situations.
- Introduce a proper oversight mechanism to ensure the accuracy of asset disclosure forms. Online management of the asset disclosure system could also reduce the administrative burden and increase transparency.
- Enhance communication on the management of conflict of interest across the public administration. Measures such as online publication of guidance and setting up an advice line/help desk for employees could increase awareness among the public administration.
- Consider the development of a government-wide monitoring and evaluation system. The Slovak Republic could conduct surveys or design an employee feedback mechanism on a regular basis to assess the implementation of conflict of interest policies.
- Strengthen the policy measures to address the practice of revolving doors. For example, the Slovak Republic could consider introducing a cooling-off period to manage post-public employment.

An emerging cause for concern in the management of conflict of interest is the practice of revolving doors. In the 2013 OECD Survey on Lobbying, one-quarter of lobbyists questioned had previously held positions in the public sector. Most said they had worked in senior managerial or advisory capacities in ministries or had been advisers to prime ministers. Revolving door practices pose a risk to fairness and impartiality in decision making. The Slovak Republic could consider establishing cooling-off periods, during which public officials are not to lobby their former government departments. Update ethics training and deliver it more systematically across the public sector

Ethics training in the Slovak public sector remains formalistic and has limited practical impact on the behaviour of public officials. More efforts are needed to update and improve the overall framework for ethics training in the public sector. Political support for ethics training could be demonstrated not only through declarations but also through practical actions, such as by setting an example of ethical behaviour and by allocating funds and staff to the implementation of ethics training and towards their positive impact on the behaviour of civil servants.

Ethics training should be a part of a broader and comprehensive anti-corruption strategy, as it helps to prioritise and focus training efforts and improve their cost effectiveness. It is also important to have a legislative or other official requirement to deliver and receive ethics training for public officials established in, for example, a Civil Service Act, a code of conduct or other appropriate regulations. Governments need to make at least one public agency responsible for the overall framework for ethics training, for central planning, co-ordination and evaluation of results. In the Slovak Republic, the Government Office could play this role. Clear formulation of responsibilities of such a central body should be complemented with proper co-ordination with other ministries and government agencies that provide ethics training as well.

Recommendations

- Ensure top-level buy-in for ethics training government wide. Political support for ethics training should be demonstrated not only through declarations but also through practical actions, such as allocation of sufficient funds and staff to the ethics training programmes.
- Establish a leading department/agency for central co-ordination of planning, delivery and evaluation of ethics trainings. The Government Office or Ministry of the Interior could play an important role in this process.
- Organise trainings based on needs assessment, targeting specific groups of public officials. At minimum, ethics training should be provided to all new public officials, senior public officials and those in areas of risk.
- Make ethics training practical and interactive with appropriately trained trainers. It is recommended to apply a combination of theoretical lectures and practical case studies into training. Dilemma exercise is one of the most effective training methods to develop practical ethical decision-making skills. Train the trainer programmes are also an effective measure to maintain and improve the quality of the trainers for ethics training.
- Conduct evaluation and follow up of the results of ethics training in order to ensure that the use of public money is producing the desired effects as well as to look for ways to improve the training approaches to make them more effective.

Notes

1. Available at: www.vlada.gov.sk/statute-of-the-government-office-of-the-slovak-republic.
2. www.finance.gov.sk/Default.aspx?CatID=8103 and www.finance.gov.sk/Default.aspx?CatID=9336.
3. www.finance.gov.sk/Default.aspx?CatID=9720.

Chapter 1.

Improving steering from the centre of government in the Slovak Republic

This chapter explores some of the keys issues of centre-of-government capacity in the Slovak Republic. It aims to assess the current situation and suggest recommendations to the government of the Slovak Republic to improve the status quo.

Introduction

The "centre of government" (CoG) can be understood as the support structure for the head of government and the Cabinet. The centre acts as a hub in order to facilitate co-ordination, collaboration and co-operation across the public administration, with the objective of securing a strong, coherent and collective strategic vision of where the country needs to go and how it will get there. The better the CoG is organised and adapted to a country's unique context and requirements, the more it enhances the strategic agility of the state, defined as the extent to which the government can identify and address internal and external challenges effectively and efficiently, and harness internal and external human and financial resources to implementing its strategy successfully (Box 1.1).

Box 1.1. Strategic agility

Governments face more and more difficulties in coping with today's complicated, multi-dimensional challenges that cross policy sectors and national boundaries. Citizens are demanding a greater say in public policy and service design and delivery, and expect these to meet their individual needs quickly and efficiently. At the same time, trust in government has declined in many countries, making it even more difficult for the state to carry out needed reforms. Governments therefore need to become more strategic and agile, to identify looming challenges and adjust quickly.

The concept of "strategic agility", which has been adapted from the private sector, refers to a public governance framework that brings coherence to government-wide decision making and enables the setting of whole-of-government priorities coherently while mobilising human and financial resources from across the government to pursue them efficiently and effectively, breaking down institutional silos in the process. Strategic agility also implies that the government can and does mobilise key stakeholders from within and outside the public sector effectively to propel society forward.

The concept of "strategic agility" can be a useful framework for reforming public sector organisations to "think" and act differently and to better prepare for the future. Strategic agility has three main dimensions:

- strategic sensitivity, or the ability of institutions to anticipate continuously evolving trends and spot new opportunities as they emerge
- resource fluidity, or the ability to redeploy and reallocate resources across institutions to where they are most needed
- leadership unity, or the ability to make collective commitments, including aligning institutions and their behaviour and engaging with the public collectively as a "single" government.

Governments can use these tools to introduce greater flexibility and responsiveness. However, to make reforms successful and sustainable, governments need to strengthen co-ordination, build trust and support, be open and transparent, and engage citizens, businesses and civil society. Performance information and evaluation, including government audit, is also important for ensuring adequate accountability and control technologies (ICT).

Box 1.1. Strategic agility (*continued*)

Figure 1.1. **Key levers of strategic agility**

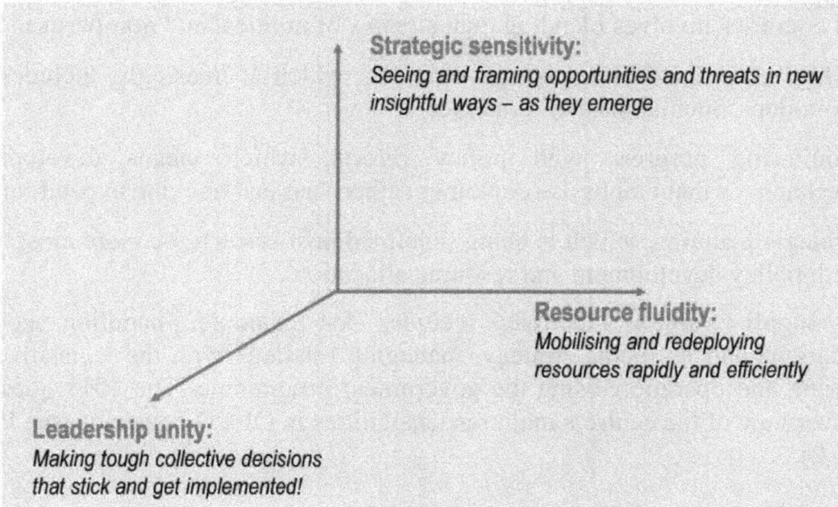

Figure 1.2. **Key capabilities enabling strategic agility**

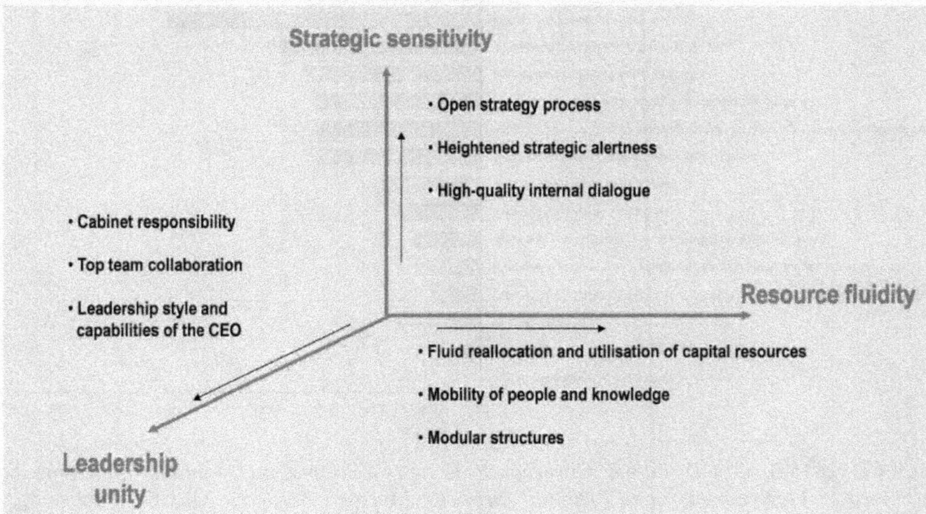

For more information on how to increase strategic agility, please see OECD (2015a and 2015c).

Sources: OECD (2015a), *Achieving Public Sector Agility at Times of Fiscal Consolidation*, OECD Public Governance Reviews, OECD Publishing, Paris, http://dx.doi.org/10.1787/9789264206267-en; OECD (2015c), *OECD Public Governance Reviews: Estonia and Finland. Fostering Strategic Capacity Across Governments and Digital Services Across Borders*, OECD Publishing, Paris, http://dx.doi.org/10.1787/9789264229334-en.

In the past, the functions of the centre of government were often limited to serving the executive on administrative matters. Today, the CoG is playing a much more active role in policy development. It provides services that range from strategic planning to real-time policy advice and intelligence; it sometimes leads major cross-departmental policy initiatives, and it monitors progress in achieving strategic objectives and outcomes. The top four priority tasks of the CoG, as identified by the OECD Questionnaire on the Organisation and Functions of the Centre of Government (OECD, 2013c), are:

- supporting decision making by the head of government/Cabinet, which in almost all countries involves blending dual streams of political and non-partisan advice
- policy co-ordination across government, which increasingly includes leading cross-departmental priority strategies
- monitoring progress with policy reform, which means developing new mechanisms that emphasise outcomes rather than just tracking expenditures
- strategic planning, which is being redefined post-crisis to be more closely aligned with policy development and resource allocation.

Other highly valued functions include, for example, handling government communications and its media strategy, managing relations with the legislative branch, and preparing and operationalising the government programme. The 2013 questionnaire gives an overview of the centre's main responsibilities in OECD countries (see Figure 1.3 and Box 1.2).

Figure 1.3. **Centre of government's main responsibilities**

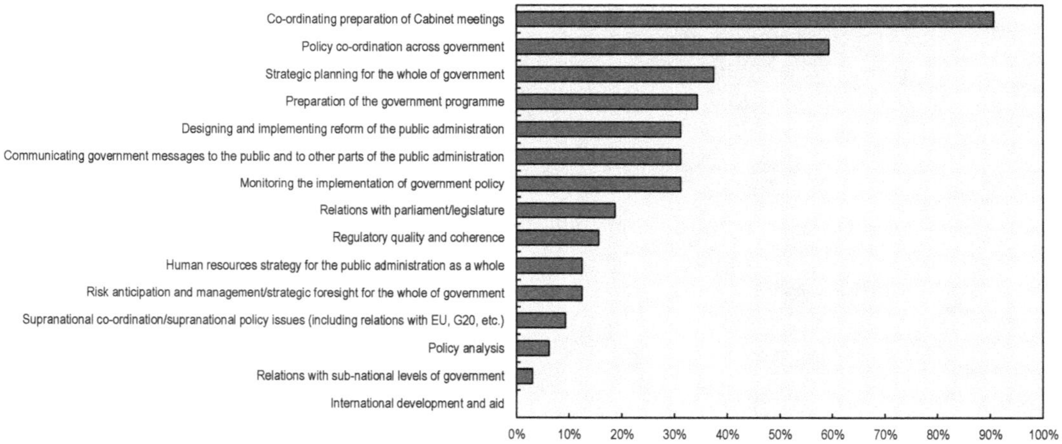

Source: OECD (2015c), *OECD Public Governance Reviews: Estonia and Finland. Fostering Strategic Capacity Across Governments and Digital Services Across Borders*, OECD Publishing, Paris, http://dx.doi.org/10.1787/9789264229334-en.

Box 1.2. **The functions of a "centre of government"**

An effective centre of government (CoG) is critical for:

- Strategic vision. The CoG needs to be able to pull together long-term, big picture objectives for the economy and society. Examples might be an objective to minimise poverty and unemployment, to promote a sustainable environment or to diversify the basis of economic activity in support of growth. These objectives both shape and reflect public sector and societal values. Constitutional requirements and objectives are likely to be relevant. The vision needs to be owned and promoted by all parts of the public sector, as a "whole-of-government" vision.

Box 1.2. **The functions of a "centre of government"** (*continued*)

- Accountability. The CoG is the steward of the strategic vision. It is accountable for overall results and oversight of delegated responsibilities. It is important, however, to avoid overly rigid "command and control" structures and micro management, and instead to work toward a system where the CoG can exert effective oversight and clarify lines of accountability. Line ministries also need to exercise leadership for the actions and policies for which they are responsible, within the overall framework of a shared or collective commitment.
- Strategic planning, policy coherence and collective commitment. The CoG needs the capacity to give the strategic vision specific shape, to secure its coherence and to make it operational. A starting point is likely to be the government programme or equivalent, giving effect to the political Manifesto of the party or parties in power. Making the strategic vision operational is key, otherwise the vision is a "dead letter". The doctrine of collective responsibility is crucial to bind line ministries as well as the CoG to a course of action. Collective commitment is also, crucially, built, developed, discussed and agreed by the whole range of actors that are engaged in public policy making, implementation and service delivery.
- Communication. The CoG needs the capacity to communicate the strategic vision, how it is being taken forward and its implementation. Transparency and openness help to promote a shared sense of purpose, for stakeholders outside as well as inside the government. Clarity of communication within the administration is important, so that, for example, local governments can understand the vision and share in its construction and so that all parts of the public sector understand their role, responsibility and accountability for results.

The sustainability of the CoG across political cycles needs attention. CoG institutions are best constructed, as far as possible, to withstand the vagaries of the political cycle and to be sustainable over the periods of time that it takes to implement long-term strategies. Stability of core functions and structures will raise confidence that the vision is taken seriously, and that the country will have the institutional capacity, over time, to carry out the vision.

External oversight and audit help to ensure that the strategic vision and its implementation stay on track and that the CoG – together with other actors – is accountable for progress, and can be challenged for the lack of it. In many European countries, the national audit office provides valuable independent perspectives not only on the efficiency but also the effectiveness of government policies. For the development of new laws and policies, some European countries have established external watchdogs (made up of stakeholders external to the government) to advise on, and challenge, proposals if these have not been developed with due care and attention.

Last but not least, the first line of engagement of an effective CoG is to project and share policy priorities in key areas with the relevant ministries, and to ensure that these policy priorities are coherent and joined up. "Joined-up government" – the capacity to ensure that complex policy objectives can be met, and that the achievement of high-level policy goals are not undermined by a failure to deal with this complexity – is often weak. Ensuring policy coherence is a major public governance challenge across all OECD member countries. A united position on cross-cutting policy goals is essential if governments are to sustain their credibility, meet their strategic objectives, and if goals are to be achieved without wasting resources. It does not serve the public interest if one part of government fails in its role in policy delivery; and it is directly contrary to the public interest if one action of government is counteracted or undermined by an action taken by another part.

Source: OECD (2015c), *OECD Public Governance Reviews: Estonia and Finland. Fostering Strategic Capacity Across Governments and Digital Services Across Borders*, OECD Publishing, Paris, http://dx.doi.org/10.1787/9789264229334-en.

While the centre of government's main functions are similar across countries, its organisation can vary considerably. Each country's centre is a product of diverse historical, cultural and political forces and has evolved incrementally over time. This diversity is further increased as governments react to the centres' expanding functions by adapting their organisational models to fit new expectations and the specific demands of the country. Over the period of 2008-12, the 2013 questionnaire shows that the size and structure of the CoG has changed in over three-quarters of OECD countries.

A centre of government may consist of a single institution or of several institutions. In polycentric CoGs (the case in the vast majority of OECD countries), the core unit, known by such names as the General Secretariat, Cabinet Office, Chancellery, Office/Ministry of the Presidency, Council of Ministers Office or Government Office, is complemented by other institutions. These can include the Ministry of Finance (responsible for the fiscal framework), the Ministry of the Interior or the Ministry of Public Administration (typically responsible for a range of whole-of-government issues, including public security, relations with sub-national authorities and whole-of-government public administration reform), the Ministry of Foreign Affairs (responsible for designing and managing international and EU relationships and advancing the country's interests on the international stage from a whole-of-government perspective), etc. The influence of the centre of government too differs among countries. The centre tends to be weaker in countries where line ministry autonomy has been highly valued, notably in reaction to historical factors relating to previous regimes having been highly centralised with strong limitations on line ministry mandates and capacity to contribute meaningfully to national strategy. Box 1.3 provides further information on institutional structures of centres of government.

The importance of the CoG has increased in recent years. Since the 2008 financial crisis, trends across the OECD point to the re-emergence of the CoG as the critical actor in leading the setting, and co-ordinating the implementation, of national development strategies. In nearly 60% of OECD countries, the number of cross-ministerial policy initiatives has grown since 2008, increasing the need for strong co-ordination. Furthermore, governments in OECD countries are currently experiencing a crisis of trust, making the environment in which necessary reforms are rolled out often one of scepticism, resistance and opposition. Success will thus depend on their ability to meet cross-cutting challenges – such as boosting growth and improving education as well as infrastructure – by delivering whole-of-government policy responses. This includes better alignment between short-term actions and long-term vision and between government priorities and budget.

Strengthening the centre of government and its co-ordinating function does not equate with centralisation. Quite the contrary, effective co-ordination of the different actors involved implies that they remain autonomous with adequate human and financial resources so that they can continue developing important sector-based expertise while at the same time willingly contribute to developing and implementing multi-sector, cross-cutting policy responses to multi-facetted, complex policy challenges. The centre's role should be a supportive and enabling one, encouraging line ministries to plan and implement their initiatives in line with whole-of-government policy, and otherwise contribute to setting and steering government-wide strategies.

This chapter will explore some of the key issues of centre-of-government capacity in the Slovak Republic. It aims to assess the current situation and suggest recommendations to the government of the Slovak Republic to improve the status quo.

Box 1.3. Institutional structures for the centre of government

It is rare to find a single institution covering all of these functions in OECD member countries. It is far more common that a small set of key players shares the task. CoG structures across OECD member countries vary significantly, depending on the historical development, cultural context and constitutional framework of a country. In most countries, however, they can be identified in a combination of units in the central administration that:

- Provide direct support to the head of the government (Prime Minister/President/ Chancellor's Office). In many countries, however, these offices are not equipped, and do not seek, to cover the whole of the CoG function. They need the capacity to protect the authority and reputation of the Prime Minister/President "above the fray", without becoming too involved in the day-to-day management of specific policies. They may also consider their role to be more political than technocratic. They are often, however, the communication hub for government policy, and their usual role in managing the agenda of the Cabinet provides them with the key authority to set priorities for the attention of the Prime Minister/President.
- Manage the budget. This is normally vested in the Ministry of Finance. The budget can be viewed as key to understanding the government's fiscal framework and its financial operating systems. It is a key allocative document affecting a significant share of a country's gross domestic product (GDP) – over half in some OECD member countries. It is an important policy tool, used by governments to establish policy priorities in concrete terms through the allocation of funding. It is an important management document, in that the basic operational costs of government ministries and agencies are established. In short, the budget provides the basic operational architecture for the work of government.
- Oversee key horizontal policies including public administration reform and central HR policy, co-ordination of law drafting and better regulation policy, and e-government. This usually involves ministries such as the Ministry of Public Administration Reform, the Ministry of the Interior and the Ministry of Justice.
- For EU member countries, manage a dedicated EU oversight unit for the negotiation and implementation (transposition) of EU directives, since these play a major part in shaping the legislative and policy landscape of member countries.

Some of these units or institutions need to co-ordinate especially closely (or be the same unit):

- There is a crucial interface between regulatory policy and the management of the Cabinet agenda, since a well-functioning regulatory policy implies the development of regulatory impact assessments (RIAs) on draft legislation. In countries where policies are usually synonymous with laws, the unit responsible for RIAs needs to work closely with (or be the same unit as) the unit that sets the Cabinet agenda.
- There is also a crucial interface between HR management and budget management, in that performance budgeting and staying within fiscal targets implies staying within budget for HR managers.

Source: OECD (2015c), *OECD Public Governance Reviews: Estonia and Finland. Fostering Strategic Capacity Across Governments and Digital Services Across Borders*, OECD Publishing, Paris, http://dx.doi.org/10.1787/9789264229334-en.

Key facts and findings

The present diagnosis builds on and deepens the analysis undertaken in 2013 and 2014, which was presented in the 2014 publication entitled: *Slovak Republic: Developing a Sustainable Strategic Framework for Public Administration Reform*. This report summarised the centre-of-government issues as follows:

- "Central government co-ordination: the transfer of some key horizontal responsibilities to the Government Office, the Slovak Republic's centre-of-government institution, has the potential to improve co-ordination; however, further improvements are needed. There is a wide network of advisory boards, usually attached to specific ministries; the line ministries lead on their policy areas and the Council of Ministers takes final decisions on key issues. This leaves a gap, where complex policies and reforms that cut across traditional ministerial lines of command need to be addressed more collectively before they can be put to the Council of Ministers.
- Strategic planning processes: ongoing efforts seek to set a planning horizon that goes beyond the electoral term of the government in office. However, some system and structure are needed. There is a range of processes for different purposes, including short and much longer term strategic plans, additional to the Programme Declaration of the Government. As line ministries are often in charge of these, timelines and methodologies can vary, which makes it particularly hard to align strategy with budget. Moreover, processes and institutions for ensuring the quality of impact assessment throughout the decision-making process are not yet well developed.
- Monitoring and evaluation: there are relatively large differences in the use of performance measurement across sectors. There is a tendency to focus on inputs and tasks rather than outputs and outcomes." (OECD, 2014c)

Through an additional questionnaire, an on-site visit to Bratislava and a series of interactive workshops supported by OECD country peers, the OECD Secretariat has been able to refine its initial assessment and identify further issues based on existing good practices in the Slovak Republic. In many cases, these good practices could be scaled up and replicated in other areas.

Centre-of-government institutions

It is important for any country to define those institutions constituting its centre of government. This not only provides a more accurate description of the CoG but facilitates comparison with other OECD countries. Most importantly, it will signal to these institutions (and to the rest of the government) that it is their joint responsibility to lead the setting and steering of national strategic policy according to the directions set by the political leadership and, consequently, to work together and with line ministries more effectively to align whole-of-government positioning coherently as the policy-making cycle advances. While this may sound straightforward, carrying this out effectively and sustaining it on an ongoing basis requires robust co-ordination arrangements and effective monitoring capacity to identify obstacles early and address them efficiently. As leadership roles and (even informal) clout shift back and forth between CoG institutions over time depending on where in the policy-making and electoral cycle the government finds itself, CoG co-ordination mechanisms need to be strengthened and simultaneously rendered flexible to drive the entire policy-making and evaluation cycle efficiently and effectively government-wide. That said, OECD evidence suggests that hardly any country "gets it right" all the time.

Based on answers to OECD questionnaires carried out for this review, the Slovak administration applies a narrow centre-of-government definition by only referring to the Government Office as its CoG institution. Rather than focusing on institutions, the administration stresses the importance of the political process (setting and implementing the Government Manifesto) as the starting point for government activities and planning, and the co-ordinating role of the government as a whole for strategy development (as defined by the Constitution, Article 119, and Act No. 575/201, i.e. the "Competence Act").

Clearly, the Slovak Republic's Government Office constitutes its main CoG institution. As defined by the Statute of the Government Office of the Slovak Republic, its main responsibilities include: checking the fulfilment of tasks in the performance of the state administration, checking the performance of tasks resulting from government resolutions, checking action taken on petitions and complaints, co-ordinating the performance of tasks for the development of the information society, and co-ordinating the implementation of policies of the European Communities and the European Union*.

The Government Office fulfils a number of key CoG functions (Table 1.1 shows the main roles of centres of government within OECD countries):

- It works with line ministries to prepare the Government Manifesto. It co-ordinates activities relating to the development of state policy:
  - It develops analytical, strategic and operational documents in all areas of the Slovak Republic's development and participates in the development and implementation of concept and strategic documents stemming from the Government Manifesto.
  - It co-ordinates with ministries and other agencies in meeting the goals of the Government Manifesto. In so doing, it monitors the development of the draft work plans of the government that aim to implement the Manifesto, providing expert and administrative services in strategy planning and steering, in economic and social policy and in matters relating to legislation.
  - It acts as the permanent advisory and co-ordination authority in the area of legislation, co-ordinating and steering ministries and other agencies in developing laws and government resolutions for consideration in the Legislative Council (parliament).
  - It provides expert support in co-ordinating big investment projects through the Government Office's Office of the Vice Prime Minister for investments.
- The Central Co-ordination Commission function for EU funds was recently transferred to the Government Office. It now acts as the government's main co-ordinating body on the transposition of EU legislation, providing expert consultation and co-ordination relating mostly to the process of developing the Slovak Republic's positions in various stages of the decision-making process; it evaluates draft EU legislation and the EU's strategic, conceptual and programme documents:

* Available at: www.vlada.gov.sk/statute-of-the-government-office-of-the-slovak-republic.

- It leads the process of transposing EU directives into national law and functions as a national co-co-ordinator for the EU 2020 strategy.
- It develops the main strategic and programming documents for using EU funds at the national and inter-ministerial level.
- It co-ordinates and steers individual managing authorities in the system of managing Structural and Cohesion Funds and offers technical assistance for managing operational programmes.
- It is itself the managing authority for the Operational Programme on the Information Society. It co-ordinates meeting the goals of the national strategic and reference framework 2007-13 in relation to horizontal priorities relating to the information society and sustainable development, and participates in the implementation of the strategy for research and innovation and for intelligent specialisation.
- It co-ordinates the development of new legislation for implementing EU cohesion policy in the Slovak Republic. It participates in developing and monitoring ministry-based plans to implement the goals of the EU Strategy for the Danube Region in the Slovak Republic.
- It acts as a national co-ordinator for financial mechanisms and bilateral co-operation, programmes; it implements, monitors and evaluates financial mechanisms for bilateral co-operation.

• It has the primary responsibility for preparing Cabinet meetings, for communicating government messages to the public and to other parts of the public administration, and for monitoring the implementation of government policy.

• It is responsible for the government's human resources management strategy in the civil service and for designing and implementing civil service reform.

The Government Office has an annual budget of around EUR 19 million and a staff of 540, consisting of 295 professional and 245 support staff. In the Slovak Republic, the Head of the Government Office is a political appointee, with the rank equivalent of a minister. This is also the case in roughly half of OECD countries, with the other half having a senior civil servant heading the main CoG institution. As in most OECD countries, professional staff within the Government Office consists mostly of civil servants, as opposed to political appointees. These civil servants are normally not seconded but are employed directly by the Government Office.

That said, after examining the functions performed by other government bodies, it is equally clear that in the Slovak Republic, the Ministry of Finance, the Ministry of Foreign and European Affairs and the Ministry of the Interior fulfil important transversal functions and can also be considered as CoG institutions:

• The Ministry of Finance is responsible for managing the national fiscal framework, including: the national budget, taxes and fees, customs, financial control, internal audit and government audit. By preparing and overseeing the fiscal framework and state budget, the Ministry of Finance fulfils a key centre-of-government function. It also oversees the Slovak Republic's digital governance agenda which is equally a whole-of-government function (see Chapter 4 for a detailed discussion on digital governance). The Ministry of

Finance's arm's-length analytical centre – the Institute for Financial Policy – prepares macroeconomic and fiscal analyses and forecasts. It also serves as the policy arm of the Ministry of Finance.

Table 1.1. **Key roles of the centre of government**

Country	Preparing Cabinet meetings	Communicating government messages	HR strategy for the public administration	Public administration reform	Strategic planning	Risk management strategic foresight	Preparing the government programme	Policy analysis	Policy co-ordination	Regulatory quality and coherence	Monitoring policy implementation	Relations with sub-national government	Relations with the legislature	International development and aid	Supranational co-ordination/policy
Australia	●	❍	□	❍	●	❍	❍	❍	❍	❍	❍	●	❍	❍	❍
Austria	●	●	❍	❍	❍	□	□	❍	●	❍	❍	●	❍	□	❍
Belgium	●	●	□	□	●	●	●	●	●	□	●	●	❍	□	❍
Canada	●	❍	❍	❍	●	●	●	❍	●	□	●	❍	●	□	□
Chile	●	❍	❍	●	●	●	●	❍	●	❍	●	❍	●	□	❍
Denmark	●	❍	□	❍	●	❍	●	❍	●	❍	❍	❍	❍	□	●
Estonia	●	●	□	❍	❍	❍	●	❍	●	❍	●	□	●	□	❍
Finland	●	●	□	❍	●	❍	❍	❍	●	❍	●	□	❍	□	❍
France	●	●	❍	●	●	●	●	❍	●	❍	●	❍	●	□	❍
Germany	●	❍	□	□	●	□	●	❍	●	□	❍	❍	❍	□	❍
Hungary	□	❍	□	□	❍	❍	●	❍	❍	□	●	□	❍	□	❍
Iceland	●	❍	□	❍	❍	❍	●	❍	●	●	●	□	●	□	□
Israel	●	❍	❍	❍	●	❍	●	❍	●	●	□	□	●	□	□
Italy	●	●	●	●	❍	❍	●	❍	●	●	●	●	●	❍	❍
Japan	●	❍	❍	❍	❍	❍	❍	□	❍	❍	□	□	❍	□	□
Korea	❍	❍	□	●	❍	❍	❍	●	●	●	●	❍	❍	❍	❍
Netherlands	●	❍	□	□	❍	□	❍	□	●	□	❍	□	❍	□	❍
New Zealand	●	❍	●	●	●	●	●	❍	●	●	●	□	●	□	□
Norway	●	❍	□	□	❍	❍	❍	●	●	□	□	□	●	□	□
Portugal	●	●	□	□	●	□	●	●	●	❍	●	●	●	❍	❍
Slovak Republic	●	●	❍	❍	❍	❍	❍	❍	❍	❍	●	❍	●	❍	❍
Slovenia	●	●	□	□	❍	❍	❍	❍	❍	●	●	□	●	□	□
Spain	□	❍	□	□	❍	●	●	❍	❍	□	❍	❍	❍	□	❍
Sweden	●	❍	□	□	●	●	●	❍	❍	❍	❍	❍	❍	□	❍
Switzerland	●	❍	□	❍	●	□	●	□	❍	❍	●	❍	❍	□	□
Turkey	●	●	❍	❍	□	□	□	□	❍	●	❍	□	●	□	□
United Kingdom	●	❍	●	●	❍	❍	❍	❍	●	❍	❍	❍	●	□	❍
United States	●	❍	❍	❍	●	❍	❍	❍	●	❍	❍	❍	❍	❍	❍
OECD total															
● Responsibility of the centre of government (CoG)	25	10	3	6	14	7	16	4	19	7	15	5	14	0	1
❍ Shared responsibility between the CoG and another body	1	18	9	13	13	15	10	20	9	14	10	12	14	6	18
□ Responsibility of another part of government	2	0	16	9	1	6	2	4	0	7	3	11	0	22	9

Note: Data for the Czech Republic, Greece, Ireland, Luxembourg, Mexico and Poland are not available. Only OECD member countries are included in the table.

Source: OECD (2013c), "Questionnaire on the Organisation and Functions of the Centre of Government", GOV/PGC/MPM(2013)3, OECD, Paris, available at: www.oecd.org/officialdocuments/publicdisplaydocumentpdf/?cote=GOV/PGC/MPM(2013)3&docLanguage=En.

- The Ministry of Foreign and European Affairs is responsible for the development of relations with other countries and co-operation with multi-national and international organisations, in particular in the area of foreign and security policy, bilateral relations, economic co-operation, culture, science, technology and education. Its CoG function includes co-ordinating the Slovak Republic's position on EU matters, for which it has 90 staff stationed at the Permanent Delegation to the European Union in Brussels. The Ministry of Foreign and European Affairs operates a government-wide commission that meets weekly to discuss proposals currently being discussed in COREPER I (Comité des représentants permanents) and COREPER II. The MoFaEA also prepares the Slovak Republic's upcoming presidency of the Council of the European Union.
  - In this connection, it will be important to clarify the mandate boundaries between the Government Office and the Ministry of Foreign and European Affairs with respect to managing relations with the EU so as to eliminate the potential for overlap and duplication; at a minimum, the Government Office's responsibility for managing the transposition of EU legislation into national law, and the Ministry of Foreign and European Affairs's mandate of advancing the Slovak Republic's national interests in Brussels before, during and after the EU decision-making process implies that these two CoG institutions need to work closely together and co-ordinate their activities *vis-à-vis* line ministries effectively on an ongoing basis.
- The Ministry of the Interior is *inter alia* tasked to protect the constitutional system, ensure public order and security, and handle migration and the protection of ethnic minorities. Furthermore, it is the authority in charge of the internal administration, including the territorial and administrative structuring of the Slovak Republic. The Ministry of the Interior co-ordinates the ongoing whole-of-government public administration reform in the Slovak Republic, which includes the ESO programme – Effective, open and reliable public administration. The ESO programme aims to streamline local state administration with the aim to make the public administration more effective and facilitate the access to services. In this context, the ministry also leads the steering committee for the co-ordination of public administration reform. Finally, the Ministry of the Interior is the managing authority for the EU Operational Programme Effective Public Administration (OP EPA). The OP EPA aims to support the government-wide public administration reform by supporting investment into the institutional capacities and into the effectiveness of public administration and public services at national, regional and local level, thus contributing to the implementation of reforms, better legal regulation and good governance (Figure 1.4).

Unlike in some OECD countries, the Ministry of Justice is not formally in charge of supporting other ministries with the legislative process and thus does not constitute a centre-of-government institution; rather, it functions as a line ministry. The other line ministries are: the Ministry of the Economy; the Ministry of Transport, Construction and Regional Development; the Ministry of Agriculture; the Ministry of Defence; the Ministry of Labour, Social Affairs and Family; the Ministry of the Environment; the Ministry of Education; the Ministry of Culture; and the Ministry of Health.

The fact that several institutions constitute the CoG in the Slovak Republic is anything but unusual, and mirrors the arrangements in many OECD countries. For example, in the United Kingdom, the Prime Minister's Office, the Cabinet Office and the

Treasury constitute the CoG (House of Commons, 2005: 7). And in Estonia, the CoG consists of the Government Office, the Ministry of Finance, the Ministry of Justice, the Ministry of Economics and the Ministry of the Interior. In any centre consisting of more than one institution, it becomes crucial to ensure effective communication channels and co-ordination mechanisms.

Figure 1.4. **Structure of the Operational Programme Effective Public Administration**

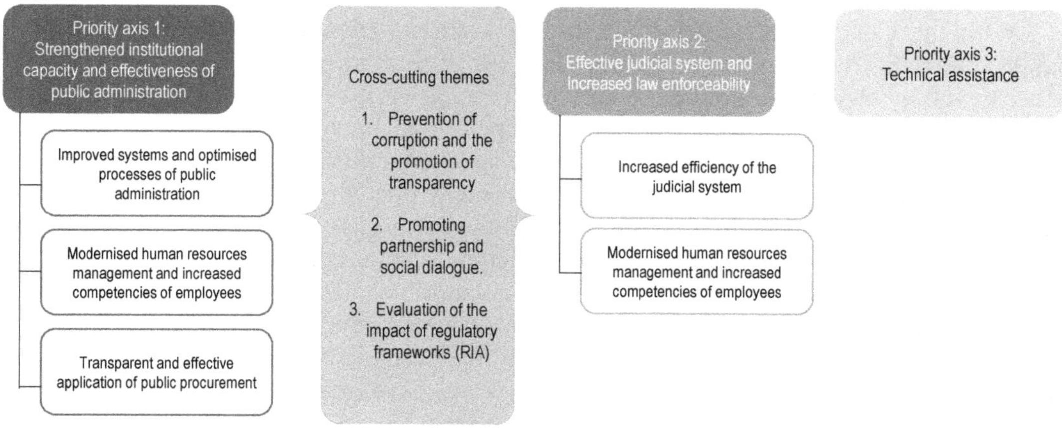

Source: Ministry of the Interior of the Slovak Republic (2015), "Operational Programme Effective Public Administration 2014-2020", www.minv.sk/?operational-programme-effective-public-administration.

Government co-ordination

Public policies usually address needs that cut across traditional ministerial areas of responsibility. Co-ordination, that is promoting coherence in the way government bodies work together, therefore lies at the "heart of the CoG's mission" (Goetz and Margetts, 1999: 436 cited in Alessandro, Lafuente and Santiso, 2013: 10). Co-ordination is crucial both among the CoG institutions themselves and with regard to the line ministries. It should be the norm and encouraged throughout the government, instead of "walking on glass" as described by a senior Slovak official.

Whereas there seem to be frequent exchanges and, generally speaking, good working relations between the four Slovak CoG institutions, their interaction seems to lack a strategic dimension. It appears there is no common understanding or willingness to steer the government systematically. The Government Office – and overall government co-ordination – could benefit from involving the other institutions more closely. It could be particularly relevant to have the Ministry of Finance actively contribute to whole-of-government steering, as it not only controls the fiscal framework but appears to be at the forefront of increasing the government's analytical capabilities (see Chapter 2 for a detailed discussion on strengthening analytical and evaluation capacity, and in particular the sections on the Ministry of Finance's Institute for Financial Policy). Without the support of the other CoG institutions, the Government Office cannot co-ordinate optimally with key line ministries the design and implementation of the political Manifesto in a way that harnesses cross-silo opportunities to achieve integrated policy outcomes for citizens and business.

In early 2015, the Government Office, the Ministry of the Interior and the Ministry of Justice jointly prepared an "Action plan for strengthening of the Slovak Republic as a legally consistent state", which was approved by Government Resolution 403/2015. The action plan consists of three parts: 1) transparency and predictability of the legislative process; 2) corruption as a negative and harmful factor; 3) transparent and effective administration of justice as a solid basis for domestic and foreign investors. While this is obviously a positive development, it remains an *ad hoc* example and is not necessarily representative of the CoG's level of co-ordination in general. Furthermore, it is still too early to tell whether this action plan's implementation has been successful.

With the CoG component institutions not working together as effectively as they could, their ability to overcome the silo-based organisation of the public sector and to steer government-wide strategies is limited. To improve interdepartmental co-operation and information-sharing, the Slovak Republic operates an extensive number of permanent or *ad hoc* co-ordination committees and working groups at the political or expert level. Yet, while ministries and other central government bodies are required to co-operate closely while fulfilling their tasks, both communication and co-operation among them often remain limited or formalistic. Interlocutors from several government bodies highlighted for the OECD review team a number of obstacles: lack of incentives to engage with other government bodies, missing accountability mechanisms and a high level of bureaucracy. Furthermore, it appears that many government officials are not motivated to undertake reforms, as past undertakings have often been poorly designed or simply discarded in favour of new ones after elections. Neither elected officials nor senior public servants provide the necessary leadership to overcome these issues.

Co-ordination is also hampered by the current organisation of the Government Office. According to the 2013 questionnaire, the Government Office's high turnover rate is only matched by Turkey's in the OECD (Table 1.2). This considerably limits the Government Office's ability to guide and steer line ministries.

Table 1.2. **Countries with particularly high levels of turnover following elections**

Country	Turnover
Belgium Chile Portugal United States	26-50%
Brazil Slovak Republic Turkey	More than 50%

Source: OECD (2013c), "Questionnaire on the Organisation and Functions of the Centre of Government", GOV/PGC/MPM(2013)3, OECD, Paris, available at: www.oecd.org/officialdocuments/publicdisplaydocumentpdf/?cote=GOV/PGC/MPM(2013)3&docLanguage=En.

However, some co-ordination arrangements in the Slovak government appear to function well, such as the development of a national position on EU draft legislation or the preparation of the upcoming Slovak presidency of the Council of the European Union, both of which are co-ordinated by the Ministry of Foreign and European Affairs (Box 1.4). Cases like this one have the potential to be scaled up and replicated in other areas. For example, the Government Office could try to apply the formal and informal elements of these well-functioning co-ordination mechanisms when setting the government's annual domestic work programmes or when monitoring their implementation.

Box 1.4. **Preparation of the Council of the European Union presidency: A good practice example from the Ministry of Foreign and European Affairs**

The EU portfolio was transferred from the Government Office to the Ministry of Foreign and European Affairs in 2010. To prepare the Slovak Republic's presidency of the Council of the European Union in the second half of 2016, the Ministry of Foreign and European Affairs created a secretariat consisting of three departments: organisation and logistics, communication and cultural presentation, and horizontal co-ordination.

Already in late 2012, the ministry had established an interdepartmental co-ordination council as an advisory, expert and initiative body for issues concerning the presidency. The council is chaired by the relevant state secretary of the Ministry of Foreign and European Affairs. The other CoG institutions provide the vice-chairmen: the Head of the Government Office, the State Secretary of the Ministry of Finance and the State Secretary of the Ministry of the Interior. All other ministries are represented via state secretaries. Under this council, there are several working groups dealing separately with:

- budget
- HRM, training
- logistics
- communications, presentations, culture, visual, media
- programme content (6 priority clusters have been identified: energy-intensive industry; youth unemployment; cohesion policy; foreign policy focus on eastern partnerships and western Balkans; digital economy; taxes).

What seems to set these co-ordination arrangements apart from others – besides an early start and thorough preparation (for example, the Ministry of Foreign and European Affairs brought all other presidencies to Bratislava so that the Slovak government could learn from their experiences) – is that the Ministry of Foreign and European Affairs managed to create a sense of "common responsibility" across ministries and to establish good personal relations with key contacts in the Ministry of Finance. While this might have been easier to accomplish within the European context, even with the added difficulty of domestic politics, this co-ordination mechanism might serve as a good practice example for other policy areas in the Slovak administration.

Strategic planning processes

Effective strategic planning is key to identifying present and future challenges and opportunities, setting a course for the country, and aligning government resources and capacities with this course of action. Effective planning starts with shared visions and strategies that set strategic objectives to guide policies and programmes. Solid evidence informs strategies and policies to maximise impact. Performance information helps allocate resources according to implementation progress and priorities.

Following each general election in the Slovak Republic, the incoming government submits its political priorities in the form of a Government Manifesto to the National Legislative Council (parliament) for approval. In the case of a single party government – as is the case at the time of writing – the Manifesto is based on the election programme. In the case of coalition governments, the Manifesto is prepared by the advisors representing the parties in the coalition that form the new government. The Government Manifesto covers the entire four-year mandate of the government and defines a series of key, high-level goals (see Box 1.5 for the 2012-16 Government Manifesto). With its goals being mostly sector-based, the Manifesto falls short, however, of developing a strategic vision for the government's term. There is no overarching rationale or organising principle around which the priorities (or "tasks") that the government has set for itself can be justified as strategic priorities for the country to be pursued using human and financial resources paid for by the public. Political guidance on what the government is aiming to achieve strategically for the country and its people and on why citizens should support the allocation of public resources in the pursuit of this endeavour could thus be strengthened. This, in turn, could enable the administration to design, prioritise and implement measures to achieve the government's overarching goals for the country more effectively, particularly if these are not articulated in the Manifesto to begin with.

Box 1.5. **The Slovak Republic's Government Manifesto (2012-16)**

The Government of the Slovak Republic has defined ten key tasks for its four-year mandate.

1. Strengthen the confidence of the people by alleviating the impacts of the crisis.
2. Consolidate public finances in order to bring the general government deficit below 3% of GDP in 2013.
3. Support economic growth and price stability.
4. Reduce the high level of unemployment among the young and systematically tackle the problem of long-term unemployment and, in particular, regional unemployment.
5. Enhance the enforceability of the law and systematically eradicate corruption at all levels of society.
6. Consolidate the public healthcare system, with a particular emphasis on its financial stabilisation.
7. Strengthen the Slovak Republic's share of responsibility for achieving the strategic objectives of the European Union, advance the legitimate interests of the Slovak Republic in the European Union, and use EU funds effectively to modernise and develop the state and society.
8. Foster the economic, social and territorial cohesion of society.
9. Establish long-term trends for the economic, social, environmental, scientific and technological development of the Slovak Republic and for the betterment of the quality of life.
10. Be a government open to all segments of Slovak society, including through the newly established Solidarity and Development Council as a platform for dialogue with social partners.

The Government Manifesto – a document exceeding 60 pages in total – provides more detailed information on each of these ten goals. The information provided is mostly contextual or related to sub-goals and secondary objectives. Concrete ways to measure progress are not specified.

At times, however, the Manifesto does point out how the government intends to achieve its goals, although on a rather general level. As part of the Slovak Republic's foreign policy objectives, for example, the Manifesto reads "The government will support EU enlargement with those countries that meet the criteria for accession. The Slovak Republic will actively contribute to this process by sharing experience from the transformation and integration processes."

Source: Government Office of the Slovak Republic (2012), "Manifesto of the government of the Slovak Republic", May, www.vlada.gov.sk/manifesto-of-the-government-of-the-slovak-republic.

While the Government Manifesto provides general guidance, by itself it is too broad a document to serve as a concrete roadmap for the public administration. The Manifesto is therefore transposed into annual governmental work programmes (which are established in addition to plans on upcoming legislation). These work programmes include information on why each specific measure is proposed, thus illustrating the link to the Government Manifesto or other major (European) strategies. They do not, however, specify strategically how a specific measure would help to advance the government's overarching strategic objectives (particularly since these tend not to be articulated in the Manifesto to begin with), nor do the government work programmes provide any information as to a specific measure's level of strategic priority relative to other planned initiatives.

The transposition of the Manifesto into the work programmes is undertaken by line ministries, which propose measures within their area of competence and based on their own analysis. There seems to be very limited strategic oversight or steering by the Government Office. The Government Office simply aggregates the departmental work plans and ensures that none of their elements are mutually contradictory. There are, however, rules for inter-ministerial consultation on strategy documents, laid out in Government Resolution 645/2014. The private sector and civil society are consulted on national strategies during the inter-ministerial process. The consultation procedures can take many forms: public discussions, representation in working groups, indirect via the Chamber of Commerce, etc. The Office of the Plenipotentiary of the Slovak Government for the Development of Civil Society also contributes to making outside voices heard.

Whereas the Ministry of Finance advises during the preparation of the Government Manifesto on the Manifesto's feasibility and likely impact on the national budget, it does not fulfil a "challenge function", i.e. it cannot block a ministry's project for grounds other than surpassing the budget. In fact, the governmental work plans transfer "specific substantive responsibility" to individual ministries and heads of other government bodies. This is reflected in individual ministries being responsible for securing sufficient financial resources for single-sector or multi-sector strategies they are leading. There does not appear to be an institutionalised co-operation between the Government Office, as the main CoG institution with responsibility for planning, and the Ministry of Finance with regard to how best to align the government budget with the government strategy and priorities.As a European Union member state, the Slovak Republic also prepares an annual National Reform Programme. This document, which is prepared by the Ministry of Finance, translates the EU 2020 objectives into national targets and constitutes an important strategic document in the broad areas of economic development and structural policies. These targets are clearly identified and progress is measured over time. In fact, one section is dedicated to track the progress of measures implemented as part of the National Reform Programme from the previous year. Given that these goals and targets are quite broad and span several sectors, the document resembles a detailed Government Manifesto. Whereas the Slovak National Reform Programme makes reference to the Manifesto on two occasions, the relationship between those two documents is not made clear. In fact, the Slovak National Reform Programme does not mention the European Union at all and only refers to the EU 2020 strategy (Box 1.6).

In addition to the short- and medium-term plans, the Slovak Republic indicated that in 2010 ministries and the Slovak Academy of Sciences prepared an outlook spanning the next 30 years. This outlook, however, does not seem to have had much impact on policy making and thus falls short of a long-term strategic vision that can serve as a guiding framework for government action. Also, it appears to have been a one-off project, with no long-term strategic foresight or horizon-scanning being undertaken on a continuous basis at the central level. With the exception of a few analytical centres, such as the Ministry of Finance's Institute for Financial Policy, the necessary skills to undertake such planning do not appear to exist yet in the Slovak government.

Box 1.6. The EU 2020 Strategy

Europe 2020 is the European Union's growth strategy for the period up to 2020. It is based on five set objectives, each with concrete targets for the EU as a whole. These five objectives focus on:

1. Employment: 70% of 20-64 year olds to be employed.
2. Innovation: 3% of EU GDP (public and private combined) to be invested in R&D/innovation.
3. Education: reducing school drop-out rates to below 10%; at least 40% of 30-34 year olds completing tertiary education.
4. Poverty/social exclusion: at least 20 million less people in or at risk of poverty and social exclusion.
5. Climate/energy: greenhouse gas emissions 20% (or even 30% if the conditions are right) lower than in 1990. Twenty percent of energy from renewables; 20% increase in energy efficiency.

The EU-level targets are translated into national targets for each member country. Each member country has adopted its own national targets in each of these areas.

Achieving the goals of the Europe 2020 strategy requires reinforced surveillance to address key macroeconomic challenges, and a thematic approach to speed up growth-enhancing structural reforms. Monitoring by the European Commission and Council is organised around the so-called "European Semester". This starts with the publication of the Annual Growth Survey. The spring meeting of the European Council, based on the Annual Growth Survey, takes stock of the overall macroeconomic situation, progress towards the five EU-level targets, and progress under the flagship initiatives. It provides policy orientations covering fiscal, macroeconomic and structural reform and growth-enhancing areas, and advises on linkages between them.

Member countries then present their medium-term budgetary strategies in their Stability and Convergence Programmes and set out actions to be undertaken (e.g. in employment, research, innovation, energy and social inclusion) in their national reform programmes. In April, these two documents are sent to the European Commission for assessment. Based on the European Commission's assessment, the Council issues country-specific guidance to member countries in June/July. This means that policy advice is given to member countries before they start to finalise their draft budgets for the following year.

Where recommendations are not acted on within the given timeframe, policy warnings can be issued. There is also an option for enforcement through incentives and sanctions in the case of excessive macroeconomic and budgetary imbalances.

The EU monitors developments on three fronts: macroeconomic factors, growth-enhancing reforms and public finances.

Source: OECD (2012), *Slovenia: Towards a Strategic and Efficient State*, OECD Public Governance Reviews, OECD Publishing, Paris, http://dx.doi.org/10.1787/9789264173262-en.

These issues, in fact, represent missed opportunities for the government: clearly articulating a strategic rationale for what the government wishes to achieve for the country over the life of its mandate, notably in the context of its membership in the

European Union, for why it wishes to pursue these objectives, how it intends to pursue them and with what kind of public resources, represents an important opportunity for the government to enhance its accountability to citizens and heighten the transparency with which it intends to allocate and expend resources to achieve its objectives, thereby contributing to improving the public's trust in the government and its institutions.

Box 1.7. **Sustainable Governance Indicators: The Slovak Republic's strategic capacity**

To measure and compare countries' ability to sustainably solve the increasingly difficult problems and challenges of today's world, the Bertelsmann Foundation has developed the Sustainable Governance Indicators (SGI) project. Based on both qualitative and quantitative data, scores are allocated to countries in three broad areas (policy performance, democracy and governance), which are again divided into several sub-categories.

One of the sub-categories of governance is executive capacity, which itself includes a "strategic capacity" indicator aiming to show "How much influence do strategic planning units and bodies have on government decision making?" In line with OECD's observations, the Slovak Republic only scored four out of ten in the Sustainable Governance Indicators.

The institutional capacity for strategic planning in the Slovak Republic is weak. Capacities for planning in the ministries are limited, and there is no central policy planning unit in the Government Office. The strengthening of the expertise of the Government Office and the creation of the Solidarity and Development Council, a new advisory body, under the second Fico government failed to improve planning capacities in any substantial way. Due to the Fico government's initial emphasis on fiscal consolidation, the role of the Institute of Financial Policy, a research institute affiliated with the Ministry of Finance, has increased. However, the institute has taken a relatively narrow fiscal perspective and has focused on the short to medium term rather than on the long term.

Source: Sustainable Governance Indicators (2015), www.sgi-network.org/2015/Slovakia.; www.sgi-network.org/2015/Governance/Executive_Capacity/Strategic_Capacity/Strategic_Planning.

Implementation and evaluation

To steer and monitor policies successfully, governments need to be able to chart their course. Performance measurement tracks policy implementation, identifies successes and failures, and produces the information that is needed to allocate resources, design new policies and guide implementation. Periodic reviews of specific policies can provide more in-depth analysis of performance and help assess the continuing relevance of specific policy. In addition, monitoring and evaluation enhance transparency and contribute to strengthening the accountability bond between governments and citizens, thus helping to build trust. The need for the CoG to provide accurate information to the political level on progress with implementation – successes and failures – assumes some mastery of the detail of spending and results across a large range of policy areas.

In the Slovak Republic, the Government Office monitors progress in implementing the annual work programme and provides quarterly updates to the government. The software-supported monitoring is described as detailed, looking not only at outputs but at outcomes. While the annual work programmes should reflect the Government Manifesto, there is no systematic monitoring of the Manifesto's implementation itself. For that, the current type of Manifesto is too vague; it does not include measurable performance goals or targets.

Figure 1.5. **Responsibility for monitoring implementation in OECD countries**

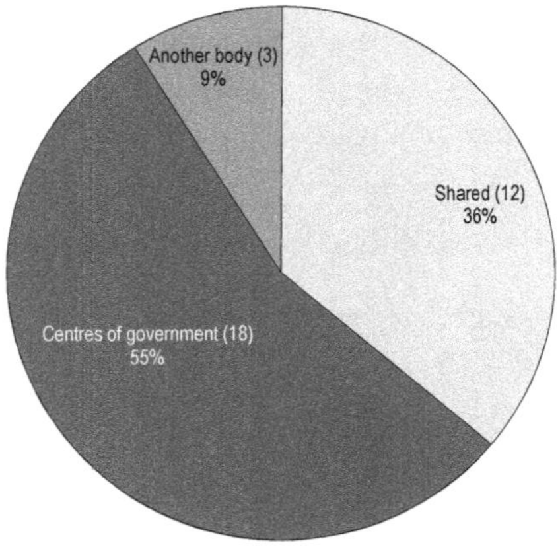

Source: OECD (2014a), "Centre stage: Driving better policies from the centre of government", OECD, Paris, www.oecd.org/gov/centre-stage-report.pdf.

There are inspections to monitor the implementation of the work programme – so-called monitoring days. These days consist of the Prime Minister – having been briefed by his/her advisors beforehand – visiting a ministry and, if necessary, drawing up an action plan. Such a high-level visit can send a powerful political message, yet could ideally be complemented by continuous engagement on the working level to make sure that both main developments and important details are on track. Currently, the Government Office seems to have limited capacity to ensure this. Unlike in some other countries, there is no dedicated body to ensure the government delivers on its key priorities through systematic performance assessment and monitoring.

Outcome-based monitoring and evaluation in general could be enhanced with more robust government-wide key indicators. Available indicators usually stem from EU requirements, but not enough useful indicators are collected at the national level. For example, the Europe 2020 strategy constitutes the main case of longer term monitoring. Participants of the OECD workshop on "Government Co-ordination and Strategy" pointed out that a strategic framework for indicators would be helpful – especially for monitoring progress achieved on meeting long-term goals. The development of such a framework and additional indicators is contingent on increasing ministries' analytical capacities; this issue thus links to Chapter 2 on strengthening analytical and evaluation capacity.

Assessment

The OECD has identified a number of issues to be addressed in order to improve the Slovak Republic's CoG's capacity to lead, set, steer and co-ordinate government activities and strategies. As reforms of the centre affect – and depend on – the administration as a whole, any such reform needs to be embedded in the wider public administration context. However, it appears that insufficient recognition of the need for comprehensive public administration reform both within the Slovak government and, most probably among citizens as well, is widespread. With the Slovak economy doing relatively well, public administration reform and its benefits do not appear to constitute a priority issue outside those administrative units that are responsible for designing and implementing it.

Box 1.8. Implementing performance budgeting in Austria: Monitoring performance and focusing on results

There are several ways in which countries carry out "performance budgeting", as illustrated by the richness of examples across the OECD. No country, however, practices it the same way or perfectly for that matter. Austria underwent reforms to develop a binding medium-term perspective for the budget and pragmatically link resources to results. Prior to the reforms, Austria had been facing traditional budgeting challenges, including:

- a short-sighted annual approach without a medium-, let alone long-, term perspective
- budget discussions that focused on ministries' expenditure, but barely on results in light of policy decisions for citizens
- a cash-based system which did not provide a full picture of public finances
- a lack of incentives and sanctions to foster appropriate fiscal behaviour in spending ministries and administrative units.

One of the most important reforms focuses on performance, linking resources to results:

- Each ministry defines a maximum of five outcomes, covered by the budget decision in parliament. These outcomes define the strategy of the ministry. Each outcome has to be justified and explained: Why has this outcome been chosen? How will it be achieved? What is the benchmark for success? The outcomes are not only addressed in the annual budget but also in the medium-term expenditure framework, which links performance information in the medium-term perspective to the annual budget.
- Each ministry contains a number of global budgets (e.g. schools in the Ministry of Education; labour market in the Ministry of Social Affairs). For each, a maximum of five outputs are defined, which form part of the budget decision. These outputs have to be directly attributable to the general outcomes of the ministry as defined in the budget.
- In order to connect resources to results at each level of the administration, resources and results are defined not only for each ministry's global budget, but for each of the ministry's discreet administrative units. Thus, resources and performance information covering all levels of the federal budget are presented within a single budget document.

To make sure that every public servant who deals with the budget is aware of the potential for improvement in the relevant general budget, the Court of Audit may add a set of brief summary recommendations. Thus, the annual budget document provides three basic types of information: resources, performance information and recommendations of the Court of Audit, thereby giving a comprehensive picture of all of the relevant information necessary for members of parliament and the public to interpret the budget documentation effectively.

To reduce the risk either of a lack of ambition when formulating the objectives or possible tensions between objectives in interrelated political areas, the Chancellery was given a co-ordinating role in formulating the objectives. This role is restricted to monitoring and advice. Due to the Austrian constitutional framework, the Chancellery cannot force line ministries to accept specific outcomes and outputs.

The Austrian reform focuses on results. This strengthens the budget as the government's central planning document. Ministers have to decide on their priorities and communicate them in a transparent and binding way. Members of parliament have to vote not only on resources, but on defined performance results. This will curb and strengthen the strategic dimension of policy making. It will be a challenge for politicians, civil servants and the public to interact with the new system to ensure that its intended effects are fully achieved.

Source: OECD (2015c), *OECD Public Governance Reviews: Estonia and Finland. Fostering Strategic Capacity Across Governments and Digital Services Across Borders*, OECD Publishing, Paris, http://dx.doi.org/10.1787/9789264229334-en.

The government could therefore consider further stepping up its communication efforts in order to raise awareness of the challenges and to convince stakeholders of the need for reform. It will be particularly important to get support from elected officials and senior civil servants across the administration, from the legislative branch more generally, and from citizens and business, as this will be crucial for the reform's successful and sustainable implementation. While limited in scope, the Ministry of the Interior's user satisfaction surveys of its redesigned services could be used as a starting point for showcasing the added value of the public administration reforms. To communicate effectively the need for more strategic governance reforms, it might be helpful to specify or even quantify the benefits and cost savings of a particular measure that will be adopted to implement them.

Centre-of-government institutions and whole-of-government co-ordination

The recognition by the government that its CoG is polycentric can have profound implications on the way in which the Government Office interacts with the other components of the CoG apparatus, because a more robust, integrated working relationship between CoG components that is sustained on an ongoing basis can improve the relationship between national strategy development, national budget setting and strategic workforce planning for the government as a whole. This, in turn, can ensure that the government's capacity to monitor and evaluate its strategic policy performance can be carried out in a way that integrates human and financial resource capacity into its performance assessment, thus providing a much more holistic view of the government's performance against the achievement of policy and financial results, while greatly enhancing its ability to remain accountable to the public.

Intra-governmental co-ordination and co-operation appears to be relatively weak. The centre-of-government institutions need to work more closely together on an ongoing basis in order to effectively steer strategy, co-ordinate the contribution of line ministries to developing and implementing this strategy, and achieve a whole-of-government approach to policy making and implementation. Most crucially, the influential Ministry of Finance could be better integrated into whole-of-government decision making as a key component of the centre of government. It would also be advisable to strengthen the Government Office, whose co-ordination capacity would benefit from additional human and financial resources. The line ministries would have to contribute to overcoming the current sectionalism and find better ways to co-operate and co-ordinate. There are good examples of co-ordination in the Slovak Republic which could be replicated, such as the Ministry of Foreign and European Affairs' co-ordination on EU matters or the Government Office's own co-ordination of EU funds (see above). In particular, it would be crucial to improve co-ordination with regard to the development and implementation of the Government Manifesto and the annual work programmes.

To increase the level of co-operation across the public administration and sustain it into the future, it would be important to invest in a more stable, professional civil service and to create a community of senior officials. The current situation in the Slovak Republic with most senior managers being replaced after a change in government and low mobility across government bodies is not conducive to a culture of productive government-wide co-operation. The government could therefore consider managing civil servants, in particular senior ones, in a way that builds collegiate leadership and fosters cross-departmental co-operation (see Chapter 3 for further information on this topic).

Box 1.9. **Reflections on the centre of government: The case of the United Kingdom**

The United Kingdom, arguably one of the leading countries with regard to public administration and governance, has repeatedly reflected upon its centre of government.

In 2005, a House of Commons report examined "the institutional structure of the Cabinet Office, no 10 Downing Street and HM Treasury in the period since 1997, and look[ed] at the debate about whether the government needs a strong centre."

In 2014, a Committee of Public Accounts report added to the assessment and issued a series of recommendations:

However, there is a lack of clarity about the centre's precise role, particularly the respective responsibilities of the Cabinet Office, HM Treasury and the Prime Minister's Office (Number 10), and how they work together as a coherent centre. The centre sometimes intervenes to address issues with high-priority government programmes, but has too often failed to do so effectively or at an early enough stage. In part, this is because the centre does not have a joined-up single view of strategic risks across government, meaning it is often reactive in its response rather than able to anticipate potentially serious problems. There are gaps in key skills at the centre and across departments, such as financial management capability and contracting expertise, which are compounded because government repeatedly fails to learn lessons and share good practice from past experience. (House of Commons, 2014)

The report recommends to clearly define:

- the role of the centre as one integrated capability
- the respective roles and responsibilities of the Cabinet Office, the Treasury and the Prime Minister's Office
- how these three bodies work together
- how the centre works with other central government departments.

Source: House of Commons (2005), "The centre of government – No. 10, the Cabinet Office and HM Treasury", *House of Commons Library Research Papers*, No. 05/92, London, available at: http://researchbriefings.parliament.uk/ResearchBriefing/Summary/RP05-92; House of Commons (2014), "The centre of government", Committee of Public Accounts, 19th Report of Session 2014-15, London, available at: www.parliament.uk/business/committees/committees-a-z/commons-select/public-accounts-committee/news/report-on-centre-of-government.

Strategic planning processes

The Slovak centre of government, in particular the Government Office, could take a more strategic and proactive approach to implementing the Government Manifesto and to monitoring its performance. In this regard it:

- The centre of government could prepare the annual work programmes in co-operation with line ministries. Moving this leadership responsibility from the line ministries to the CoG while enhancing the partnership relationship between the CoG and the line ministries could not only foster a whole-of-government approach but also allow for the definition and adjudication of clearer whole-of-government strategic priorities. Line ministries obviously need to be closely involved in this process so that the government's work plan reflects sector issues and priorities, and so that line ministries can effectively translate the government's work programme into individual institutional work plans.

- Both the government-wide work programme as well as the individual work plans could be based on more robust, outcome-based performance information and informed by the results of strategic foresight. These could be tasks for the emerging analytical centres, potentially also for an analytical centre of the Government Office, which could also engage in co-ordinating the strategic foresight efforts of line ministry analytical centres and integrating the results of this activity coherently into medium-term whole-of-government strategy (for more information, see Chapter 2).

Box 1.10. **Breaking up governmental silos: The case of Slovenia**

There are many causes for governmental silos, which can be defined as public bodies working on their own without having established efficient communicating and co-operation measures. In Slovenia, the following causes – both of administrative or political nature – have been identified:

Administrative/managerial reasons include:

- strong line ministries' bureaucracies, following their own agendas
- lack of awareness and lack of a culture of co-operation – "silo mentality"
- lack of competence
- lack of procedural and organisational arrangements.

Political reasons include:

- unclear, vague or weak coalition agreements, government strategies, etc.
- lack of prioritisation
- political ambitions of individual ministers
- lack of team spirit and/or lack of a culture of co-operation in the government
- lack of strategic leadership by the head of government and the CoG
- strong lobbies imposing their agendas.

To mitigate the risk of governmental silos, Slovenia correspondingly took countermeasures on both the administrative and political levels. The government established clear working arrangements and accountability structures for priority cross-cutting areas. These procedures included, for example, the requirement to report on inter-ministerial co-ordination when tabling new legislation. Furthermore, the government invested in team building, training and improving competence within civil service in order to constantly improve a culture of co-operation and mutual trust. On the political level, both the Prime Minister and senior civil servants provided support and helped to raise awareness across the administration.

Source: Virant, G. (2015), Presentation by former Minister of Public Administration, OECD Workshop on Government Co-ordination and Strategy, Bratislava, 9-10 April.

Improving co-ordination and strategy-setting could better align budgetary allocations with government priorities. In line with the 2015 OECD *Recommendation of the Council on Budgetary Governance* (Box 1.21), the Slovak government could task the Government Office and the Ministry of Finance with ensuring that strategic priorities are sufficiently financed in the national budget. It is here that the co-ordination deficits among CoG institutions, as identified in the section above, are most evident. The Ministry of

Finance – in close co-ordination with the Government Office – could play a much stronger and more strategic role.

Box 1.11. **OECD Principles of Good Budgetary Governance, Principle 2**

Closely align budgets with the medium-term strategic priorities of government, through:

- developing a stronger medium-term dimension in the budgeting process, beyond the traditional annual cycle
- organising and structuring the budget allocations in a way that corresponds readily with national objectives
- recognising the potential usefulness of a medium-term expenditure framework (MTEF) in setting a basis for the annual budget, in an effective manner which: 1) has real force in setting boundaries for the main categories of expenditure for each year of the medium-term horizon; 2) is fully aligned with the top-down budgetary constraints agreed by government; 3) is grounded upon realistic forecasts for baseline expenditure (i.e. using existing policies), including a clear outline of key assumptions used; 4) shows the correspondence with expenditure objectives and deliverables from national strategic plans; and 5) includes sufficient institutional incentives and flexibility to ensure that expenditure boundaries are respected
- nurturing a close working relationship between the central budget authority and the other institutions at the centre of government (e.g. Prime Minister's Office, Cabinet Office or planning ministry), given the inter-dependencies between the budget process and the achievement of government-wide policies
- considering how to devise and implement regular processes for reviewing existing expenditure policies, including tax expenditures [...], in a manner that helps budgetary expectations to be set in line with government-wide developments.

Source: OECD (2015d), *Recommendation of the Council on Budgetary Governance*, OECD, Paris, www.oecd.org/gov/budgeting/Recommendation-of-the-Council-on-Budgetary-Governance.pdf.

Implementation and evaluation

The principal planning document of the Slovak Republic, the Government Manifesto, is currently not being closely monitored against the achievement of strategic outcomes as it is being implemented by the government. The Government Office could therefore be tasked to monitor and report on progress toward achieving specific strategic policy outcomes on a regular basis to the political leadership, parliament and the general public. This could enable the government to adjust policies and measures in the case of unsatisfactory success. A similar monitoring system, on a more detailed basis, could be established for the annual work programmes, building on the work the Ministry of Finance's Institute for Financial Policy (IFP, see below) has been pursuing in developing sets of indicators to monitor progress in different areas. For example, to monitor and evaluate progress in the education system, the IFP has proposed a detailed set of indicators as a supporting mechanism to measure the impact of budgetary expenditures in education. It would appear, however, that these indicators are not yet used extensively by policy makers. Lessons learnt could be communicated and fed into the development of future Government Manifestos and annual work programmes.

In order to strengthen the Government Office's monitoring capacities, it could be beneficial to establish a dedicated monitoring unit. This unit would build on and support the existing practice of implementation days by measuring progress on a continuous basis. It would be important not to give such a unit too broad a scope but rather to have it focus on a limited number of key cross-governmental priorities. As the success of such a unit depends very much on its support from the political leadership and its ability to establish reliable and trusted relationships with other government bodies, it is crucial to select a well-connected and able Head of Unit and to provide him/her with direct access to either the Head of the Government Office or the Prime Minister himself/herself.

Box 1.12. **Delivery units: Finding new ways to improve implementation**

To improve policy implementation and achieve the government's main goals, the United Kingdom developed an approach dubbed Deliverology. The initial approach had three key components: "establishing a small team focused on performance [the delivery unit], gathering performance data to set targets and trajectories, and having routines to drive and ensure a focus on performance" (Barber, Kihn and Moffit, 2011). More than 15 countries have established delivery units at the national level, but there are also a few at state level (e.g. Maryland, United States) and at local level (Borough of Haringey, London). The World Bank, too, established a President's Delivery Unit in 2014.

While delivery units can be a useful tool to increase implementation, they are no panacea. In fact, they need to be adapted most carefully to the institutional framework within a country in order to have a positive impact. Gold (2014) has identified both the main types of delivery units as well as conditions for their success: Delivery units vary with regard to their scope, mostly with regard to what kind of priorities are being tracked (few vs many; service delivery vs high-priority outcomes) and how problems are being solved (stocktakes with the head of government; policy/innovation labs; in-house consultancy work). In order for a delivery unit to be successful, it is important that its scope is well-defined and, ideally, quite narrow. Most crucially, however, the success of a delivery unit depends on the ability of the centre of government to co-ordinate the work of line ministries and on the unit's own ability to establish good working relationships with the counterparts in other government bodies.

Examples of delivery units include:

- United Kingdom: In 2001, then Prime Minister Blair set up the first Delivery Unit, headed by Sir Michael Barber. The unit, which had about 40 staff, was first part of the Cabinet Office and later transferred to the Treasury (Ministry of Finance). The unit tracked progress on, and removed obstacles to, the delivery of a very limited number of policy priorities. It also worked with line ministries to identify and overcome implementation challenges. The Delivery Unit was abolished in 2010, following a change in government. In 2012, however, a new Implementation Unit was established in the Cabinet Office. The Implementation Unit adapted a more flexible approach, focusing more on departmental capability than on pure monitoring. Its scope has also been broadened.
- Australia: The Cabinet Implementation Unit in the Department of the Prime Minister and Cabinet, established in 2003 as a fairly small unit of around ten staff, works with Australian government departments and agencies to ensure that the Australian government's decisions are implemented on time, on budget and to expectations. The unit seeks to ensure that policy prepared for consideration by the Prime Minister and Cabinet has clear goals, a robust assessment of costs and benefits, and clarity about how it will be implemented. The unit helps departments and agencies to prepare their implementation plans and to identify, assess and manage implementation risks. The unit also monitors the progress of the implementation of key government decisions and reports to the Prime Minister and Cabinet on the status of these decisions.

For further information on delivery units, please see OECD (forthcoming) and Gold (2014); the World Bank's "Global Partnership for Strategic Delivery" network might also be of interest.

Sources: Barber, M., P. Kihn and A. Moffit (2011), "Deliverology. From idea to implementation", McKinsey & Company; Gold, J. (2014), "International delivery: Centres of government and the drive for better policy implementation", *Mowat Research Papers*, No. 96, Mowat Centre, School of Public Policy & Governance, University of Toronto, Toronto, Ontario, Canada, www.instituteforgovernment.org.uk/sites/default/files/publications/International%20Delivery%20report.pdf.

In order for any monitoring to be effective, it would be necessary to invest in high-quality outcome-based indicators. Again, the Slovak Republic can build on the experience of existing good practices within its own administration. For example, the Ministry of Finance uses a series of very useful indicators, including time series, to track progress on the National Reform Programme. Other EU indicators might also be adapted to the Slovak context. It would then also be necessary to improve the quality of data collection across the government, a task that the ministries' analytical units could be mandated to pursue. While each ministry would obviously develop indicators within its field of competency, it would be important to agree on a set of common principles in order to allow for comparisons. For a detailed description of how to measure progress on pre-defined objectives, please see Chapter 2, in particular Box 2.3, and OECD (2013b).

Box 1.13. **Monitoring government performance: The case of Colombia's SINERGIA**

Colombia has developed and refined a comprehensive information system to monitor and evaluate whether the country is reaching its main goals. This system has allowed the country to discuss its priorities as well as to identify its biggest challenges. Through it Colombia has integrated all of the information from the different entities and sectors, with diverse indicators, clear guidelines and targets. Through a complete set of indicators, the government has developed user-friendly dashboards and traffic lights to display the information.

The Colombian Constitution requires that all public policies be monitored and evaluated, and SINERGIA is the national system responsible for these tasks. SINERGIA is led by the Directorate of Public Policy Evaluation within the National Planning Department and the Presidency of the Republic. SINERGIA must be implemented by all sub-national governments, with the aim of aligning municipal and departmental policy interventions and investment agendas with those of the National Development Plan (this monitoring component is called SINERGIA TERRITORIAL). SINERGIA measures the progress and goals of the projects included in the National Development Plan through three main tools:

1. SISMEG (monitoring): A set of performance indicators which measures policy outputs and outcomes as identified by the National Development Plan (roughly the Colombian equivalent to the Slovak Government Manifesto). The system is built following a pyramidal structure with three main levels: strategic, sector and management. Strategic indicators are at the top and are related to the main government pillars as stated in the National Development Plan. These are followed up by the President and the Council of Ministers. Sector indicators describe sector-specific goals and are monitored by the President and each minister in bilateral meetings and within each ministry. Finally, management indicators are standard indicators that are measured for all of the entities to track institutional efficiency.
2. SISDEVAL (*Sistema Nacional de Evaluaciones*): A system to evaluate the outcomes of the main public policies and programmes implemented within the framework of the National Development Plan. Every year, the policies that will be evaluated are elected by a committee of the Department of National Planning (DNP) and approved by the National Commission on Economic and Social Policy (CONPES). Policies are evaluated by a recognised, experienced third party (consultancy) so as to guarantee objectivity and transparency in the process. Since the creation of SISDEVAL, the number of evaluations has increased significantly, from one evaluation in 2003 to 32 in 2011.
3. Polls: Nation-wide polls are carried out periodically so as to compare public perception and government results. The results of the polls are public and can be found on the SISDEVAL website. Surveys measure perception of the way the government is achieving the goals it has set.

Box 1.13. **Monitoring government performance: The case of Colombia's SINERGIA** *(continued)*

In the beginning, SINERGIA focused on central government management only; in 2004, its scope was broadened to include the monitoring of territorial management and decentralised entities. It now provides information on the overall performance of public policies across all levels of government in Colombia. However, at the territorial level, performance management implementation remains relatively underdeveloped. In 2009, methodological guidelines were approved focusing on performance management at the sub-national level; a network of regional officials was created to encourage the exchange of good practices in the field of performance management.

Through SINERGIA, follow-up is readily available. The presidency, the government and citizens can follow up on the government's performance. It is an essential tool for building trust in government.

Source: OECD (2013d), *Colombia: Implementing Good Governance*, OECD Public Governance Reviews, OECD Publishing, Paris, http://dx.doi.org/10.1787/9789264202177-en.

Recommendations

Based on the assessment above, the OECD recommends strengthening the core centre-of-government institution – the Government Office – so that it can take a more systematic and active approach to co-ordinating whole-of-government policy making. However, this approach by no means implies creating in the Government Office some sort of overbearing, centralised "task-master" bent on concentrating power, whose mandate would be to "dictate" policy and actions to the rest of the government. This is also not meant to imply that line ministry competencies or line ministry enabling legislation be modified in any way. To the contrary, increasing the competencies and capabilities of the Government Office will only result in better government co-ordination if the Government Office manages to become a valued partner and interlocutor for the other CoG institutions as well as for line ministries. To achieve this, it will be crucial to communicate the necessity for reform and to invest in building and sustaining a government-wide culture of co-operation and collaboration.

Improved co-operation in turn can greatly facilitate addressing the other three main challenges the Slovak CoG is currently facing: 1) improving strategic planning to achieve multi-dimensional policy outcomes; 2) linking strategy to budget considerations to make sure that financial resources are properly assigned to achieve strategic results – and seen by the public as being so assigned; and 3) supporting and monitoring policy implementation to improve the government's capacity to achieve these results.

Pursuing these tasks effectively could benefit from the creation of a dedicated unit within the Government Office, such as an analytical unit in charge of advising the incoming government on the Manifesto, managing its translation into government work programmes, and monitoring and supporting their implementation government-wide. This unit could work in partnership with its analogous units in the other CoG institutions and in the key line ministries across the government.

The OECD thus makes the following recommendations in order to improve the Slovak Republic's centre-of-government policy-setting, steering and performance monitoring capacity:

Whole-of-government co-ordination

- Define the Slovak Republic's centre of government as polycentric, in recognition of the fact that in addition to the Government Office, the Ministry of Finance, the Ministry of Foreign and European Affairs, and the Ministry of the Interior also fulfil important transversal functions. This definition could be communicated broadly across the public administration to ensure that the CoG as a polycentric driver of whole-of-government strategy is well understood in line ministries and agencies across the system – and more generally by citizens and business.
- Strengthen and reinforce co-operation and co-ordination among the CoG institutions and between the CoG institutions and the public administration as a whole. Crucially, this could contribute to overcoming the existing silo-based approach to government, while ensuring that policy and spending are better linked and potential overlap and duplication reduced, thus improving the government's capacity to assess spending performance against the achievement of strategic policy outcomes. This could also ensure that a strengthened Government Office is not perceived by other government bodies as an adversary but as a true partner.
  - In this connection, ensure that the mandate boundaries between the Government Office and the Ministry of Foreign and European Affairs with respect to managing relations with the EU are clear and well communicated across the public administration; at a minimum, the Government Office's responsibility for managing the transposition of EU legislation into national law, and the Ministry of Foreign and European Affairs' mandate of advancing the Slovak Republic's national interests in Brussels before, during and after the EU decision-making process, implies that these two CoG institutions need to work closely together and co-ordinate their activities *vis-à-vis* line ministries effectively on an ongoing basis.
- Strengthen the Government Office's co-ordination capacity by explicitly confirming its mandate and leadership role in this area, allowing it to lead whole-of-government strategy and priority policy setting and steering exercises effectively. Enabling the Government Office in co-operation with the other CoG institutions to lead the co-ordination function of defining and steering of government-wide policy priorities could contribute to improving overall government coherence and implementation capacity.
- Develop a communication strategy to explain the co-ordination role of the centre-of-government institutions and the need for CoG reform so as to ensure that line ministries understand that they are exercising their sector-specific mandates as part of a coherent, integrated government-specific strategy. At the same time, confirm to line ministries that their competencies as set down in legislation are not being affected in this process. Mandate the Government Office to lead this exercise. It would be important to target this strategy at both citizens and the public administration, particularly the senior civil service. This could raise awareness of the CoG's institutional make up and mandate, and stimulate understanding and buy-in for greater cross-silo co-operation on important

multi-sector national strategic initiatives, including the design and implementation of the Manifesto itself.

Strategic planning processes

- Strengthen the Government Office's role with regard to strategic planning and the work programme. While the Government Office is in charge of planning and the work programme, many tasks are *de facto* being carried out by the line ministries. A more proactive Government Office could continue to gather inputs from line ministries but could set the work programme according to whole-of-government priorities.
- Consider framing the Government Manifesto around a small number of key, overarching strategic priorities under which the "tasks" could be organised. Such a narrative can be both a powerful communication tool and a way to evaluate progress at the end of a political term.
- Develop the annual work programmes with a clear, strategic hierarchy of goals in mind. Not all tasks in a government work programme are of equal importance. Stating the priorities creates clarity about the intentions of the government and contributes to focusing efforts on, and allocating human and financial resources against, the most important priority tasks.
- Make explicit how a specific measure in the work programme is supposed to achieve the strategic priorities identified in the Government Manifesto. The Government Manifesto could thus play an important role after its adoption. Furthermore, policy makers would need to convince the CoG that the proposed measure indeed contributes to the implementation of the whole-of-government strategy.
- Create linkages between strategic planning and budgeting, thus strengthening the means by which the government can achieve its policy agenda through the judicious allocation of human and financial resources. This can only be achieved through close co-operation between the Government Office and the Ministry of Finance.
- Use strategic foresight and horizon-scanning to inform government strategies and work programmes. Capacity could be vested in an analytical centre at the Government Office (see immediately below), working in close co-operation with the other analytical centres (see Chapter 2).

Strategic planning governance

- Consider establishing an analytical unit in the Government Office, focusing on whole-of-government strategy as well as the work programme. Such a unit could be staffed partly by Government Office and Ministry of Finance experts. It is important to stress that such an analytical unit would need to be built up slowly and carefully. It could first manage the translation of the Government Manifesto into the annual work programmes. At a later stage, it could look at strategic foresight.

Implementation, evaluation and public accountability

- Strengthen whole-of-government performance monitoring and assessment capacity. For the centre of government, in particular the Government Office and the Ministry of Finance, to exercise its mandate in strategy setting and implementation, it needs reliable outcomes-based performance information to be able to determine whether policies are working, and if not, change course so that they do end up achieving the results they were designed and adopted to achieve. High-quality, comparable indicators could be developed to monitor progress and evaluate the impact of government policies and measures against expected results for citizens and businesses. The Government Office could thus reinforce its existing monitoring unit (or create a new one within the analytical unit – see above), mandating it to track policy implementation against the achievement of strategic outcomes for citizens and businesses, in addition to assessing implementation against annual outputs, as it does now. This unit could be mandated to act as the government's central co-ordination and communication hub; in so doing, it could monitor on an ongoing basis progress being made on the small number of key government-wide priorities identified in the Manifesto using the performance monitoring evidence it generates, while drawing upon performance data provided by the analytical centres. The data generated by such a monitoring unit could provide the political leadership with real-time information on the government's performance and enable it to address potential difficulties earlier and more effectively.
- Mandate the Government Office to provide parliament and the general public with annual reports on the implementation of the Government Manifesto. These reports could embed analytical units' quantitative and qualitative outcomes-based performance analysis within a whole-of-government policy narrative. Debates on these reports, in turn, could increase citizens' engagement on the Government Manifesto and would represent a means to hold the government publicly accountable.

Bibliography

Alessandro, M., M. Lafuente and C. Santiso (2013), "The role of the centre of government: A literature review", *IDB Technical Note*, IDB-TN-581, Inter-American Development Bank, September, available at: www.iadb.org/wmsfiles/products/publications/documents/38051851.pdf.

Barber, M., P. Kihn and A. Moffit (2011), "Deliverology. From idea to implementation", McKinsey & Company.

European Commission (2015), "Country report Slovakia 2015", Commission Staff Working Document, COM(2015)85 final, European Commission, Brussels, available at: http://ec.europa.eu/europe2020/pdf/csr2015/cr2015_slovakia_en.pdf.

Goetz, K.H. and H.Z. Margetts (1999), "The solitary center: The core executive in Central and Eastern Europe", *Governance: An International Journal of Policy and Administration*, Vol. 12, No. 4, pp. 425-53.

Gold, J. (2014), "International delivery: Centres of government and the drive for better policy implementation", *Mowat Research Papers*, No. 96, Mowat Centre, School of Public Policy & Governance, University of Toronto, Toronto, Ontairio, Canada, available at: www.instituteforgovernment.org.uk/sites/default/files/publications/International%20Delivery%20report.pdf.

Government Office of the Slovak Republic (2012), "Manifesto of the government of the Slovak Republic", May, available at: www.vlada.gov.sk/manifesto-of-the-government-of-the-slovak-republic.

House of Commons (2014), "The centre of government", Committee of Public Accounts, 19th Report of Session 2014-15, London, available at: www.parliament.uk/business/committees/committees-a-z/commons-select/public-accounts-committee/news/report-on-centre-of-government.

House of Commons (2005), "The centre of government – No. 10, the Cabinet Office and HM Treasury", *House of Commons Library Research Papers*, No. 05/92, London, available at: http://researchbriefings.parliament.uk/ResearchBriefing/Summary/RP05-92.

Ministry of the Interior of the Slovak Republic (2015), "Operational Programme Effective Public Administration 2014-2020", www.minv.sk/?operational-programme-effective-public-administration.

OECD (2015a), *Achieving Public Sector Agility at Times of Fiscal Consolidation*, OECD Public Governance Reviews, OECD Publishing, Paris, http://dx.doi.org/10.1787/9789264206267-en.

OECD (2015b), "Delivering from the centre: Strengthening the role of the centre of government in driving priority strategies", GOV/PGC/MPM(2015)4, OECD, Paris.

OECD (2015c), *OECD Public Governance Reviews: Estonia and Finland. Fostering Strategic Capacity Across Governments and Digital Services Across Borders*, OECD Publishing, Paris, http://dx.doi.org/10.1787/9789264229334-en.

OECD (2015d), *Recommendation of the Council on Budgetary Governance*, OECD, Paris, available at: www.oecd.org/gov/budgeting/Recommendation-of-the-Council-on-Budgetary-Governance.pdf.

OECD (2014a), "Centre stage: Driving better policies from the centre of government", OECD, Paris, available at: www.oecd.org/gov/centre-stage-report.pdf.

OECD (2014b), "Reforming the public sector", in: OECD, *OECD Economic Surveys. Slovak Republic 2014*, OECD Publishing, Paris, pp. 49-81, http://dx.doi.org/10.1787/eco_surveys-svk-2014-5-en.

OECD (2014c), *Slovak Republic: Developing a Sustainable Strategic Framework for Public Administration Reform*, OECD Public Governance Reviews, OECD Publishing, Paris, http://dx.doi.org/10.1787/9789264212640-en.

OECD (2013a), *Poland: Developing Good Governance Indicators for Programmes Funded by the European Union*, OECD Public Governance Reviews, OECD Publishing, Paris, http://dx.doi.org/10.1787/9789264193543-en.

OECD (2013b), *Poland: Implementing Strategic-State Capability*, OECD Public Governance Reviews, OECD Publishing, Paris, http://dx.doi.org/10.1787/9789264201811-en.

OECD (2013c), "Questionnaire on the Organisation and Functions of the Centre of Government", GOV/PGC/MPM(2013)3, OECD, Paris, available at: www.oecd.org/officialdocuments/publicdisplaydocumentpdf/?cote=GOV/PGC/MPM(2013)3&docLanguage=En.

OECD (2013d), *Colombia: Implementing Good Governance*, OECD Public Governance Reviews, OECD Publishing, Paris, http://dx.doi.org/10.1787/9789264202177-en.

OECD (2012), *Slovenia: Towards a Strategic and Efficient State*, OECD Public Governance Reviews, OECD Publishing, Paris, http://dx.doi.org/10.1787/9789264173262-en.

Sustainable Governance Indicators (2015), www.sgi-network.org/2015/Governance/Executive_Capacity/Strategic_Capacity/Strategic_Planning; www.sgi-network.org/2015/Slovakia.

Virant, G. (2015), Presentation by former Minister of Public Administration, OECD Workshop on Government Co-ordination and Strategy, Bratislava, 9-10 April.

Chapter 2.

Strengthening analytical and evaluation capacity in the Slovak Republic

This chapter examines the Slovak government's use of evidence-based decision making and its analytical capacities. It argues that the decisions of the Slovak administration on policies, legislation or spending are often insufficiently based on evidence and sound analysis. There have been attempts to improve the situation; however, progress remains slow, especially due to the lack of demand on the side of the decision makers. This chapter also provides a set of recommendations on how to strengthen the analytical capacities of the Slovak administration to better support the government's decision making.

Introduction

Governments are responsible for taking policy decisions to improve the quality of life of citizens and the competitive position of the country's businesses. Using a scientific approach to investigate all available evidence can lead to policy decisions that are more effective in achieving the desired outcomes, as decisions are based on accurate and meaningful information.

Evidence-based decision making requires a systematic and rational approach to researching and analysing the available information and turning it into evidence to inform the policy-making process. It can produce more effective policy decisions and, as a result, better outcomes for the community. When evidence is not used as a basis for decision making, or the evidence that is used is not an accurate reflection of the "real" needs of the targeted population, the proposals for change are likely to produce ineffective outcomes and could even affect outcomes negatively for those that they are seeking to benefit.

OECD experience suggests that whole-of-government evidence-based decision making tends to lead to greater effectiveness and efficiencies in achieving strategic outcomes (Box 2.1). A robust, joined-up knowledge base that informs whole-of-government strategic decision making allows for a wide range of policy benefits, including a deeper understanding of the policy challenges and opportunities facing society (on different time horizons), the impact of proposed policy "solutions" and whether policy interventions are achieving the expected results for society. A broader definition of public outcomes should be considered, one that encompasses results for a given ministry or agency, system-wide results and societal outcomes – which are most meaningful for citizens. To this end, the effective integration of evidence into all aspects of the policy cycle, i.e. *ex ante* and *ex post*, can help governments achieve strategic outcomes while guiding strategy setting and implementation over the medium and long term.

There are many methodologies for evidence-based policy, but they all share the following characteristics:

- test a theory as to why the policy will be effective and what the impacts of the policy will be if it is successful
- include a counterfactual: what would have occurred if the policy had not been implemented?
- incorporate some measurement of the impact the policy will have on the economy, society, environment, preferably in quantitative terms (i.e. a cost-benefit analysis)
- examine both direct and indirect effects that occur because of the policy
- separate the uncertainties and controls for other influences outside of the policy that may have an effect on the outcome
- should be able to be tested and replicated by a third party.

For an efficient use of analytical capacities in the government, a demand from those responsible for taking decisions for analytical information must exist as well as a willingness to use this information as an important source of evidence. Inevitably, though, decision-making procedures will also still be strongly influenced by political and other factors. This is the case in most, if not all, OECD countries. On the "supply" side, there must be sufficient capacity in individual ministries and agencies. The analysts need to have sufficient skills and must have access to reliable data sources. In case such sources do not exist, government has to have a capacity to gather such information through other means. There should be a clear separation between providing analytical information to the ministries and implementing policies. To keep their "autonomy", analytical units should not be involved in implementing the policies.

Box 2.1. Evidence-based decision making: A key aspect of a strategic state

Since the launch of the first of *Government at a Glance* in 2009, the OECD has been advocating evidence-based policy making with the view that coherent policies require governments to take account of all pertinent information. This implies that governments assess the benefits of policy proposals in relation to the future costs as well as their interaction with structural reforms. Evidence-based policy analysis allows for decisions aimed at implementing and steering strategy to be taken in the country's medium- and long-term interests, based on evidence derived from strategic foresight and environmental scanning that correctly identify domestic and international short- and long-term challenges and opportunities, on performance assessment that allows for judicious prioritisation of expenditures to achieve the best results with the least resources, and on individual issues being analysed within a broader strategic framework.

Insights from recent OECD Public Governance Reviews identify key areas for evidence-based decision making:

- performance-informed budgeting as a means to support evidence-based decisions on resource allocation
- analytical capacity within ministries to carry out evidence-based policy analysis and implementation
- use of evidence-based impact assessment to secure the coherence and effectiveness of policies, laws and regulations
- prioritisation of key issues for assessment
- internal (and external) consultation to share issues and secure feedback.

Across the OECD, good governance practice suggests that policy should be based on sound evidence derived from rigorous analysis of the available facts. Governance practices determine how evidence contributes to identifying policy options. The OECD *Recommendation of the Council on Regulatory Policy and Governance* (2012b) provides a framework for the making and updating of rules and regulations. This evidence needs to be available at the right time and be seen by the right people. OECD practice suggests that the following major ingredients are needed to obtain and use the "right evidence":

- a sound methodology that allows for proper consideration of the immediate and long-term nature of the issue and of the rationale supporting different options for policy intervention (including doing nothing)
- good data for analysis
- public access to the data, assumptions and methodologies used to frame the issue and identify options to address it, so that scrutiny can be brought to bear and the analysis replicated independently
- time to carry out this analysis properly and to consult the general public on its results

Box 2.1. **Evidence-based decision making: A key aspect of a strategic state** *(continued)*

- a capable and skilled public service, including people skilled in quantitative methods
- a "receptive policy-making" environment: that is political leaders who are willing and able to decide on the basis of the evidence presented.

Sources: Banks, G. (2010), *An Economy-wide View: Speeches on Structural Reform*, Australian Government, Productivity Commission, Melbourne, Victoria, available at: http://papers.ssrn.com/sol3/papers.cfm?abstract_id=1614664; OECD (2009), *Government at a Glance 2009*, OECD Publishing, Paris, http://dx.doi.org/10.1787/9789264075061-en; OECD (2012), *Recommendation of the Council on Regulatory Policy and Governance*, OECD, Paris, www.oecd.org/gov/regulatory-policy/recommendations-guidelines.htm; OECD (2013b), "Strategic insights from the Public Governance Reviews: Update", GOV/PGC(2013)4, OECD, Paris, www.oecd.org/officialdocuments/publicdisplaydocumentpdf/?cote=GOV/PGC%282013%294&docLanguage=En.

Key facts and findings

Using analytical capacities in the Slovak administration

The culture of using evidence and analytical support in the decision-making process is not yet firmly embedded in the functioning of the Slovak government. There seems to be a lack of demand for evidence and analysis on the part of decision makers when discussing government policies, programmes and/or regulations, beyond assessing narrow budgetary impacts as part of the regulatory impact assessment (see below).

Specialised units that should focus on providing analytical background for a ministry's decision making have only been established in some Slovak ministries. Their structures, competences and their position in the organisation of the ministry vary. There are also big differences in staffing and overall capacity in these units.

Probably the best known and most-often cited example of an analytical unit is the Institute for Financial Policy (IFP),[1] which operates within the portfolio of the Ministry of Finance. The IFP's mission is to provide reliable macroeconomic and fiscal analyses and forecasts for the Slovak government, especially the Minister of Finance, as well as for the general public. The IFP serves as a centre of excellence, having sufficient personnel capacities with necessary skills (Box 2.2).

Another example of a functioning analytical unit is the Methodological and Analytical Unit of the Ministry of the Interior. This unit mostly focuses on public administration reform; therefore it is not used by the ministry as a whole. Currently, its main task is to gather data on administrative procedures (timing issues, number of affected subjects, etc.) and carry out process analysis of these procedures. The main aim is to simplify administrative procedures and reduce administrative burden for citizens, especially in connection to an extensive project on building physical one-stop shops across the Slovak Republic. Some performance indicators, such as the time spent on dealing with administrative procedures per citizen, are used in this process to measure its performance with one of the goals being to reduce this time.

Similar bodies exist or are currently being established as part of several other ministries, namely the Ministry of Education with its Educational Policy Institute, the Analytical Centre of the Ministry of Labour and Social Affairs, the Department of Economic Analyses of the Ministry of Environment, the Department of Analyses and Planning of the Ministry of Economy, the Institute of Health Policy of the Ministry of

Health and the Institute of Strategy of the Ministry of Transport, Construction and Regional Development. However, these analytical units are much smaller in scale; in many cases, their influence on the decision-making process of their ministry is rather limited compared to the IFP. Perhaps most tellingly, the Government Office does not have a formally established analytical unit and there is no central co-ordination of analytical units across the administration.

In most of cases, the analytical units report directly to their minister or to the State Secretary. Despite their sometimes exclusive names (e.g. institute, centre), they usually do not have any specific statute in the organisational chart of the ministry, do not operate at arm's length from the political level and therefore are not protected from political influence related, for example, to changes in the political leadership of the ministry. They also do not use any specific procedures for recruitment or other specific human resources policies to attract highly skilled personnel.

Box 2.2. Institute for Financial Policy of the Slovak Ministry of Finance

The Institute for Financial Policy (IFP) is a special unit of the Slovak Ministry of Finance with a status of a section. The Head of the institute reports directly to the State Secretary of the Ministry of Finance. It currently has 30 employees including the Head, 3 directors and 16 analysts. The IFP's mission is to provide high-quality, transparent and reliable macroeconomic and fiscal analyses and forecasts for the government. The IFP's main goals are to contribute to the transparency of the budgeting process in the Slovak Republic, the sustainability of public finances and the effectiveness of public finances, including taxation and public expenditure.

The IFP's main activities are:

- macroeconomic analyses and forecasts
- tax analyses and forecasts
- fiscal analyses and forecasts
- expenditure analysis
- structural reforms
- analytical service for the management of the Ministry of Finance.

The IFP provides inputs to the government for its strategic documents such as the Stability Programme or the National Reform Programme and for its medium-term budgets. In addition, the institute is also known for publishing its own economic analyses, working papers and commenting on recent developments and economic indicators.

The IFP contributed substantively to lowering the tax wedge for low-wage earners, tax reforms in the Slovak Republic in 2012 and 2013, a pension reform in 2012, measures to combat tax frauds and cutting down excessive solar subsidies.

Source: Based on information from the Slovak government.

There are no systemic, formalised procedures on how to involve the analytical units in the decision-making process inside their ministry. While the IFP produces a significant number of policy briefs and working papers, including economic forecasts and inputs for medium-term budgets, it is at the discretion of the Minister of Finance or the government whether to use these analyses to support their decisions. The IFP is regularly asked to provide the Minister of Finance with advice and supporting analysis; however, this only occurs in an *ad hoc* manner without any formal rules, and may change with every new minister. In the case of other ministries, the practice of involving analytical centres in the decision-making process is even rarer.

These analytical units also seem to be struggling for resources, especially to attract skilled people, but also to conduct analyses that demand data that are not immediately available to the administration, to conduct large surveys, etc. Getting access to relevant data that exist elsewhere and the quality of some of that data seem to represent significant challenges. Only in a few cases do ministries systematically gather data on relevant sectors; often, the only source of reliable information is the statistical office. Its resources are nevertheless also limited, especially in connection with the austerity programme. External analytical capacities that could be used by the administration are also rather limited and the practice of using external think-tanks or academics for such work is not widespread.

Significant problems exist on the side of the demand for analytical information and evidence. Many senior decision makers do not seem to be aware of the ways in which analytical capabilities in their institutions could help in their particular context, other than meeting conditionality for receiving EU funding. There were cases in the past when one minister was discredited when an analysis by another ministry raised arguments against the course of action he was planning to take. He then decided, rightfully, to create an analytical unit in his ministry.

There is an apparent lack of interest and engagement from the centre of government (CoG), including the Ministry of Finance, in demanding evidence and analysis from line ministries supporting their programmes and/or decisions, beyond the narrow short-term budgetary impacts of policy or legislative changes within the regulatory impact assessment (RIA) process. For example, the Ministry of Finance does not seem to request evidence on unit costs of outputs delivered by line ministries. Broader *ex post* evaluation evidence of cost effectiveness of existing programmes – either as part of the annual budget process or as part of regular progress monitoring – is neither demanded nor conducted by individual ministries nor by the CoG when controlling if the strategic goals of the government are being met (this is, however, planned as part of the government's public administration reform agenda).

In principle, the fact that the Ministry of Finance controls the budget and allocates resources to line ministries gives the ministry sufficient leverage to require this kind of evidence. In the United Kingdom, Treasury "spending teams", which mirror each line ministry, place emphasis on their own analytical capability and see part of their role as demanding good-quality evidence to underpin decisions in line ministries. This leverage does not seem to be used in practice in the Slovak Republic.

The Ministry of Finance is currently preparing an EU-funded project on introducing bi-annual spending reviews conducted by every minister to assess the effectiveness of ministries' spending programmes. The reviews should be linked to budget preparations; capacity in all ministries should be strengthened to enable them to conduct these reviews to provide input for reviewing and amending spending programmes and projects, linking budget allocations to the performance of these programmes and projects – in order to assess programme performance against results achieved.

Strengthening the capacity for conducting analysis and producing and using data to inform policy proposals is recognised as a priority by the government, namely the

Ministry of the Interior. A key component of the current public administration reform focuses on strengthening the analytical capacities of central government institutions. The objective is to have, at a minimum, analytical units in all economic and social ministries as well as in the Government Office. A project on building analytical capacities has been developed to guide this process, which includes the following elements:

- a review of existing analytical centres
- strengthening and development of analytical centres
- implementation of a system of performance evaluation of analytical centres, with a special emphasis on linking objectives to the Europe 2020 strategy in the context of the Slovak Republic
- networking and co-ordination among the analytical centres
- creation of a system to support the collection of valuable data and analysis.

In addition to strengthening analytical capacities in participating ministries (including the Government Office) through hiring and financing additional experts, this project would include an element focusing on developing a methodology for evaluating the performance of these analytical units.

Use of performance information and indicators

The capacity of governments to assess the performance of policies and regulations is essential for understanding whether a given policy, regulation or action plan is contributing to achieving wider national strategic objectives, or alternatively if it is hindering them. The process of performance measurement includes a definition of concrete and measureable objectives and an evaluation of whether these have been achieved. It helps to ensure that strategies inform daily decision making, to enhance accountability and credibility and to communicate progress (Box 2.3).

Box 2.3. **From setting objectives to measuring results: A seven-step process**

Performance measurement and evaluation need to be integrated into all major policy initiatives, both *ex ante* and *ex post* – these tools are critical to evaluate policies to identify success and failures, and to improve policies accordingly. The process of performance measurement includes the definition of concrete and measurable objectives and the evaluation of whether these objectives have been achieved. It helps to ensure that strategies inform daily decision making, to enhance accountability and credibility, and to communicate progress. Performance measurement works best if it builds on clear objectives, good-quality data and is embedded in a culture of constant learning and improvement.

There are risks, however. If measurements are not complemented with more in-depth qualitative analysis, these indicators lead to a situation in which reward is given to programming that is not achieving its intended result, or is achieving perverse outcomes. Moreover, an exclusive focus on "what is measurable" leads to the discounting or non-measurement of other important performance objectives.

The OECD has developed a seven-step methodology to help policy makers set objectives for their policies and assess whether they have been achieved. Figure 2.1 provides a concrete illustration of the application of the seven-step method to a policy on strengthening the enforcement of traffic regulation to reduce traffic causalities.

Box 2.3. **From setting objectives to measuring results: A seven-step process** *(continued)*

Step 1: Establish priority policies

For indicators to provide valuable information, they must be properly rooted in policy itself. At the sametime, it is unrealistic – and perhaps undesirable – to link indicators to all policy initiatives. Thus, policies need to be prioritised according to their ability to help government meet its strategic objectives. A priority policy should be articulated as a consistent course of action expressed as a causal and concrete statement (see example below).

Step 2: Define the targets

A target is a concrete goal that states the degree or level of achievement expected with respect to its associated priority policy. Targets are most directly linked to results indicators, and the degree or level of achievement that a target measures can be based on a variety of comparative parameters, depending on the base comparator and the results being sought.

Step 3: Identify key activities

An activity is a specific programme, initiative or project that clearly supports reaching a target. Activities must be systematically and clearly linked to targets and should be expressed as action verbs. Thus, "train", "implement" and "build" all work well to lead an "activity statement" but "improve", "strengthen" or "enhance", for example, do not.

Step 4: Build output indicators

An output indicator measures progress with an activity, and thus these two components should be clearly linked. A well-constructed output indicator is measurable. Thus, it must be quantitative (i.e. expressed in physical or monetary units) and time bound (i.e. limited to the lifetime of the corresponding activity). One key question to ask when establishing an output indicator is: what will be produced by the activity being measured?

Step 5: Build results indicators

A results indicator measures the results of activities in terms of their contribution to corresponding targets. Thus, they are closely associated with targets.

Step 6: Identify the desired impact

An impact indicator sets a longer term perspective and provides insights on the effect that one or more key activities has on the priority policy, and ultimately on the strategic objective. Impact indicators are particularly difficult to develop because attribution or causality is hard to establish – i.e. making a direct and complete link between the activity's impact and policy objective can be difficult. This is because other factors, often not within the control of government, may be involved with meeting a strategic or policy objective. Thus, it may be more rewarding and appropriate to identify desired impact – the desired impact of an activity on a priority policy and, more fundamentally, the desired impact of a priority policy on a strategic objective. Such a conversation can: 1) help focus policy thinking by providing a framework or an orientation within which other decisions can be taken; 2) inspire extended institutional and individual effort.

Step 7: Identify appropriate qualitative research methods

There are many approaches to determining the effectiveness of activities and/or priority policies. Output, result and impact indicators may signal problems and trigger governments to "dig deeper" to find the causes of the problem and identify the appropriate actions. Qualitative research methods can add value to the indicators and an understanding of policy effectiveness. Such research methods can include case studies, focus groups, interviews and reviews (e.g. OECD peer reviews).

Box 2.3. **From setting objectives to measuring results: A seven-step process** (*continued*)

Figure 2.1. **Illustration of the seven-step methodology**

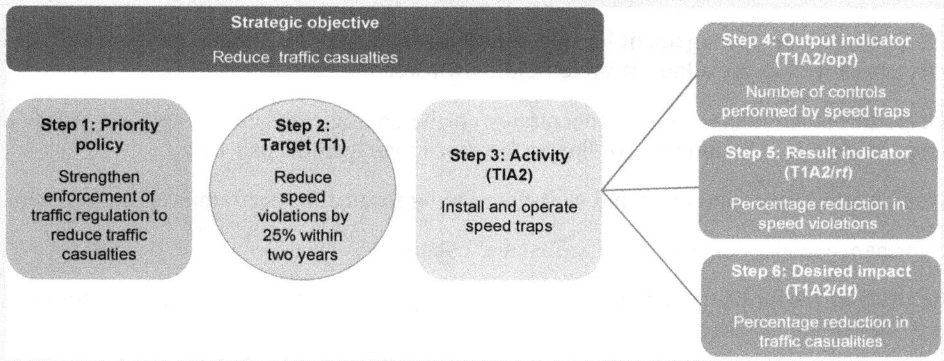

Source: OECD (2013a), *Poland: Developing Good Governance Indicators for Programmes Funded by the European Union*, OECD Public Governance Reviews, OECD Publishing, Paris, http://dx.doi.org/10.1787/9789264193543-en.

There is no government-wide policy on the use of performance-related information in developing and implementing public policies or regulations, including the creation of feedback loops to ensure that this information is used to evaluate the performance of such policies or regulations with the aim to improve their design to make them more effective in achieving the government's goals. There are relatively large differences in the use of performance measurement across sectors and there is a tendency to focus on inputs and tasks rather than outputs and outcomes.

There have been some attempts to use performance indicators to monitor the progress of implementation of some policies, especially those relating to the use of EU funds, such as the National Reform Programme. The Institute for Financial Policy has been advocating the use of performance indicators for some time and is using such indicators in some of its studies.

As another example, the Ministry of Economy is using the World Bank's Doing Business indicators and the OECD Product Market Regulation indicators to assess the quality of the business environment. There have been attempts to set strategic goals as a certain ranking in the Doing Business table. However, it is not clear to what extent those international indicators are used to evaluate the performance of government policies – i.e. whether these policies help (or not) to achieve the strategic goals.

Attempts also exist at using performance indicators in particular sectors (e.g. implementation of the Information Society Strategy – Digital agenda scoreboard, measurement of satisfaction of Slovak citizens and business in the main areas of the digital agenda; Operational Programme Integrated Infrastructure – priority axis Technical Assistance, etc.).

Several sets of indicators are used by the Ministry of Environment (indicators of green growth; environmental indicators; sector-based indicators – those of the effects of economic activity on the environment) and key indicators. The use of indicators is also mandatory for all programmes using EU funding.

Box 2.4. Common principles for performance management in Finland

Performance management is one part of the Finnish state administration's steering system.

- Societal effectiveness is a result of co-operation between different actors in the society.
- The performance management of the administrative field is based on common guidelines and practices as well as the administrative field's own steering practices.
- The performance management concentrates on the strategically most important issues and on those that need change. The intensity of the performance management can vary.
- There are clear roles and tasks and well-functioning forums for performance management.
- Performance management is professional and coherent.
- The basis of performance management is clear targets, indicators that describe them and monitoring the achievement of targets.
- Performance management is based on a structured and genuine dialogue and partnership between leaders and experts.
- Joint information systems and tools support these principles.

Source: Finnish Ministry of Finance (2012), "Common principles of performance management", ULOS-ohjaus, Fact Sheet No. 4, 30 November, http://vm.fi/documents/10623/1150432/4+Common+principles+of+performance+management.pdf/ea68e775-b499-417c-b6e6-038e2c39bdeb.

Strategic foresight

Independent data analysis and research informing whole-of-government decision making is a key ingredient in evidence-based decision making. The policy environment faced by governments is no longer dominated by predictability. It has become ever more complex, unpredictable and immediate, with multiple actors taking concurrent action both domestically and internationally. Such an environment requires governments to be proactive in scanning, gathering and analysing information to guide decision making and priority setting. Strategic foresight reporting helps governments look ahead to identify future risks and opportunities as a means of prioritising and focusing government policies; it is an essential component of achieving strategic insight.

Strategic foresight reporting is another essential component of achieving strategic insight. By scanning ahead to identify future risks and opportunities, governments can better prioritise and focus policies (see the example of Finland in Box 2.5). With the exception of some work conducted by the IFP, Slovak ministries do not seem to be engaged in conducting strategic foresight and in futures reporting.

One of the IFP's tasks is preparing and updating economy-wide short- and medium-term macroeconomic forecasts for the Slovak Republic. This is done in co-operation with the Macroeconomic Forecasting Committee and Tax Revenue Forecasts Committee with the participation of external stakeholders (Box 2.6). Medium-term forecasts serve as a basis for compiling a multiple budget of public finance and for preparing or updating the Convergence Programme of the Slovak Republic.

Box 2.5. Strategic foresight in Finland

Finland's strategic foresight practices have served as a benchmark for many OECD countries. There is a comprehensive foresight framework carried out by the government, including both the once-per-term horizontal government foresight report as well as the ministries' Futures Reviews, which are prepared to inform the incoming government of sector-based challenges and opportunities over an eight- to ten-year planning horizon.

Government foresight reporting has been in practice in Finland since 1993, when the first horizontal government foresight report, entitled *Finland's Options*, was tabled in parliament. This initial report presented views on major future developments and optional scenarios for Finland posited in the context of future research and the then-government's priorities; it also provided a plan for the kind of future society that the government was seeking to create through its actions in office. Since then, a horizontal government foresight report has been submitted to parliament during every electoral period.

Horizontal government foresight reports set forth the Finnish government's long-term views and proposed objectives and policies on selected issues.

- Presented to parliament as government proposals, they outline the government's aims while serving as policy statements directing administrative actions. The initial proposals are assessed and discussed by the Committee for the Future, a parliamentary committee assigned to research and comment on matters associated with futures studies, including the methodology. For each report, the government passes a resolution in its plenary session to give parliament a report addressing a topical or otherwise important subject.
- Although the report is prepared by the Prime Minister's Office and under the authority of the Prime Minister, the subject of evaluation in the foresight reports has, to date, been selected by the Prime Minister in consultation with Cabinet members. Finland's coalition government system ensures that the plenary session reaches consensus on the selected foresight issue, which, in principle, should secure commitment across the coalition parties to the issue under investigation.

In addition to the horizontal reporting, the government disseminates vertical futures reviews at the end of each term of government for consideration by parliament in the preparation of a new Government Programme. These reports are sector-based and are produced by individual ministries. Before parliamentary elections in 2003, 2007, 2011 and now in 2015, ministries prepare future reviews outlining sector prospects and proposing optional strategic policies. The reviews are sent to all political parties represented in parliament as a means of increasing transparency in the preparation of the Government Programme.

Source: OECD (2015a), *OECD Public Governance Reviews: Estonia and Finland: Fostering Strategic Capacity across Governments and Digital Services across Borders*, OECD Public Governance Reviews, OECD Publishing, Paris, http://dx.doi.org/10.1787/9789264229334-en.

Box 2.6. Macroeconomic Forecasting Committee and Tax Revenue Forecasts Committee

In order to increase the transparency and objectivity of macroeconomic forecasts, the Ministry of Finance has addressed ten independent institutions (ING Bank, Tatra banka, SLSP, CSOB, INFOSTAT, VÚB, UniCredit, Volksbank, the Slovak Academy of Sciences and the NBS) achieving good results in this area, and set up a Macroeconomic Forecasting Committee. The committee holds its sessions regularly on a bi-annual basis before preparing the starting points-related information and finalising the draft state budget and, when so required, prior to preparing or updating the Convergence Programme (Stability Programme) of the Slovak Republic. The committee sits in order to discuss preliminary forecasts delivered by the Ministry of Finance, whose predictions can be subsequently modified respecting the prevailing opinion of the committee. The outcome of such discussions includes, among other things, an overall evaluation of the character of the said forecasts, i.e. whether a conservative, realistic or optimistic

Box 2.6. **Macroeconomic Forecasting Committee and Tax Revenue Forecasts Committee** *(continued)*

forecast is concerned. The Ministry of Finance's medium-term macroeconomic forecasts thus accepted are the basis for preparing background information on starting points for a multi-year budget for the next three years and for updating the Convergence Programme of the Slovak Republic.

The Tax Revenue Forecasts Committee exploits the outcome of activities performed by the Macroeconomic Forecasting Committee. Tax revenues and social insurance contributions account for most of the public administration expenditure and the estimation thereof is marked by a considerable degree of uncertainty, as it is in the case of the economic environment. Any such uncertainty opens room for potential suspicions that the revenues have been deliberately overestimated or underestimated by the institutions accountable for the preparation of public budgets. The Tax Revenue Forecasts Committee is therefore required to contribute to strengthening public control over the process of constructing the public administration budget, such a contribution being achieved by engaging the expert public in the relevant discussions.

Committee members include representatives of the following institutions: MF SR, ARDAL, State Treasury, NBS, INFOSTAT, ING Bank, SLSP, Tatra banka and CSOB. The committee holds its sessions at least three times a year during the main stages of the preparation of the national budget. It sits in order to discuss preliminary forecasts delivered by the Ministry of Finance, whose predictions can be subsequently modified respecting the prevailing opinion of the committee. The outcome of such discussions includes, among other things, an overall evaluation of the character of said forecasts, i.e. whether a conservative, realistic or optimistic forecast is concerned. The evaluating criterion is a 1% interval around the Ministry of Finance's ultimate forecast for the total income from taxes and social insurance contributions.

Source: Ministry of Finance of the Slovak Republic (2014), "Macroecnomic forecasts", 17 June, www.finance.gov.sk/en/Default.aspx?CatID=340.

Regulatory impact assessment

Regulating, along with spending and taxing, is a key tool of government. It is of particularly high importance for implementing government strategies. Well-designed, evidence-based legislation tends to help governments achieve policy goals; on the other hand, poorly designed legislation tends to undermine the operation of the economy and impede people's lives. Ill-conceived regulation can stifle innovation and entrepreneurship, reduce welfare and slow growth. Whether legislation is well- or poorly designed depends to a large extent on the quality and use of evidence in the rule-making process.

Ex ante impact assessment of new regulations is one of the most important regulatory tools available to governments. All OECD countries have committed themselves to integrating regulatory impact assessment into their decision-making procedures through the 2012 *Recommendation of the Council on Regulatory Policy and Governance* (Box 2.7). OECD experience shows that a robust administrative responsibility centre with adequate resourcing can help ensure that impact assessments find an appropriate and timely place in the policy- and rule-making process and can raise the quality of these assessments.

- Co-ordination of rulemaking and regulatory impact analysis is in most OECD countries first and foremost a responsibility of CoG institutions (Figure 2.2).

- Effective strategic whole-of-government oversight by the CoG over rulemaking is central to enhancing the efficient functioning of national strategies and achieving national strategic outcomes.

Figure 2.2. **Location of oversight bodies in OECD countries**

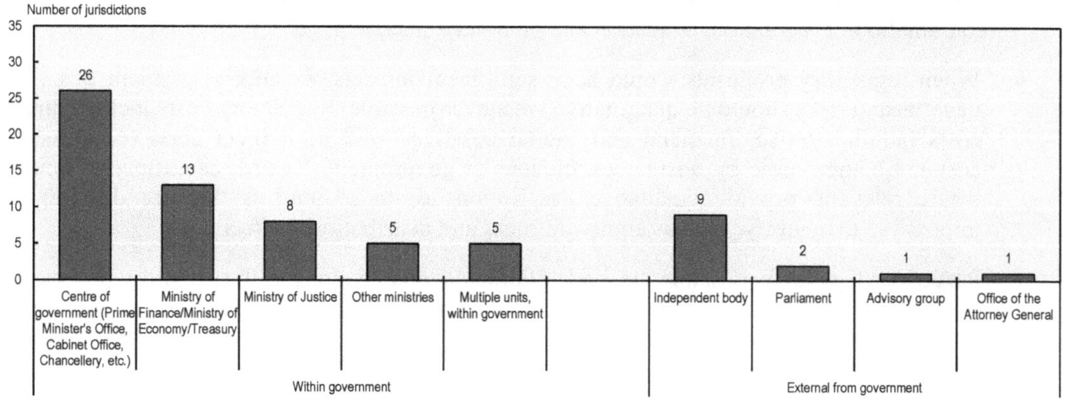

Source: OECD (2015b), *OECD Regulatory Policy Outlook 2015*, OECD Publishing, Paris, http://dx.doi.org/10.1787/9789264238770-en.

In the Slovak Republic, according to the government's rules of procedure, all legislative and non-legislative documents submitted to the government must include an evaluation of impacts in five main areas: 1) impacts on public budgets; 2) business environment; 3) social impacts (impacts on citizens' financial situation, social exclusion, equality of opportunities and gender equality, impacts on employment); 4) environment; and 5) the "informatisation" of the society. This information should be summarised in the so-called "*doložka vybraných vplyvov* – Clause on selected impacts" obligatorily attached to the draft.

Box 2.7. **Recommendation of the Council on Regulatory Policy and Governance**

Recommendation No. 4

Integrate regulatory impact assessment (RIA) into the early stages of the policy process for the formulation of new regulatory proposals. Clearly identify policy goals, and evaluate if regulation is necessary and how it can be most effective and efficient in achieving those goals. Consider means other than regulation and identify the trade-offs of the different approaches analysed to identify the best approach.

- Adopt *ex ante* impact assessment practices that are proportional to the significance of the regulation, and include cost-benefit analyses that consider the welfare impacts of regulation, taking into account economic, social and environmental impacts, including the distributional effects over time, identifying who is likely to benefit and who is likely to bear the costs.
- *Ex ante* assessment policies should require the identification of a specific policy need, and the objective of the regulation, such as the correction of a market failure or the need to protect citizens' rights, that justifies the use of regulation.
- *Ex ante* assessment policies should include a consideration of alternative ways of addressing the public policy objectives, including regulatory and non-regulatory alternatives to identify and select the most appropriate instrument, or mix of instruments,

Box 2.7. **Recommendation of the Council on Regulatory Policy and Governance** *(continued)*

achieve policy goals. The "no action" option or baseline scenario should always be considered. *Ex ante* assessment should, in most cases, identify approaches likely to deliver the greatest net benefit to society, including complementary approaches such as through a combination of regulation, education and voluntary standards.

- When regulatory proposals would have significant impacts, ex ante assessment of costs, benefits and risks should be quantitative whenever possible. Regulatory costs include direct costs (administrative, financial and capital costs) as well as indirect costs (opportunity costs), whether borne by businesses, citizens or government. Ex ante assessments should, where relevant, provide qualitative descriptions of those impacts that are difficult or impossible to quantify, such as equity, fairness and distributional effects.
- RIA should, as far as possible, be made publicly available along with regulatory proposals. The analysis should be prepared in a suitable form and within adequate time to gain input from stakeholders and assist political decision making. Good practice would involve using the RIA as part of the consultation process.
- *Ex ante* assessment policies should indicate that regulation should seek to enhance, not deter, competition and consumer welfare, and that to the extent that regulations dictated by public interest benefits may affect the competitive process, authorities should explore ways to limit adverse effects and carefully evaluate them against the claimed benefits of the regulation. This includes exploring whether the objectives of the regulation can be achieved by other less restrictive means.
- When carrying out an assessment, officials should:
  - assess economic, social and environmental impacts (where possible in quantitative and monetised terms), taking into account possible long-term and spatial effects
  - evaluate if the adoption of common international instruments will efficiently address the identified policy issues and foster coherence at a global level with minimal disruption to national and international markets
  - evaluate the impact on small- to medium-sized enterprises and demonstrate how administrative and compliance costs are minimised.

RIA should be supported with clear policies, training programmes, guidance and quality control mechanisms for data collection and use. It should be integrated early in the processes for the development of policy and supported within agencies and at the centre of government.

Source: OECD (2015d), *Recommendation of the Council on Regulatory Policy and Governance*, OECD Publishing, Paris.

RIA, in fact, consists of several separate documents. The so-called "Clause on selected impacts" serves as a summary and quick test for preliminary impact estimation. It contains a table indicating whether the impacts in the five areas will be positive or negative. In addition, potential alternative solutions may be mentioned ("in case the drafting institution considered any"). It also has to include opinions of relevant ministries responsible for evaluating the quality of impact assessments (see below). When the impact (positive or negative) is expected in any of the five areas, further specific impact analyses should be elaborated for each of the areas where there will be potential impacts, whether positive or negative. The impact assessment should be carried out before submitting the material to the inter-ministerial comments procedure and for public consultation.

While the formal obligation to conduct RIA has been in place since 2001, with major modifications added in 2008 (when a methodology was introduced and responsibility for quality control was given to four ministries) and again in 2010, it does not seem to be complied with as a general rule. The only exception is the assessment of budgetary impacts obligation, which is strictly enforced by the Ministry of Finance. The existence of sound formal procedures for conducting RIA is the main reason why the Slovak Republic ranks slightly above average in the OECD 2015 Regulatory Policy Indicators (Figure 2.3), which focus mostly on the *de jure* situation.

Figure 2.3. **Regulatory impact analysis for developing primary laws at the executive government**

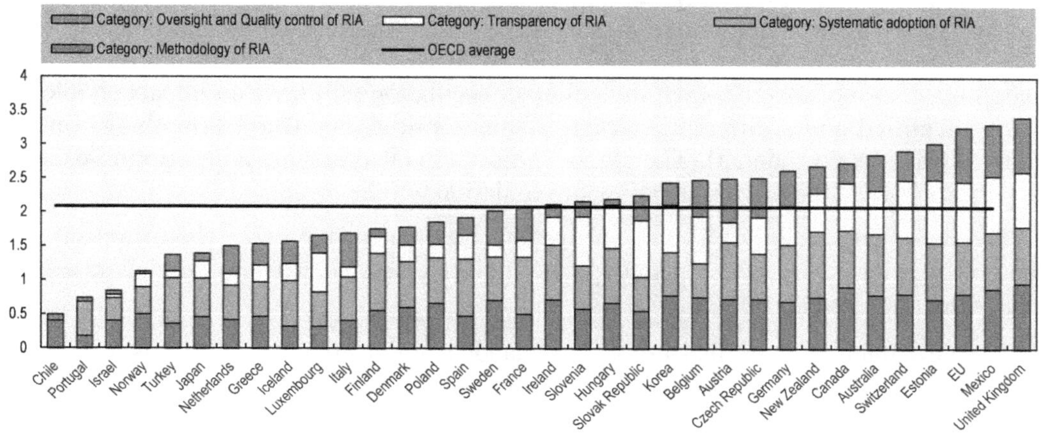

Notes: Canada and the United States are not included in this figure because for these countries all primary laws are initiated by congress or parliament and therefore are out of the scope of this survey. All other countries reported that the majority of primary laws are initiated by the executive, apart from Mexico, which for the period of 2009-12 reported 96% of regulations originated with the federal Congress.

Source: OECD (2015b), *OECD Regulatory Policy Outlook 2015,* OECD Publishing, Paris, http://dx.doi.org/10.1787/9789264238770-en.

There might be several reasons for the discrepancy between formal rules and the reality, one of them being insufficient oversight over the quality of RIAs submitted to the government. The oversight function is, according to the current rules, spread among several ministries (the Ministry of Environment is responsible for assessing the quality of environmental impacts; the Ministry of Labour, Social Affairs and Family for social impacts; the Ministry of Finance for budgetary impacts and "informatisation" impacts; and the Ministry of Economy for business impacts). These ministries have only limited capacity to check the content of RIAs. In addition, impacts are assessed in an isolated way and so is the quality of these assessments.

As already mentioned, the lack of available data and a lack of public consultation on impact assessments are among other issues causing a low level of compliance. In addition, RIA is usually conducted at the end of the regulation-making process when the decision on the preferred solution has already been taken. Therefore, RIA cannot serve its main purpose – to contribute to better quality government regulatory decisions.

The Ministry of the Economy is the main body co-ordinating impact assessment across the administration; however, it lacks sufficient capacity to enforce the obligation to conduct RIA, since it is simply one of the various line ministries without any specific competences in overseeing the quality of RIA. In addition, the Ministry of the Economy does not seem to have a strong enough voice in the government and therefore its objections against a low quality of impact assessments are often not taken into account. This is, however, not the case of the Ministry of Finance when its position points to an insufficient analysis of budgetary impacts. This is usually taken seriously with the aim of a sustainable public debt.

The "Unified methodology for the assessment of selected impacts", the government resolution setting the rules for conducting impact assessments of legislative and non-legislative documents, was amended in January 2015 with the aim to improve the RIA process. It was to enter into force on 1 October 2015 (postponed from April 2015 to give ministries more time to prepare). The amendments introduce important changes in the methodology. From 1 October 2015, the "Clause on selected impacts" should follow a slightly different structure (Box 2.8). It should, among other things, clearly state a definition of the problem the material is trying to solve and a description of the goals and desired results. Subjects on which the policy or regulation will have an impact should be clearly identified and a different alternative solution described (the "do nothing" option should always be considered). The clause should now also include a description of how the performance of the discussed policy or regulation will be evaluated.

The new methodology will not change the fact that in the case where impacts are identified in any of the five areas, a special impact assessment has to be elaborated for each of the impacted areas.

The new methodology also introduces mandatory consultations with businesses (or their associations) as a firm part of the RIA process whenever the proposal has potential impacts on the business sector. The Ministry of Economy should decide whether these consultations are necessary based on the work plan of the government or, when a document submitted is not included in the plan, based on the information that the policy or regulation is being developed (see also the following section on stakeholder engagement).

According to the new methodology, a new Permanent Working Committee of the Legislative Council of the Slovak Republic for Assessing Selected Impacts was set up as of 1 October. It gathers representatives of the four co-ordinating ministries and representatives of businesses associations. The statement of the committee on the quality of impact assessment will be submitted to the government as part of the dossier. The ministries will assess the quality of the impact analysis in their sectors respectively but the decision should be taken collectively.

Box 2.8. **Clause on selected impacts**[1]

1. Basic data (title, status, procedure, timeline)
2. Problem definition
3. Goals and status to be achieved
4. Subjects that will be impacted (directly and indirectly)
5. Alternative solutions considered and analysed
6. Subordinate regulations and their short description
7. Transposition of the EU legislation (identification of where the draft goes beyond the minimum requirements set by EU law, including justification)

Box 2.8. **Clause on selected impacts**[1] *(continued)*

8. Review (optional; when and how the regulation will be reviewed and based on which criteria)
9. Impacts of the proposal

Impacts on public budgets	☐ Positive	☐ None	☐ Negative
– of which impacts covered by existing resources	☐ Yes	☐ No	☐ Partially
Impacts on business environment	☐ Positive	☐ None	☐ Negative
– of which impacts on small and medium-sized enterprises	☐ Yes	☐ No	☐ Partially
Social impacts	☐ Positive	☐ None	☐ Negative
Environmental impacts	☐ Positive	☐ None	☐ Negative
Impacts on informatisation	☐ Positive	☐ None	☐ Negative

10. Notes
11. Contacts
12. Sources of information
13. Statement of the commission in the preliminary comment procedure.

Note: 1. Working translation, shortened.

Source: Based on information provided by the Slovak government.

This is an important step forward, as it should strengthen the process of quality control over the impact assessments submitted to the government. Nevertheless, these changes will most likely not solve the issue of an atomised approach to RIA, as individual ministries will still look at the impacts in their area of competence in an isolated manner. For example, the Ministry of the Environment will look at the quality of environmental impacts, the Ministry of Finance at the budgetary impacts, etc. What will be lacking will be an integrated view on the trade-offs, for example, between positive impacts on environmental protection and negative impacts on the business environment.

The new methodology also specifies different stages for consulting RIA inside the administration which were introduced in 2008 but often not complied with. There will be a "preliminary comment procedure" when the ministry or agency which plans to submit a policy or regulation to the government will have to first fill in the clause on selected impacts and send it to the Permanent Working Committee (see below). The annex has to be accompanied by the analysis of specific impacts in case the clause identifies impacts in the five selected areas (impacts on public administration budgets, business environment, social impacts, environment and the "informatisation" of the society). The committee will provide its statement and consult with the drafting ministry in case of disagreements. This new process should help solve issues with the quality of the impact analysis before it is sent around for comments and give an opportunity to the drafting institution to discuss the analysis with the responsible ministries.

After that, the draft policy or regulation, including the impact assessment, is submitted to the inter-ministerial comment procedure as well as for public consultations (see the following section). During this process, again, individual ministries can comment on the quality of impact assessment. Finally, if the document is changed substantively as part of the inter-ministerial comment procedure from the point of view of potential impacts, the drafting ministry has to present and update the clause on impacts and if necessary the specific impact assessments to the Permanent Committee for a final statement. The government may still decide in advance when approving the Legislative Plan, in exceptional cases, that RIA does not have to be conducted (this will not concern the assessment of budgetary impacts).

The new methodology should also improve the quality of the analysis of impacts through introducing the "SME Test". Again, it is the Ministry of Economy which decides on the necessity of doing the SME Test based on the existence of potential impacts on small- and medium-sized enterprises (SMEs). The test itself and the analysis of impacts on SMEs are then conducted by the Better Regulation Centre of the Slovak Business Agency.[2]

Despite the obligation to assess various options as part of the impact assessment procedure, it has rarely been conducted so far. The new impact assessment methodology should be stricter in this aspect and ministries should always at least take into consideration a "do nothing" option (what would happen if no action was taken).

Risk assessment is not part of impact assessment or regulatory management policy. The methodology also only vaguely touches upon the issue of implementation and enforcement of a given regulation. This should be a standard part of an impact assessment, as many additional burdens might be caused in the implementation process (Figure 2.4 shows the proportion of OECD countries actually evaluating and/or quantifying impacts of enforcement mechanisms).

Figure 2.4. **Number of OECD countries focusing on enforcement mechanisms as part of their impact assessment procedures**

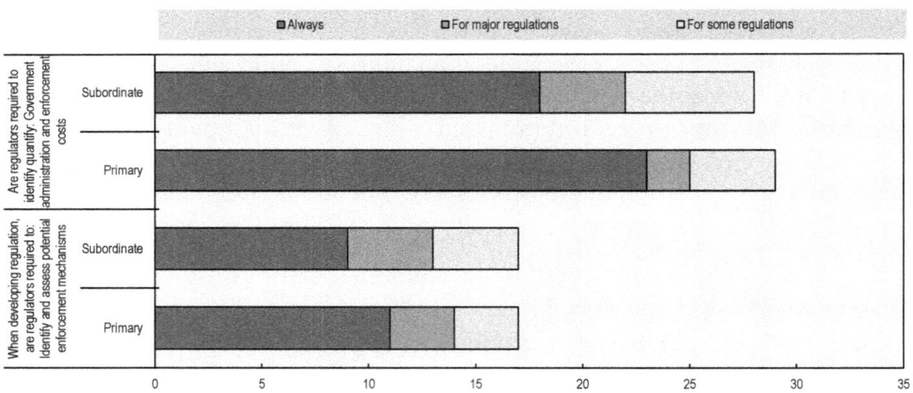

Source: OECD (2015b), *OECD Regulatory Policy Outlook 2015*, OECD Publishing, Paris, http://dx.doi.org/10.1787/9789264238770-en.

Consultation and participation of the civil society in policy making

Effective consultation is crucial to ensuring that the interests of citizens and business are taken into account in the development and design of government policies and regulations. It improves the effectiveness of regulation by drawing on the information that regulated entities have about the likely impacts of regulation. The positive effect of increased transparency and stakeholder engagement is not just confined to regulation, but also enhances policy and programme development and delivery. It is critical that the government consults with civil society on the drafting of all relevant legislation. This is consistent with the principle of open government, as per the OECD *Recommendation of the Council on Regulatory Policy and Governance* (Box 2.9). In addition, citizen participation and inclusive decision making is equally beneficial in terms of budget processes as well as in building a longer term strategic vision for the country.

Box 2.9. **OECD Recommendation of the Council on Stakeholder Engagement in Regulatory Policy**

Adhere to principles of open government, including transparency and participation in the regulatory process to ensure that regulation serves the public interest and is informed by the legitimate needs of those interested in and affected by regulation. This includes providing meaningful opportunities (including online) for the public to contribute to the process of preparing draft regulatory proposals and to the quality of the supporting analysis. Governments should ensure that regulations are comprehensible and clear and that parties can easily understand their rights and obligations.

- Governments should establish a clear policy identifying how open and balanced public consultation on the development of rules will take place.
- Governments should co-operate with stakeholders on reviewing existing and developing new regulations by:
  - actively engaging all relevant stakeholders during the regulation-making process and designing consultation processes to maximise the quality of the information received and its effectiveness
  - consulting on all aspects of impact assessment analysis and using, for example, impact assessments as part of the consultation process
  - making available to the public, as far as possible, all relevant material from regulatory dossiers, including the supporting analyses and the reasons for regulatory decisions as well as all relevant data
  - structuring reviews of regulations around the needs of those affected by regulation, co-operating with them through the design and conduct of reviews including prioritisation, assessment of regulations and drafting simplification proposals
  - evaluating the competitive effects of regulation on various economic players in the market.
- Introduce regular performance assessments of regulations and regulatory systems, taking into account, among other things, the impacts on affected parties and how they are perceived. Communicate the results of these assessments to the public.
- Make sure that policies and practices for inspections and enforcement respect the legitimate rights of those subject to the enforcement, are designed to maximise the net public benefits through compliance and enforcement, and avoid unnecessary burdens on those subject to inspections.
- All regulations should be easily accessible by the public. A complete and up-to-date legislative and regulatory database should be freely available to the public in a searchable format through a user-friendly interface over the Internet.
- Governments should have a policy that requires regulatory texts to be drafted using plain language. They should also provide clear guidance on compliance with regulations, making sure that affected parties understand their rights and obligations.

Source: OECD (2015c), *Recommendation of the Council on Regulatory Policy and Governance*, OECD Publishing, Paris, http://dx.doi.org/10.1787/9789264209022-en.

From the formal point of view, many procedures for public consultations are in place. This explains a high position in the OECD Regulatory Policy Indicators survey (Figure 2.5). Public consultations are required for every legislative and non-legislative proposal submitted to the government, including legislative intents (an initial stage of a legislative draft in a non-paragraph wording). All drafts submitted to the government are automatically published on the government consultation portal (Legal Documents Portal)[3] at the same time as they are submitted to the inter-ministerial comment procedure. The deadline for comments is usually 15 working days from the date of publication on the portal. Whenever a comment receives support from 500 individuals or organisations, ministries are obliged to provide written feedback on such comment, which is then part of the dossier submitted to the government for discussion.

Figure 2.5. **Stakeholder engagement on developing primary laws in the executive government**

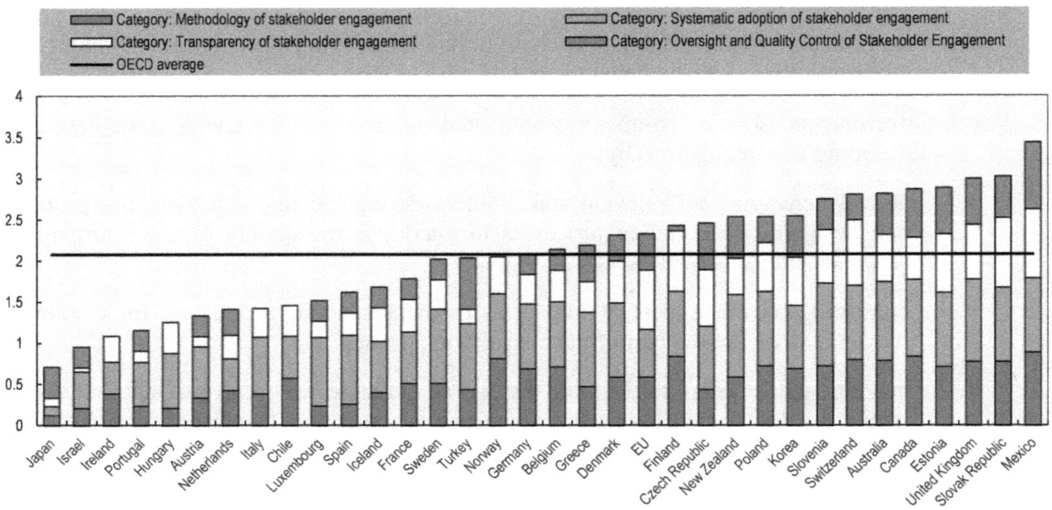

Note: 1. Canada and the United States are not included in this figure because for these countries all primary laws are initiated by congress or parliament and therefore are out of scope of this survey. All other countries reported that the majority of regulations are initiated by the executive, apart from Mexico, which for the period of 2009-12 reported 96% of regulations originated with the federal Congress.

Source: OECD (2015b), *OECD Regulatory Policy Outlook 2015*, OECD Publishing, Paris, http://dx.doi.org/10.1787/9789264238770-en.

To be able to submit a comment through the portal, a user has to be registered. The registration also enables signing up for receiving alerts whenever a document from a selected area(s) is published on the portal for consultation.

The number of comments received through the consultation portal varies. In general, it seems that the general public is still poorly informed on how to take part in the consultation process. Some of the users also complained about the low user-friendliness of the portal. A new portal is currently being developed by the Ministry of Justice. This is a good opportunity to broaden its functionalities and launch an information campaign aimed at outside stakeholders and the general public on the possibilities to become engaged in the government's decision-making process.

Legislative drafts having economic and social impacts are also obligatorily the subject of consultations with the Economic and Social Council of the Slovak Republic (tripartite).

There is currently no systemic policy on conducting early consultations;[4] however, these sometimes take place through informal consultations with non-governmental stakeholders, the creation of *ad hoc* working groups and advisory committees, ongoing or *ad hoc* co-operation with academics, think tanks, non-governmental organisations (NGOs), etc. While the Slovak government almost never uses green papers to initiate a discussion with the public, organising public meetings, informal consultations with external stakeholders and creating special advisory bodies or working groups is a more common practice. Preliminary consultations via the website of an agency or ministry also sometimes take place. For many legislative drafts, a so-called legislative intent (a non-paragraph summary of the prepared draft describing the main goals of the draft and its planned content) is elaborated and submitted to the government (and therefore also consulted with the public via the consultation portal).

Another platform that can be used to engage outside stakeholders in the decision-making process in the government is the Government Council for Non-Governmental Non-Profit Organisations (NGOs). This council consists of representatives of ministries and more than 30 NGOs.[5] It is chaired by the Plenipotentiary of the Slovak Government for the Development of Civil Society. One of the aims of the council is "to contribute to the development of participative democracy in Slovakia" to make sure that government policies and regulations are "not only efficient, fair and democratic, but also adopted based on a wide consensus of the government and non-governmental sector and its implementation was controlled by the civil society".[6] This platform is, however, more used to discuss general policies, strategies or projects on co-operation with NGOs than to find NGOs' views on particular specific policies or regulations.

The new RIA methodology aims at improving the situation regarding early consultations through introducing obligatory consultations with stakeholders early in the decision-making process. As described in the previous section, consultation with the business sector should be a firm part of RIA and should be conducted before the draft is submitted to the "preliminary comment procedure" (see previous section).

Assessment

The use of robust evidence and sound evidence-based analysis in government decision making with respect to policies, legislation and spending appears to be limited when compared to other OECD countries. Decisions tend to be based on political priorities and the relative strength of individual ministers rather than on rational analysis of costs and benefits and potential outcomes. There are attempts to improve the situation; however, progress remains slow, especially due to the lack of demand on the side of the decision makers. The procedures for stakeholder engagement in policy- and regulation-making in the Slovak Republic are well-established; however, many consultations take place solely on an informal basis or too late in the process, when it has become difficult to change the policy or regulation substantively.

Using analytical capacities in the Slovak administration

Analytical capacity in most of the Slovak line ministries is insufficient with only rare exceptions. The Institute of Financial Policy of the Ministry of Finance stands out as an example of good practice; however, even its statute is not formalised and the institute can be abolished at any moment. Basic analytical units exist or are being built in some ministries, but they usually struggle for resources and often do not have direct access to top-level decision makers and their inputs are not regularly used in the decision-making process of their ministry.

Relatively unusual among OECD countries is the lack of demand on the side of the centre of government for evidence and analysis from line ministries. This is connected to the issue of insufficient policy co-ordination from the CoG: performance of government-wide policy and/or spending programmes is neither measured nor evaluated; neither *ex ante* nor *ex post* (see Chapter 1).

Lack of demand for analytical information accompanying government decisions on spending programmes or *ex post* evaluation of performance of its regulations and policies, may well reflect wider systemic challenges, namely that:

- The Ministry of Finance sees its priority as controlling aggregate spending to meet deficit targets rather than having responsibility for driving the efficiency and effectiveness of public spending in achieving strategic policy outcomes. This should be a responsibility of the government as such, controlled by the CoG. The lack of such a function might be connected to the low level of horizontal co-ordination and reluctance of individual ministries to centralised control and/or co-ordination of their work.
- Line ministries are not clear about specific output or outcome priorities, with a lack of relevant performance indicators to drive focus on priorities, and to form the basis for progress monitoring, including co-ordination by the CoG (including *ex post* accountability to the parliament for the public resources they are spending).
- External stakeholders also insufficiently call for more evidence and analytical information to support government decisions. Some external subjects, such as think tanks, could use this kind of information as an input for their own analyses. They should also get more engaged in providing inputs to the analytical units.

All analytical units face the wider recruitment and retention problems endemic in the civil service as a whole (see Chapter 5). It is increasingly difficult to attract skilled personnel and to motivate employees to stay in analytical units for longer periods. Many existing units are by-passing the standard selection procedures by carrying out their own, "pre-selection" processes. Unless these issues are addressed, it is hard to see how analytical capability can become self-sustaining.

The existing analytical units are not co-ordinated and rarely collaborate on analyses that would require the co-operation of several ministries. The current EU-funded project on strengthening analytical capacities in selected ministries is an important and useful step forward. It focuses on the supply side – improving the capacity of analytical units in selected ministries. Nevertheless, the demand must also be strengthened, albeit it is more difficult. The IFP's involvement in co-ordinating the project might seem logical regarding its experience and informal statute and prestige; nevertheless, there is a danger that the IFP might nudge the other analytical units towards conducting mostly macroeconomic analyses instead of work tailored to the needs of their parent ministries. It would therefore be advisable that the project be co-ordinated by the Ministry of the Interior in close co-operation with the Ministry of Finance and the Government Office.

Conditions should be created to attract skilled personnel with the necessary analytical skills. The current EU-funded project should certainly help in this aspect. At the same time, clear procedures must be established government-wide and at each line ministry on how to use these analytical capacities to improve the decision-making process. Stricter rules for conducting RIA and providing evidence on the effectiveness of spending programmes, both *ex ante* and *ex post*, will force ministries and agencies to strengthen their analytical capacities. The project currently being prepared by the Ministry of Finance should set the basis for introducing regular spending reviews in all ministries linked to the budget cycle and represents an important step forward in the right direction.

The units in line ministries would benefit from more co-ordination and sharing of recruitment, training, etc. Co-ordination from the CoG should be strengthened for using evidence and sharing it across the administration. The basic model of centres of excellence reporting directly to the minister is sensible. While analytical capability is being built up, it is best for it to be concentrated in a central team or unit. In the longer term, as analytical capability becomes more established, a more "bedded out" model, with analysts sitting in policy and delivery teams, might become appropriate. The IFP should be taken as an example of good practice; however, the specific needs of individual line ministries should be taken into account.

Use of performance information and indicators

Quantitative information on the performance of policies, programmes and regulations is used very sporadically. Such performance indicators are rarely set up front – in the stage when a policy, spending programme or law is adopted by the government. This makes it impossible to measure whether these policies/programmes/regulations are achieving their goals. *Ex post* evaluation of policies/programmes/regulations should be conducted more often to find out whether there is a need to change them or to abolish them and/or replace them with more effective ones.

When drafting new regulations, it should be made obligatory to set the goals the given regulation should achieve in quantitative terms, wherever possible. The drafting institution should also set a timeframe during which the regulation's performance has to be reviewed (mandatory reviews policy). A mandatory five-year horizon for regulatory reviews could also be set across the administration. Before adopting such a policy, it should be pilot-tested on several selected important pieces of legislation, to make sure the implementation is smooth. A similar procedure might be applied to government policies. In case of spending programmes, the Ministry of Finance should demand *ex post* evaluation of the cost effectiveness of existing programmes as part of the budgetary cycle.

Strategic foresight

The Government Manifesto is the leading document in setting a strategy for the next electoral term (see Chapter 1). It is the programme of the government based on the government's political priorities. No long-term, strategic foresights are usually prepared to inform the preparation of the Manifesto, with the exception of macroeconomic short- and medium-term forecasts prepared by the IFP. No other foresight activities are regularly conducted by any other institution. OECD experience demonstrates that foresight efforts are more effectively integrated into whole-of-government decision making when they are tightly linked to the CoG, notably the unit reporting to the head of government (Table 2.1). The purpose of such foresights should be to give politicians a clear view of the future, to make their planning more evidence based and less prone to conventional lobbying by interest groups.

Table 2.1. **Interdisciplinary foresight projects: Overview from selected initiatives**

Country	Body responsible for co-ordination	Foresight effort	Main purposes	Time horizon
Finland	Prime Minister's Office (PMO)	Government Foresight Report	To identify likely development trends and set objectives and strategic outlines for government work	10-20 years
Flanders, Belgium	Advisory Board reporting to the Prime Minister's Office and Cabinet	Future Search	The Flemish government undertook a three-day "future search" exercise to identify and "co-create" five priority roles for centre-of-government focus and capacity building. These were: large government-wide priorities (e.g. climate issues, etc.); improving the flexibility and agility of government; promoting innovation; developing long-term vision; and legal quality and transparency	Not specified
France	Prime Minister's Office	France in 10 years?	To show a pathway to advance the country with indicators and clearly identified benchmarks; to engage in clearly identified common choices that organise major transitions; to adapt policies and instruments in view of the desired objectives; to engage a large debate with all stakeholders	10 years
Netherlands	Commission for Consultation of Sector Councils (COS)[1]	Horizon Scan Report 2007	To help decision- and agenda makers, researchers and developers think about future societal problems, threats and opportunities	Open (long-term)
Sweden	Prime Minister	Commission on the Future of Sweden	To identify long-term challenges and contribute to a more future-oriented public debate, enabling government and society to improve preparedness	40 years
United Kingdom	Cabinet Office (PMO) with the Government Office for Science	UK Foresight Major Projects	To assist decision makers in understanding how their decisions today might affect the future, and to help policy makers to reach more stable decisions that are more likely to survive the uncertainties of the future	20-80 years

Note: 1. Independent commissions of representatives from research, society and government.

Source: OECD Secretariat desk-based research and interviews; OECD (2015a), *OECD Public Governance Reviews: Estonia and Finland: Fostering Strategic Capacity across Governments and Digital Services across Borders*, OECD Public Governance Reviews, OECD Publishing, Paris, http://dx.doi.org/10.1787/9789264229334-en.

In the future, analytical units should be able to provide the government with strategic foresights. This work should be co-ordinated by an analytical unit within the CoG – preferably within the Government Office. This co-ordination would help build both horizontal and vertical coherence in the development and implementation of the government's agenda. The Slovak Republic could learn from Finland in relation to setting up a foresight activity, particularly at the centre of government. The key to a shared vision is active engagement of society's actors in its development – which requires embedding a culture of open and transparent government at all levels of the public administration.

Regulatory impact assessment

The obligation to conduct regulatory impact assessment when developing new regulations is in place in the Slovak Republic; the major issue is the enforcement of these obligations and the non-compliance of line ministries and agencies.

Recent changes aimed at improving the RIA system are an important step forward. The creation of a semi-independent advisory body overseeing the quality of impact assessments should enable putting more pressure on line ministries to take RIA more seriously. At the same time, thanks to the new rules, external stakeholders, especially businesses, should be consulted concerning draft legislation sufficiently early in the process.

On the other hand, the fact that budgetary, economic, social and environmental impacts will be assessed in an isolated manner and the quality of such analyses will be evaluated by four different institutions (though members of the same commission) might not contribute to an integrated view on the assessment of potential impacts of draft regulation.

Sufficient analytical capacities are crucial for the administration to be able to conduct such evaluations both *ex ante* and *ex post*. The highest level political support and a clear demand from the government for high-quality analysis accompanying all legislative and policy drafts submitted to the government are equally necessary. Independent control over the quality of impact assessments is nonetheless important. The new commission should evaluate individual impact assessment as a whole, not in an isolated matter. It would be preferable if the chair of the commission represent a neutral institution, such as an academic body or come from the Office of the Government.

Concerning the methodology, there is certainly room for better integration of the individual impact assessment. The methodology in its current version also focuses on the impacts on businesses and the business environment rather than on the impacts on citizens, NGOs and the public sector. This might reflect the priorities of the government in this area; however, in the future, these impacts should also be evaluated. More attention should also be paid in the RIA methodology to the issue of implementation end enforcement.

It is too early to evaluate the current system before it is actually implemented. Even though the changes represent important improvements, there are still some potential issues that remain to be solved. It would be, however, unwise to recommend any substantive changes at this stage. The quality of the new impact assessment should therefore be evaluated after two years with the aim to improve the overall RIA system. A programme on training in RIA techniques should be launched as soon as possible to help ministries and agencies to develop capacities to conduct RIA. Examples of good impact assessment should be gathered and disseminated across the administration. Potentially, the competence for co-ordination of RIA across the administration should be transferred to the Government Office.

Consultation and participation of the civil society in policy making

As in the case of RIA, the necessary formal obligations to engage stakeholders are partially in place and should be strengthened by implementing the new RIA methodology. What lags behind is enforcement and some kind of quality oversight as well as the sufficient demand from the government for engaging stakeholders in the decision-making process. Therefore, stakeholders are insufficiently consulted, especially in the early stages of the process of developing policies and/or regulations. The consultation portal is not used to the optimal extent by external stakeholders due to the low user-friendliness and lack of awareness. There is also a potential to use the Government Council for Non-Governmental Non-Profit Organisations to get NGOs more engaged in the decision-making process, especially on strategic government policies and programmes.

Recommendations

The OECD recommends the Slovak government undertake the following measures to enhance analytical and evaluation capacity:

- Consider strengthening analytical capacity in key ministries. Create conditions to attract and keep personnel with the necessary analytical skills. Use the current EU-funded project to raise awareness in line ministries on the need to strengthen analytical capacities.
- Increase the demand for analysis and evidence to support government decisions by establishing formal procedures for *ex ante* and *ex post* assessment of government policies, programmes and regulations. Clear procedures could be established government-wide and at each line ministry on how to use the analytical capacities to improve the decision-making process.
- Make the use of performance indicators more widespread when adopting policies, programmes or regulations. Adopt a government-wide policy on *ex post* evaluation of these policies/programmes/regulations. When drafting new regulations, make it obligatory to set the goals the given regulation should achieve, preferably in quantitative terms, wherever possible. The drafting institution should also set a timeframe during which the regulation's performance has to be reviewed (mandatory reviews policy).
- Use the analytical units to engage in strategic foresight activity and share its results with the government. While ministerial analytical units could conduct horizon scanning as well as take into account results of private sector-led foresight activity in their sector, this activity could be co-ordinated by the CoG to provide a synthesis of these sector-specific scans and to maximise the impacts of foresight activities on whole-of-government strategy setting and implementation, notably with respect to designing and implementing the Government Manifesto and its corresponding government-wide and ministry-specific programmes of work.
- Implement the approved changes in the RIA process without further delay. Ensure full compliance, including the obligation to always assess several alternatives (including the "do nothing" option and non-regulatory alternatives, where appropriate). Evaluate the system after two years to assess whether it is working in an efficient manner and adopt necessary changes if this is not the case.
- Adopt a methodology for early-stage consultations. Enforce the obligation to consult all legislative proposals with all relevant stakeholders including civil society organisations as part of RIA. Train civil servants in consultation techniques.
- Make the new consultation portal more user-friendly and inform the general public better on the functionalities of the portal as well as on the possibilities to become engaged in the government's decision-making process.

Notes

1. www.finance.gov.sk/en/Default.aspx?CatID=629.

2. The Slovak Business Agency is a non-profit organisation for the support of small- and medium-sized enterprises. It was founded in 1993 through a common initiative of the EU and the government of the Slovak Republic. It is a unique platform of public and private sectors. The founding members include the Ministry of Economy of the Slovak Republic, the Entrepreneurs Association of Slovakia and the Slovak Association of Crafts. For more information, see: www.sbagency.sk/en/slovak-business-agency.

3. https://lt.justice.gov.sk/Default.aspx.

4. Engaging with stakeholders before the draft is finalised, usually through a form of publishing green papers, establishing advisory bodies with external stakeholders, working groups, public hearings, surveys, etc.

5. www.tretisektor.gov.sk/index.php?cms_location=rada-pre-mimovladne-neziskove-organizacie (in Slovak).

6. The website of the council.

Bibliography

Banks, G. (2010), *An Economy-wide View: Speeches on Structural Reform*, Australian Government, Productivity Commission, Melbourne, Victoria, available at: http://papers.ssrn.com/sol3/papers.cfm?abstract_id=1614664.

Banks, G. (2009), *Evidence-based Policy Making: What Is It? How Do We Get It?*, ANU Public Lecture Series, Australian Government Productivity Commission, Canberra, February, available at: www.pc.gov.au/news-media/speeches/cs20090204/20090204-evidence-based-policy.pdf.

Cabinet Office (2013), "Review of cross-government horizon scanning", London, available at: www.gov.uk/government/uploads/system/uploads/attachment_data/file/79252/Horizon_Scanning_Review_20121003.pdf.

Finnish Ministry of Finance (2012), "Common principles of performance management", ULOS-ohjaus, Fact Sheet No. 4, 30 November, available at: http://vm.fi/documents/10623/1150432/4+Common+principles+of+performance+management.pdf/ea68e775-b499-417c-b6e6-038e2c39bdeb.

Ministry of Finance of the Slovak Republic (2014), "Macroecnomic forecasts", 17 June, www.finance.gov.sk/en/Default.aspx?CatID=340.

OECD (2015a), *OECD Public Governance Reviews: Estonia and Finland: Fostering Strategic Capacity across Governments and Digital Services across Borders*, OECD Public Governance Reviews, OECD Publishing, Paris, http://dx.doi.org/10.1787/9789264229334-en.

OECD (2015b), *OECD Regulatory Policy Outlook 2015*, OECD Publishing, Paris, http://dx.doi.org/10.1787/9789264238770-en.

OECD (2015c), *Recommendation of the Council on Regulatory Policy and Governance*, OECD Publishing, Paris, http://dx.doi.org/10.1787/9789264209022-en.

OECD (2013a), *Poland: Developing Good Governance Indicators for Programmes Funded by the European Union*, OECD Public Governance Reviews, OECD Publishing, Paris, http://dx.doi.org/10.1787/9789264193543-en.

OECD (2013b), "Strategic insights from the Public Governance Reviews: Update", GOV/PGC(2013)4, OECD, Paris, available at: www.oecd.org/officialdocuments/publicdisplaydocumentpdf/?cote=GOV/PGC%282013%294&docLanguage=En.

OECD (2012), *Recommendation of the Council on Regulatory Policy and Governance*, OECD, Paris, available at: www.oecd.org/gov/regulatory-policy/recommendations-guidelines.htm.

OECD (2009), *Government at a Glance 2009*, OECD Publishing, Paris, http://dx.doi.org/10.1787/9789264075061-en.

Chapter 3.

Strengthening the capability of the state civil service in the Slovak Republic

This chapter focuses on strengthening the capability of the state civil service in the Slovak Republic through strategic human resources management (HRM) practices that build on the legal and institutional reforms currently planned or underway. The analysis supports the findings and proposals contained in the Slovak government's HRM Strategy to 2020, underlining the need for HRM practices that ensure merit, professionalism, continuity and the development of human capital in the staffing of the civil service. The chapter highlights how the consistent application of basic HRM procedures and standards across the civil service, supported by the Government Office and the planned establishment of an impartial and independent Council of the Civil Service, will create scope to develop strategic HRM based on competencies, performance and workforce planning.

Introduction

This chapter focuses on strengthening the capability of the state civil service in the Slovak Republic to steer and lead policy development and implementation and to deliver public services at the central and deconcentrated levels. Key lessons from experience in OECD countries point to the creation of a modern, strategic human resource management (HRM) system as an essential part of reforms aimed at improving public governance. OECD experience suggests that HRM reforms should be well integrated with other public governance reforms, and that HRM reforms are a long-term process which requires ongoing commitment and incremental steps forward. In the end, strategic HRM will contribute significantly to the efficiency of government, its capacity to deliver public services effectively and the agility to implement reforms in all areas of government.

It is important to recognise that the assessments and recommendations of this chapter are set against a backdrop of ongoing work aiming to improve HRM in the Slovak civil service. The HRM reform agenda is composed of two positive elements: the drafting of the new Civil Service Act to replace the 2009 legislation currently in force and the completion of the HRM Strategy to 2020 (see Box 3.1). The adoption of a new Civil Service Act by 2016 is part of *ex ante* conditionality for EU funds. Together, these will establish the framework for comprehensive HRM reforms. Following from the completion of the first phase of optimisation reforms, which required tough decisions on restructuring the civil service, a path has now been paved for the government to focus on the HRM policy reform agenda, including building a longer term roadmap for implementation and using strategic HRM to shape the civil service for the future. The new Civil Service Act and HRM Strategy are significant positive advancements, not only in terms of their content, but also in terms of the effective collaboration which took place between the Government Office and ministries in shaping the reform agenda, demonstrating that co-operation with regard to HRM is possible and that the Government Office is capable of leading these efforts. This provides a platform for an ongoing partnership that will be essential in putting the reforms into practice. The recommendations made in this chapter seek, therefore, to contribute to the work in progress and, in many cases, mirror or amplify elements that have already been included in the HRM Strategy to 2020.

Ensuring a stable, capable, well-managed and well-trained civil service will be critically important in the Slovak Republic if the government is to meet the needs of citizens and deliver on its ambitious public administration reform (PAR) agenda over the period 2014-20. HRM reform is recognised as a priority by the government, signaled by placing leadership responsibility for the reforms in the Government Office. In this context, the government's approach to HRM reform will have significant consequences for the success of the overall PAR, including the government's capacity and ability to effectively use EU funds and to achieve sustainable improvements in government performance over time.

HRM practices that ensure merit, professionalism, and stability and continuity in staffing provide the foundations for an efficient and effective public sector that can promote strong, sustainable and inclusive growth. Systematic adherence to basic merit-based processes and standards in key areas such as recruitment, promotion and compensation in turn creates scope to develop strategic HRM based on competencies, performance and more flexible management of the public sector workforce according to the evolving needs of government. Strategic workforce planning is an essential component of high-performing public administrations. It is indispensable if the government is to maintain a well-structured and representative workforce of appropriate size, which is able to meet the changing needs of citizens and business in a cost-efficient manner. Good workforce planning requires high-quality information and discussion that are linked to whole-of-government priorities, as well as organisational strategies and efficiency concerns, and accountability arrangements that support workforce decisions.

In the short term, many of the envisioned reforms – both in terms of HRM and the overall PAR agenda – will affect most employees in some way. With any organisational change, there is a risk that low employee morale or engagement will decrease individual employee productivity. This demands immediate consideration of issues related to employee and institutional capacity, morale and change management, demonstrating and communicating the benefits of reform and recognising public employees as strategic partners in the reform process.

On a medium- to long-term basis, the Slovak Republic stands to benefit from a better functioning, more strategic HRM system that builds a stable, professional, independent and skilled civil service capable of steering and leading policy development, engaging effectively with partners within and outside the public administration, and designing and delivering effective services that meet the needs of citizens, regardless of where they reside in the country.

This chapter focuses on the following areas of HRM and public employment policy which will be particularly important for strengthening the capacity of the state civil service:

- Strategic workforce planning and management across the public sector. Knowing the size and shape of the workforce is an essential prerequisite to planning and better aligning capacity with organisational and service demands. Improving the quality of workforce data collected across the Slovak central government will be essential in providing an accurate picture of the level, composition and trend in public employment; in turn creating a solid foundation for effective workforce planning and more flexible and efficient management of the workforce.
- Building a professional, educated and stable workforce managed through fair, rule-based and transparent practices. Modern, merit-based recruitment methods are key to acquiring the talent and competencies needed by the public service. The retention of talented staff, avoidance of high levels of turnover and insulating staffing from political influence are also critical for building professionalism and continuity, and for ensuring that the public service has the necessary skill base.
- Enhancing performance management and accountability, and building leadership capacity to steer strategic policy development and implementation. Developing an integrated performance management framework can contribute towards more outcome-focused public organisations and motivate employees to use their competencies to their maximum potential by connecting their efforts to organisational and service delivery success. Senior leaders play a key role in ensuring organisational performance and are often held accountable for results.
- Strengthening government capacity to deliver on an ambitious HRM reform agenda, building on insights from OECD countries on how to make government-wide HRM reform happen. The success and sustainability of reforms of public employment and civil service HRM require both political support and institutional capacity building. Modernising HRM in the central government of the Slovak Republic involves not only legislative changes and the development of

strategic HRM, but also an evolution in core public service values to underpin changes in the way staff are recruited and managed. The reforms and the values they represent are more likely to take root and flourish if they are widely communicated and discussed with public servants and more broadly across society so as to create a shared understanding of how they aim to contribute to better public governance and improvements in public services.

Key facts and findings

Strategic workforce planning and management across the public sector

The experience of OECD countries shows that strategic workforce planning and management are essential for governments to ensure that the public sector workforce is able to meet the changing needs of citizens in a cost-efficient manner. This requires an appropriately structured workforce with the right competencies and the flexibility to deploy the workforce in line with operational requirements. It also requires governments to look to the future, thinking strategically about the right mix of people and skills that will be needed to respond to changing societal needs.

Workforce planning and management involve:

- the ability to track employee numbers, costs and competencies (compensation policy and pay management are also key tools for managing the cost of the workforce)
- alignment of workforce planning with the strategy and planning of each government organisation so that the workforce is fit for purpose
- flexibility in workforce management to adapt to changing needs and priorities
- a whole-of-government perspective on allocations across sectors and on the overall size and cost of the workforce, enabling better control of scarce resources
- managerial accountability for the strategic management of the workforce.

Size and composition of the government workforce of the Slovak Republic

Workforce planning and management start with good accounting in terms of numbers and costs of public employees. Most national governments in OECD countries know how many employees they have. Data are usually collected and maintained centrally by the Ministry of Labour and the national statistical agency.

The Slovak Republic has not up until now maintained a central database on public employment, although developing standardised data in a central civil service register is now a priority for the Government Office and work has already begun. Until such a central civil service register is completed, workforce data must be treated with caution, particularly in terms of seeking to draw international comparisons or to examine trends over time.

Data collected by the International Labour Organization (ILO) suggest that employment in the Slovak Republic's general government and public corporations (the "public sector" in the System of National Accounts) accounts for a relatively high share of total employment compared to other OECD countries, exceeded only by the Scandinavian countries. Public sector employment represented 26.5% of total employment in 2009, rising to 27.2% in 2013 (Figure 3.1). A somewhat different picture emerges when employment in general government is separated out from employment in public corporations (Figure 3.2). General government is defined as comprising all levels of government (central, state, local and social security funds) and includes core ministries, agencies, departments and non-profit institutions that are controlled by public authorities. Data for 2011 indicate that general government employment as a percentage of the labour force in the Slovak Republic was below the OECD average and very close to the Central and Eastern European country average.

Figure 3.1. **Public sector employment as a percentage of total employment**

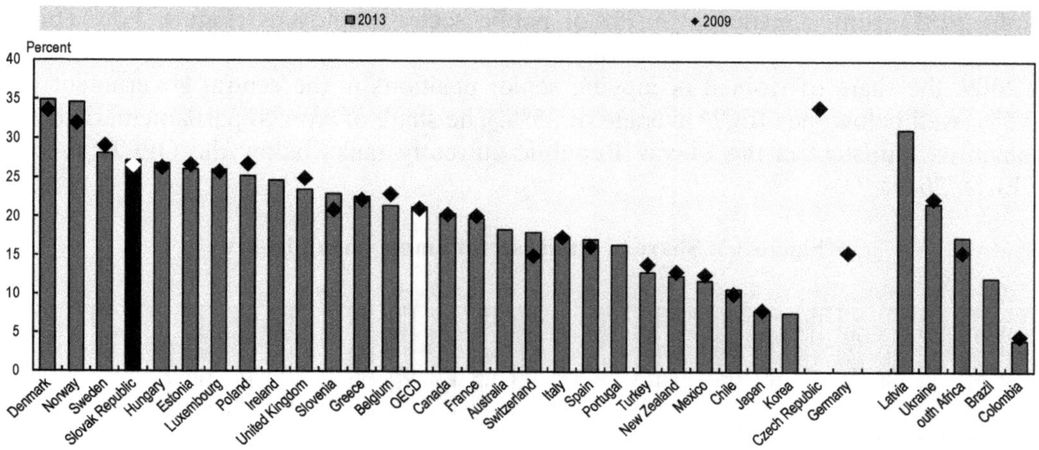

Note: Data were collected by the International Labour Organization, ILOSTAT (database). Public sector employment covers all employment of the general government sector as defined in the System of National Accounts (SNA) plus employment of public corporations. The general government sector comprises all levels of government (central, state, local and social security funds) and includes core ministries, agencies, departments and non-profit institutions that are controlled by public authorities. Public corporations are legal units producing goods or services for the market and that are controlled and/or owned by government units. Public corporations also include quasi-corporations. Data represent the total number of persons employed directly by those institutions, without regard for the particular type of employment contract.

Source: ILO (2014), ILOSTAT (database), www.ilo.org/ilostat.

Figure 3.2. **Employment in general government and public corporations as a percentage of the labour force, 2011**

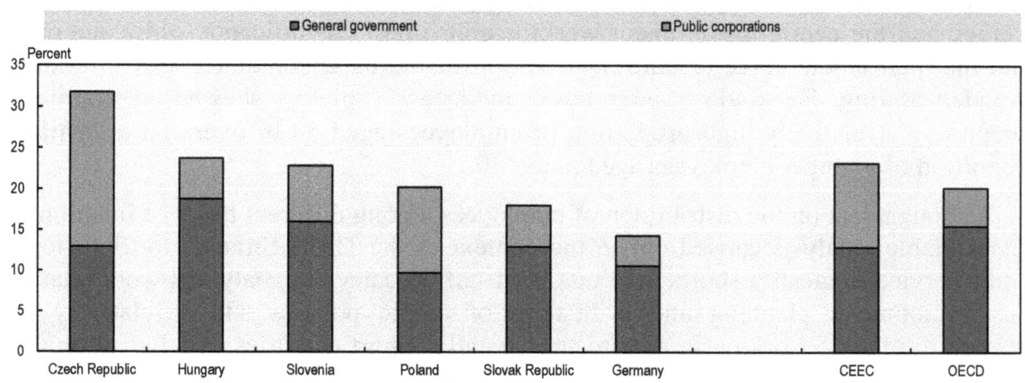

Note: CEEC: Central and Eastern European countries.

Source: ILO (2014), ILOSTAT (database), www.ilo.org/ilostat; OECD (2014a), "Labour Force Statistics", *OECD Employment and Labour Market Statistics* (database), http://dx.doi.org/10.1787/lfs-lfs-data-en (accessed on 21 March 2015).

Government employees are governed by two main employment frameworks: the Civil Service Act (CSA) and the Public Service Act (PSA). Survey data collected by the Government Office for 2014 indicate that civil servants employed under the CSA made up 36% of central government employees (Government of the Slovak Republic, 2014). Civil servants employed in ministries make up only 14% of the public service. Public services are highly decentralised and most central government employees come under the Public Service Act and are located in district offices at the territorial level and in social and health insurance funds.

In 2013, women made up 59.7% of public sector employees (Figure 3.3). This is above the OECD average and represents a slight increase from 58.4% in 2009. However, in 2009, the share of women occupying senior positions in the central government was 22.5%, well below the OECD average of 35%. The share of women parliamentarians and women as ministers in the Slovak Republic currently ranks below the OECD average (OECD, 2015).

Figure 3.3. **Share of public sector employment, by sex**

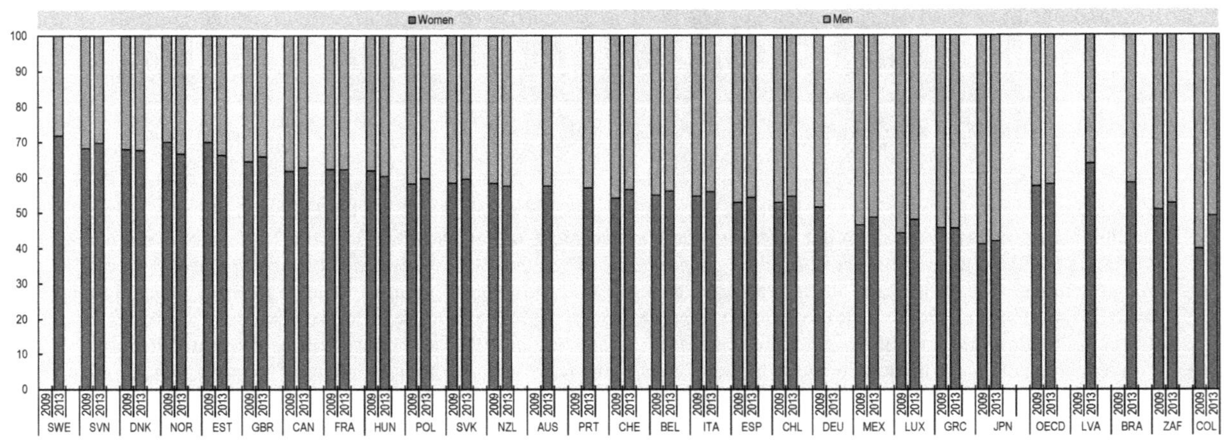

Source: ILO (2014), ILOSTAT (database), www.ilo.org/ilostat.

While data on the age composition of the workforce are scarce, the Slovak central government has a larger percentage of employees 50 years or older than the OECD average and the central government workforce also has a significantly older age profile than the total labour force (Figure 3.4). The available data, combined with information provided during fact-finding interviews, indicates a highly skewed age structure, comprising a relatively high proportion of employees aged 50 or over and a significant proportion of younger employees aged under 30.

Although data on the distribution of employees among different types of functions are not available, analysis carried out in the context of the HRM Strategy to 2020 for the public service suggests a shortage of qualified staff to carry out analytical work related to the development, planning and evaluation of public policies and a relatively high proportion of staff working in administrative and support activities. Analytical units are being established in ministries to start to address this imbalance.

Figure 3.4. **Percentage of employees 50 years or older in central government and total labour force, 2009**

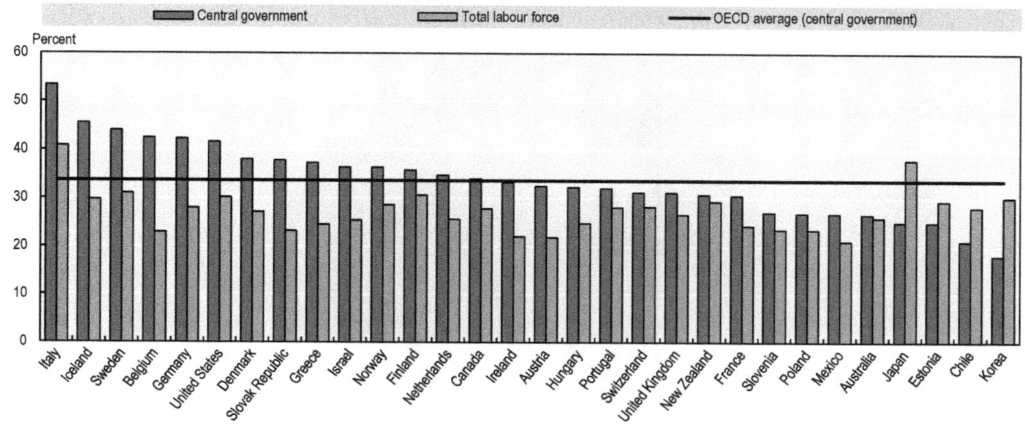

Source: OECD (2011b), *Government at a Glance 2011*, OECD Publishing, Paris, http://dx.doi.org/10.1787/gov_glance-2011-en.

Compensation costs of public employees

Compensation of government employees in the Slovak Republic as a percentage of GDP in 2010 was one of the lowest of all OECD countries at 7.7% (OECD 2012a). In 2012, compensation of general government employees as a share of total public expenditure was below both the OECD and Central and Eastern European country (CEEC) average (Figure 3.5). The government has sought to reduce the state wage bill by maintaining tight control over the level of central government employment and has reported a moderate decrease in employment in the central public administration (Figure 3.6). The Ministry of Finance does this via limits on the number of positions allocated to ministries. In addition, a hiring freeze has been in operation for several years. In the absence of reliable time series data on public employment, it is unclear what impact this policy is having. The experience of OECD countries highlights that unless it is combined with strategic, whole-of-government workforce planning, a hiring freeze leaves little room to manoeuvre in terms of being able to align workforce capacity to deliver on the government's priorities and is likely to result in rigidities which can hinder the effective and efficient management of the workforce (OECD, 2011a).

Figure 3.5. **Compensation of general government employees as a share of total public expenditure**

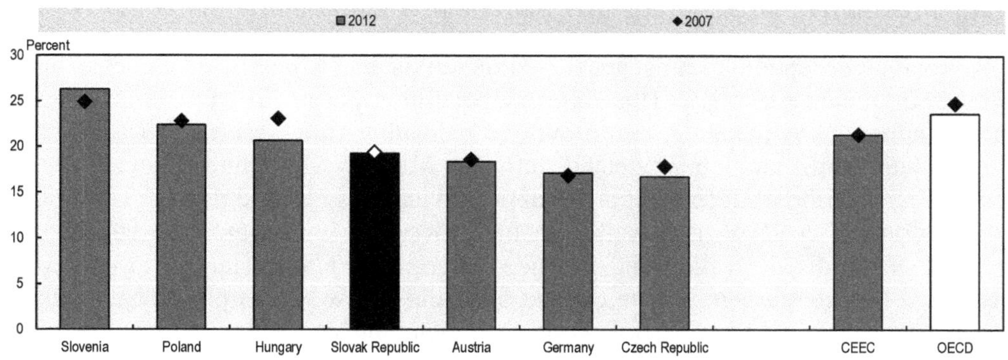

Note: CEEC: Central and Eastern European countries.

Source: OECD (2014b), *OECD National Accounts Statistics* (database), http://dx.doi.org/10.1787/na-data-en (accessed on 21 March 2015).

Figure 3.6. **Changes in central public administration employment levels, 2008-13**

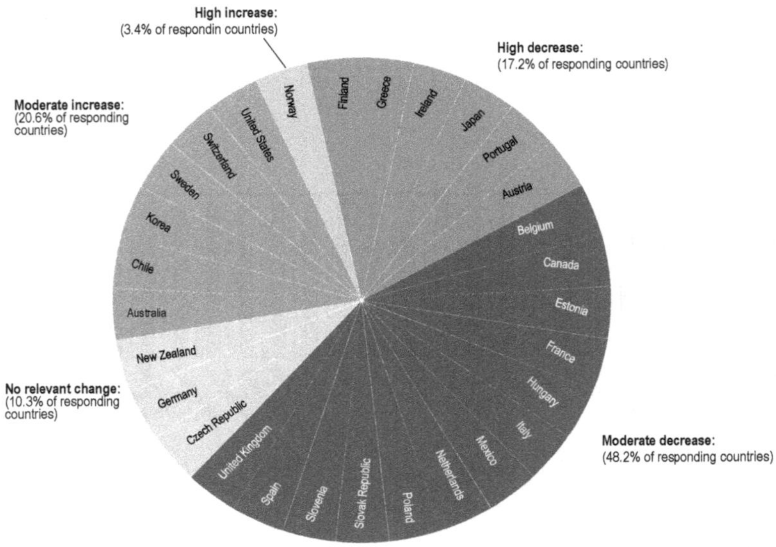

Source: OECD (2015), *Government at a Glance 2015*, OECD Publishing, Paris, http://dx.doi.org/10.1787/gov_glance-2015-en.

Strategic workforce planning and strategic human resources management tools

Until robust workforce data are built up, practicing strategic workforce planning and aligning essential competencies with organisational objectives will remain a challenge for the Slovak government. A large majority of central government ministries, as well as organisations at the deconcentrated level of the central government, lack comprehensive HR plans that are integrated into the management framework of the organisation itself.

The number of civil service positions is determined year by year through the budget process. The Ministry of Finance collects the number of proposed positions from ministries and makes adjustments in relation to the budget. However, frequent restructuring seems to be a feature within many ministries and this tends to make it difficult to track the numbers of civil servants accurately. The focus of personnel offices within the majority of ministries appears to be on preparing the annual staffing plan for the budget submission and allocating available positions within the ministry rather than on strategic workforce management activities.

A notable exception to this general situation is the Ministry of Finance and its Institute for Financial Policy. This ministry portfolio appears to have adopted a more strategic approach to planning, recruiting and managing staff, resulting in an enhanced ability to build skills and retain talented staff. The Ministry of the Interior, which under a recent reorganisation of deconcentrated public services has become the employer of staff at the district office level, is currently in the process of implementing a staffing table based on standardised position and function descriptions and is starting to use this for workforce planning purposes in the context of its three-year budget plan. That said, there does not appear to be any general, systematic planning or analysis to ensure that the government as a whole has an adequate workforce to deliver on current or future strategic objectives in an efficient and effective manner.

This state of affairs is also illustrated through the responses provided by the Slovak government to the 2010 OECD Survey on Strategic HRM: the Slovak Republic ranked last among OECD countries in terms of use of strategic HRM tools in central government. The 2010 survey data point to the lack of a general accountability framework, no regular reviews of ministries' HRM capacities, the absence of performance management tools and little planning and forecasting of HR needs (Figure 3.7). Based on additional information received during interviews with Slovak officials in 2015, it would appear that little has changed in this regard since the survey was conducted. However, the Ministry of the Interior has recently begun to implement performance indicators for front line services in district offices. This is a positive development which could serve as a good practice example for other parts of the public service.

Figure 3.7. **Use of strategic human resources management tools in central government**

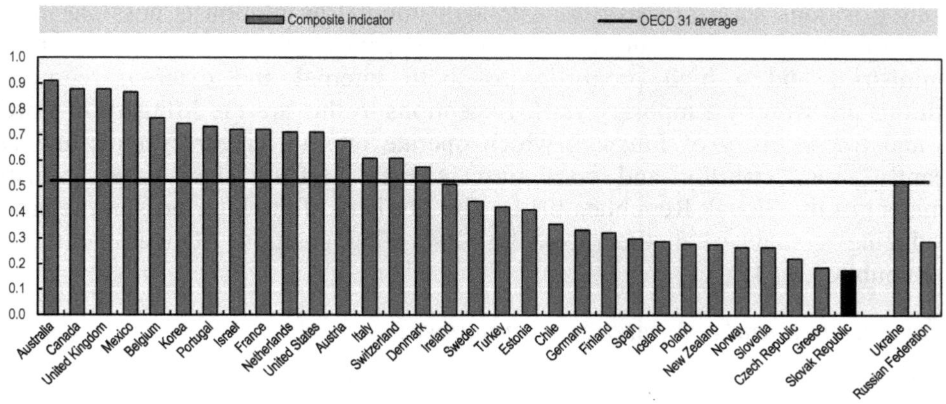

Notes: Data for Brazil, Hungary and Japan are not available. The index is composed of the following variables: the existence of a general accountability framework; the existence of HRM targets built into the performance assessments of top and middle managers; elements that top and middle management should take into account when planning and reporting within the general accountability framework; regular review and assessment of ministries'/departments' HRM capacity; existence of forward planning to adjust for adequate workforces to deliver services; and elements considered in governments' forward planning. The index ranges between 0 (low utilisation of strategic HRM practices) and 1 (high utilisation of strategic HRM practices). For further details on the methodology and factors used in constructing this index, see OECD (2011b), *OECD Government at a Glance 2011*, Annex E, available at: www.oecd.org/gov/indicators/govataglance; http://dx.doi.org/10.1787/gov_glance-2011-en.

Source: OECD (2010), "OECD Survey on Strategic Human Resources Management in Central/Federal Governments of OECD Countries", questions 35, 36, 37, 38, 39 and 41, OECD, Paris.

Mobility and career structures

The organisation of jobs and career structures is an important element of workforce flexibility, in that it can enable the efficient redeployment of staff and the reorganisation of how work gets done, as well as lead to increased mobility across institutional silos. It can heighten efficiency, by reducing transaction costs associated with managing employees, by introducing results-based management and by improving performance incentives. Flexibility can be enhanced through the creation of broader occupational groups and standard job profiles based on common sets of competencies, as well as by redesigning jobs to provide for more functional flexibility. Additionally, improving mobility arrangements for public employees is an important tool for strategic workforce planning and management, as well for fostering a whole-of-government perspective and collaboration among staff in different organisational units. Clear career structures and transparent promotion procedures can be a significant motivating factor for staff and enhance to the attractiveness of the public service as an employer, thereby contributing to the recruitment and retention of good staff.

Slovak government officials interviewed for this review indicated that mobility within the public service appeared difficult. That said, mobility programmes (in support of support both horizontal and external mobility) as well as exchange programmes to international and non-governmental organisations are outlined in the HRM Strategy to 2020. Currently, no formal job rotation or redeployment programmes exist and the lack of a co-ordinated approach to HRM across the civil service results in significant barriers to mobility between ministries. Further rigidities in workforce management result from the lack of a standardised set of job profiles or a standard way of describing and classifying positions across ministries. Although internal promotion is possible through competitive recruitment procedures, there do not appear to be clear career structures in most ministries and a high proportion of both internal and external recruitment competitions are won by temporary staff. Exceptions to this are the Ministry of Foreign Affairs and the Ministry of Finance, which operate internal career systems and have significantly more stability and continuity in their staffing than other ministries (Government of the Slovak Republic, 2014). The Ministry of the Interior is in the process of introducing a standard methodology for describing positions (Government of the Slovak Republic, 2014).

Skills development and competency management

Ensuring the right skills and competencies are available for government to achieve its strategic priorities relies partly on acquiring talent through effective recruitment and selection arrangements; but it also involves training and developing the skills and competencies of current employees. Developing the skills of public employees is important in order to continuously improve and adapt the competencies of the workforce and build human capital. At the same time, training and development have taken on increased importance as governments find themselves in competition for scarce skills in the knowledge economy. The drive for innovation and new ways of delivering public services calls for new or improved competencies, while the restructuring of the public service which is going on in many countries has increased the need to reskill staff in order to enable redeployment.

Civil servants in the Slovak Republic have a statutory entitlement to five days in-service training per year. In practice, however, training tends to be under-resourced (Government of the Slovak Republic, 2014). While in most OECD countries a central HRM body co-ordinates training policy and sets general guidelines for departments to follow when developing and delivering training, the Slovak public service does not have an overarching strategy or co-ordination system. The majority of training is developed and run by individual ministries, without reference to strategic planning for necessary organisational or whole-of-government competencies. Indeed, planning for the longer term development of competencies of civil servants is often not possible because of high turnover. Whole-of-service training is limited to employees entering the permanent civil service and consists of "adaption training" administered entirely by self-study. However, research carried out in the context of developing the HRM Strategy to 2020 found that there is no systematic and consistent approach to induction training for new employees.

The use of competency management and a common competency framework can be an effective tool for workforce planning and management, as a means also to promote mobility and improve recruitment and training. Most OECD countries have made efforts to develop competency management to adapt the public sector workforce to the needs of public policy setting and implementation and of service design and delivery. Competency frameworks help organisations to identify competency gaps and develop strategies to fill them. In this way, competency management has become an important instrument for building the capacity of the workforce.

Currently the Slovak government does not have a common competency framework, nor does it use competency management to guide strategic workforce planning and management. Competency-based job profiles and the use of common job profiles – which can help identify and fill the competencies needed by organisations – are not tools currently used in the Slovak central government.

Arrangements to provide continuity in staffing

Building a professional and stable civil service is essential for the overall effective functioning of government. Keeping the public administration in a constant state of flux works against the reliability and capacity of the public administration and makes the public service unattractive for good and well-qualified individuals. A certain level of tenure and employment guarantees for civil servants is necessary for continuity in the public administration and works in favour of stability and professionalism. Most OECD countries have laws that regulate civil servants' employment contracts. Continuity of employment is based on tenure (i.e. security of employment with dismissal only in cases of misbehaviour) or employment for an unspecified duration. There are also generally provisions regulating redeployment, retraining and redundancy to create scope for adaptation of the workforce (OECD, 2011a).

While the Slovak Republic's Civil Service Act of 2009 introduced a service contract between the civil servant and the Civil Service Office (CSO) and stronger employment protection for civil servants, these provisions have been slow to take effect. Civil servants in the Slovak Republic can be dismissed by the head of office, which is the highest management position in a ministry or other public service organisation. The Civil Service Act provides that dismissal can take place for organisational reasons or a breach of discipline. However, the definition of a serious breach of discipline and the procedures attached to this are left to the internal regulations of ministries (Government of the Slovak Republic, 2014). A 2006 amendment to the Civil Service Act made the post of head of office subject to political nomination and heads of office enjoy a high measure of discretion over recruitment, remuneration and termination of appointment of civil servants within their ministry. Politically influenced turnover in management positions continues to be an issue for the Slovak government, where data from 2010 show that even relatively junior management positions change with a change of government (Figure 3.8). This trend does not appear to have changed since 2010 and affects continuity within ministries, careers, staff motivation and the independence of policy advice, among other things.

The issue of high turnover among staff was mentioned by multiple ministries during the fact-finding interviews. Aside from politically influenced turnover, factors mentioned as possibly contributing to turnover include unpredictable career structures, salary levels that are insufficiently attractive compared to the private sector and the insecurity of employment that comes from lack of tenure. Frequent reorganisations, which tend to create uncertainty among staff, may also be a factor contributing to turnover (Government of the Slovak Republic, 2014). High turnover carries a whole set of disadvantages for organisations. It is expensive in terms of added recruitment costs and inefficient in terms of constant loss of skills and institutional knowledge; high turnover makes it very difficult for organisations to effectively plan their workforce on any meaningful timeframe, particularly if there is a risk that sweeping changes in personnel will occur with a change of government. Turnover also reduces the incentive for organisations to invest in the training and development of their staff as the resulting skills will be lost when staff leave.

Figure 3.8. **Turnover of civil servants with a change in government, 2010**

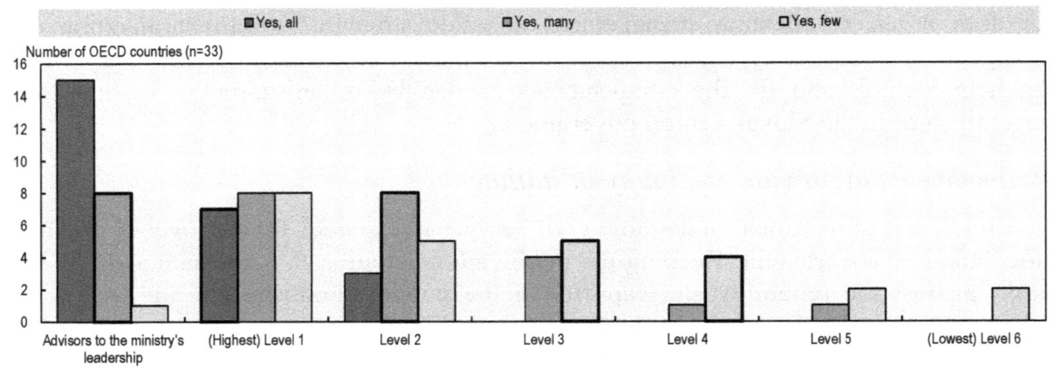

Note: Bars outlined with a thicker black line signify where the Slovak Republic answered yes.

Source: OECD (2010), "Survey on Strategic Human Resources Management in Central/Federal Governments of OECD Countries", OECD, Paris.

Using employees other than tenured civil servants

All OECD countries allow temporary employment for different short-term needs. In the Slovak Republic, the Civil Service Act 2009 provides for both permanent and temporary categories of employment. Discussions with officials during the course of this review suggest that there is significant recourse to the use of temporary employees, although this varies across ministries. This seems to be driven in part by frequent reorganisations and also by the need to bring in skills that are not available within the ministry. While this in itself is not necessarily a disadvantage, an over-reliance on temporary staff undermines the ability of an organisation to build up competencies and to plan its workforce over the medium to longer term. A major issue, however, is that temporary employment appears to often be used as an inside track to recruitment to the civil service, thereby undermining merit-based processes (Government of the Slovak Republic, 2014).

Recruitment and selection arrangements in the Slovak central government

Merit-based recruitment is one of the cornerstones of an effective, representative public service in OECD countries. Rules on merit-based recruitment and promotion are normally embedded in constitutional documents and public service legislation to ensure that public employees are selected on fair and objective grounds and to prevent all forms of patronage – personal as well as political. While arrangements vary widely across OECD countries, common features are strong merit-protection arrangements and use of modern, well-validated recruitment methods to ensure that the public service selects the best candidates.

In the Slovak Republic, recruitment is decentralised to ministries, which enjoy a large measure of discretion in organising their recruitment and selection procedures. The system of recruitment in the Slovak public service today leans towards a position-based rather than a career-based system, where applicants apply to specific posts that are mainly open to external recruitment (Figure 3.9). Nevertheless, there is a significant use of internal recruitment. Research carried out in the context of the development of the HRM Strategy to 2020 found that 69.5% of recruitments were through external competitions, while the remainder were through internal selection procedures. Internal selection was used particularly in the Ministry of Foreign Affairs, the Ministry of Finance and the Ministry of the Interior, suggesting that these ministries have a stronger element of career structure and career management than other ministries (Government of the Slovak Republic, 2014).

Figure 3.9. **Position verses career-based systems of recruitment across OECD countries**

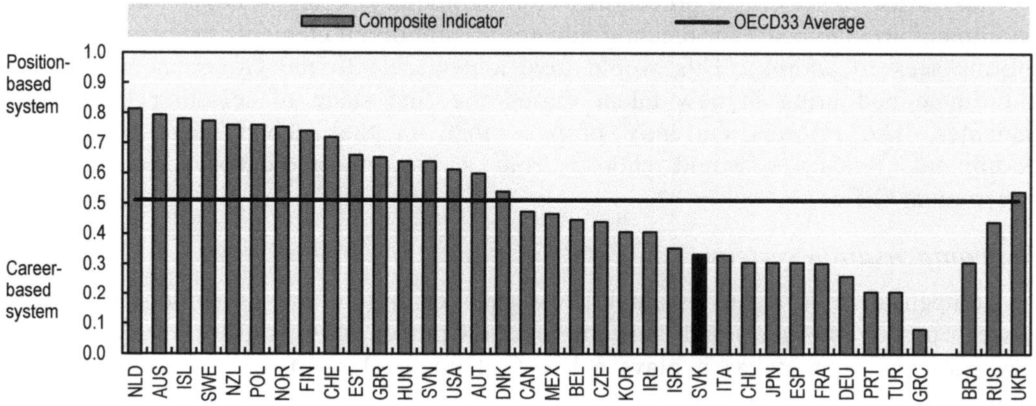

Source: OECD (2010), "Survey on Strategic Human Resources Management in Central/Federal Governments of OECD Countries", OECD, Paris.

Recruitment and selection procedures are laid down in the Civil Service Act 2009. In practice, it would appear that ministries often do not adhere fully to these common standards as, in contrast to the majority of OECD countries, there is no central HRM unit responsible for standardising recruitment, designing job profiles and competency frameworks and overseeing the recruitment process. Nor is there an independent merit-protection agency, such as exists in a number of OECD countries, and unsuccessful candidates do not have recourse to appeal procedures. However, the proposed new Civil Service Act includes the establishment of a Civil Service Council as a politically independent authority to oversee compliance with the legislation.

Vacancies in the permanent civil service must be advertised in the press and the Official Gazette. In contrast to most OECD countries, there is no central Internet portal or webpage to publish all public service positions. As no common competencies or job profiles exist, job requirements are defined by individual ministries and vary in terms of elements such as the content of written tests, the structure and composition of selection committees, interview procedures and ranking of candidates. Most ministries have no objective standards for validating the skills and personal characteristics of candidates and most do not organise training in selection procedures for members of selection commissions (Government of the Slovak Republic, 2014). In the absence of competency management, the content of examinations and interviews is not structured around well-defined competency requirements for particular positions. Selection is through a written examination and an interview with a selection commission. Temporary employment in the civil service, which is not subject to any merit requirements and is often done on an informal basis, appears frequently to be used as a stepping stone to recruitment to the permanent civil service. Research carried out in the context of the development of the HRM Strategy to 2020 found that almost three-quarters of all recruitment competitions (71%) were won by temporary employees, although there were variations between ministries.

These findings highlight inequality in the opportunities for recruitment, as well as weaknesses in selection procedures which bring into question whether the principle of merit is effectively upheld in recruitment, and whether selection is based on objective, well-validated and documented grounds that result in the selection of the best candidates. In any country, weaknesses in the recruitment and selection system leave the staffing of the civil service potentially open to cronyism, patronage and political influence.

Standardised selection procedures for temporary civil servants and specific recruitment arrangements for recent graduates are important elements the proposed HRM reforms seek to address. This would give a new role to the Government Office to co-ordinate and bring in new talent during the first stage of selecting from recent graduates. The reforms currently propose that, in the second stage of graduate recruitment, ministries would choose from a list of candidates selected by the Government Office.

The compensation system

Compensation is a fundamental HRM area central to the psychological contract between public employers and their employees. Compensation is also directly related to organisational capacity, as it plays a key (but not exclusive) role in determining the number and quality of employees attracted to work in public sector institutions. Part of this attractiveness rests on employees' perception that levels of pay fairly reflect merit: the skills and competence of employees and the difficulty of the work they do.

In the Slovak government, line ministries and managers are responsible for the majority of decisions regarding compensation. The basic wage is determined by the salary grade of the employee, according to the law. Currently there are 11 salary grades for civil servants, defined under the Regulation of the Government of the Slovak Republic. In most OECD countries, job content is the most important factor in determining base salary. Relevant experience is a key factor in determining base salary for middle management and professional positions as well as for secretarial and technical support staff. Educational qualifications are also particularly important for professionals (OECD, 2012b).

Table 3.1. **Elements for determining base salary in OECD countries**

	Top management	Middle management	Professional	Secretarial staff	Technical support
Job content	27	26	27	25	22
Relevant experience	23	25	26	25	25
Educational qualifications	22	22	25	23	23
Performance appraisals	22	22	23	21	19
Seniority in the position	18	22	24	18	17

Source: OECD (2012b), *Public Sector Compensation in Times of Austerity*, OECD Publishing, Paris, http://dx.doi.org/10.1787/9789264177758-en.

Bonuses complement the basic wage and constitute a large part of total compensation. Discretionary personal performance bonuses can account for up to or exceeding 100% of the basic salary grade established in the Civil Service Act. This makes for a complicated and opaque remuneration system with a high element of discretion for managers to augment the salaries of their staff.

Decisions regarding personal bonuses are delegated to individual managers of civil servants. However, there are no standardised objective performance assessment criteria on which managers base their decisions for personal bonuses. While the trend in OECD countries points toward greater use of performance-related pay, with less emphasis on seniority-based pay, this is usually accompanied by standardised and objective assessment criteria, the use of performance appraisals and objectives setting (Figure 3.10). Performance appraisals, which are common in the majority of OECD countries, were abolished in the Slovak Republic when the current Civil Service Act came into force in 2009. The OECD understands that the new Civil Service Act proposes to streamline the number of salary grades as well as bring back performance appraisals on which performance-related pay will be based.

Figure 3.10. **The use of performance-related pay**

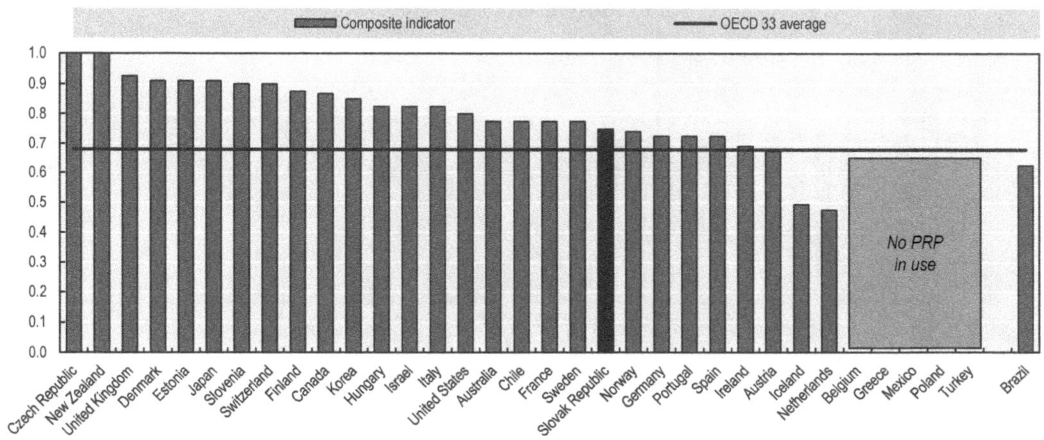

Source: OECD (2010), "Survey on Strategic Human Resources Management in Central/Federal Governments of OECD Countries", OECD, Paris.

On average, salary levels are seen to be low in comparison to private sector wages, posing a severe challenge for ministries to attract and retain talent. In addition, there appear to be two remuneration systems running in parallel. Previous civil servants were granted increments of 4% per annum, while increments have been cut back to 1% in recent years. This has created salary gaps, where younger staff who have recently joined the civil service are less well paid than longer serving civil servants. This creates difficulties for motivating and retaining young professional staff. It is not clear that the proposed, relatively limited reforms to the salary system will adequately address this issue.

Institutional arrangements for human resources management

Almost all OECD countries have a central HRM body. The Slovak Republic is one of only two OECD countries which do not have a central human resources management body. Most commonly, the scope of the central HRM authority extends over the core ministries and their direct operating agencies. While the mandate and tasks of central HRM institutions vary, they are generally responsible for designing and overseeing core HRM policies, leaving a degree of implementation flexibility to line ministries and line managers. A move towards increased delegation of HRM is seen across many OECD countries. Central HRM authorities increasingly delegate HRM responsibilities to managers across the administration, providing them with guidance and support, as well as providing shared systems; however, the extent of HRM delegation varies among OECD member countries (Figure 3.11). Experience in OECD member countries shows that effective delegation of HRM authority has to be accompanied by:

- strengthening of the capacity of the central HRM body to monitor the implementation of HRM policy
- effective systems to hold managers accountable for their handling of delegated authority
- adequate managerial capacity and competence in ministries and other institutions.

Figure 3.11. **Extent of delegation of human resources management practices to individual ministries**

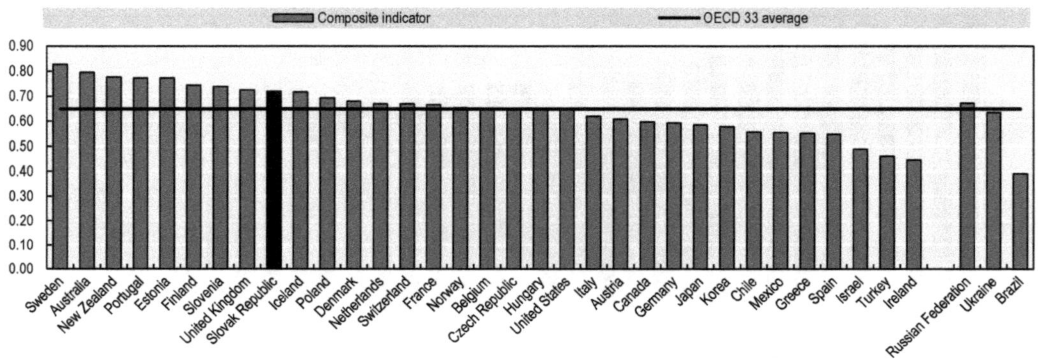

Notes: The index is composed of the following variables: the existence of a central HRM body, and the role of line ministries in determining: the number and types posts within organisations; the allocation of the budget envelope between payroll and other expenses; staff compensation levels; position classification, recruitment and dismissals; and conditions of employment. The index ranges from 0 (no delegation) to 1 (high level of delegation). Missing data for countries were estimated by mean replacement. For further details on the methodology and factors used in constructing this index see OECD (2011b), *Government at a Glance 2011*, Annex E, available at: www.oecd.org/gov/indicators/govataglance; http://dx.doi.org/10.1787/gov_glance-2011-en.

Source: OECD (2010), "Survey on Strategic Human Resources Management in Central/Federal Governments of OECD Countries", OECD, Paris.

HRM is highly decentralised in the Slovak central government, with limited co-ordination or common standards implemented across ministries. Ministries' service offices are delegated significant responsibility for most HRM functions including salary, recruitment, training, career management and dismissal. Yet, unlike most OECD countries, this delegation has not been accompanied by guidelines, common frameworks or an effective oversight body at the central level to create some consistency and coherence across the system. None of the elements highlighted above for effective delegation of HRM authority exist in the Slovak system. Attempts to achieve greater co-ordination in the mid-2000s proved unsuccessful, with a short-lived Civil Service Office abolished in 2006. A degree of central oversight has been reinstated with the

Government Office taking over responsibility for oversight of compliance with civil service legislation from the Ministry of Labour, Social Affairs and Family in November 2013. Recently, the Government Office has taken the lead in co-ordinating the development of the HRM Strategy to 2020 and is also taking steps to set up a central personnel registry for the civil service. If adopted, the proposed new Civil Service Act would build central oversight and co-ordination responsibilities in the Government Office. It is not clear, however, whether this would also entail building capacity within the Government Office to cope with its proposed new responsibilities.

Performance management, accountability and leadership capacity to steer strategic policy development and implementation

Performance management and accountability frameworks in the Slovak central government

Improving the efficiency and effectiveness of government is a high priority for OECD countries, particularly in the current economic environment. Efforts to strengthen performance orientation involve creating government-wide frameworks to drive organisational performance, as well as constant efforts to improve HRM systems for motivating staff and managing the performance of individuals and teams. A central issue that countries have to deal with in this context is the balance between giving government organisations sufficient managerial freedom to enable them to function as efficiently as possible and maintaining sufficient control and oversight to satisfy the requirements of public accountability and probity that are essential to good governance. The general trend in OECD countries has been to delegate more authority to managers, including for HRM, while increasing their accountability for results and strengthening accountability through reporting and performance management arrangements.

Performance management should link the management of people with organisational goals and strategies and, ultimately, with the government's programme and objectives. This involves four levels of performance management:

- At the highest level, the government develops performance-oriented practices and procedures, including a government-wide framework for developing performance information (evaluation and performance measures), integrating performance information into budget and accountability processes, using it in decision making, and monitoring and reporting on results (OECD, 2009).
- At the programme level, performance management is focused on the desired output of government programmes and on what has been accomplished, such as volume and value of service take-up, upward trends for inclusion and user satisfaction.
- At the organisational level, performance enhancement is part of long-term strategic planning and focused on impact, resource utilisation and improvement of public services and is also focused on improving organisational performance through better management, organisational reforms and process improvements to deliver improved services and outputs.
- At the level of teams and individuals, performance management is about motivating employees, setting performance objectives within the framework of organisational objectives and strategies, using performance assessment to improve performance and dealing with issues of poor performance.

The index in Figure 3.12 reflects the existence of a formalised performance assessment; use of performance assessment tools such as meetings with supervisors, frequency of meetings and written feedback; the performance assessment criteria used; and the importance of good performance assessments for career advancement, remuneration, contract renewal on the same job/remaining in the same job and employment contract renewal. The Slovak Republic does not rank in this figure as no formalised performance assessment exists. At the individual level, there is no use of performance assessment tools (such as setting and reviewing performance objectives and having performance meetings with supervisors) and no performance management framework to set and link individual objectives with organisational and whole-of-government ones. However, the new Civil Service Act includes provision for individual performance assessment (Box 3.1).

Figure 3.12. **The use of performance assessment for human resources management**

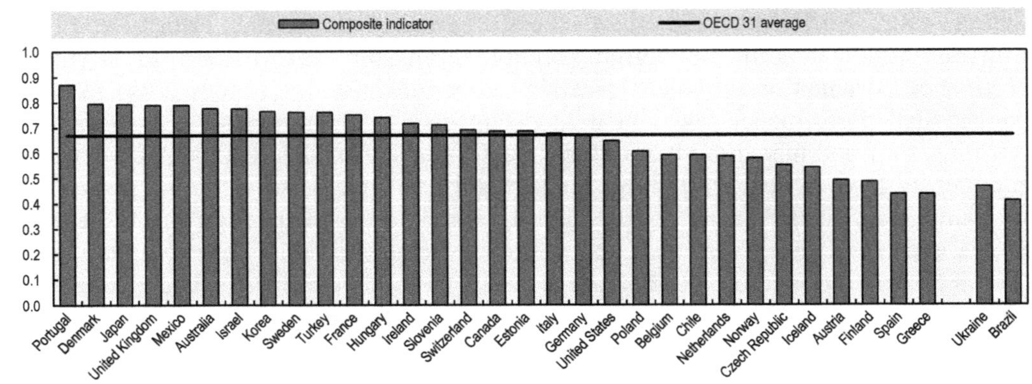

Source: OECD (2010), "Survey on Strategic Human Resources Management in Central/Federal Governments of OECD Countries", OECD, Paris.

Leadership capacity and managing the senior civil service

Strengthening the capability of the civil service to steer and lead policy relies on a well-managed and competent cadre of senior civil servants and reasonable continuity at senior management levels. Senior leaders also play a key role in ensuring organisational performance and are often held accountable for results. Currently, there are no dedicated practices for managing or developing the competencies of the senior civil servants in the Slovak government (Figure 3.13). As mentioned above, politically influenced turnover in the senior civil service is very high, which affects, among other things, the independence of policy advice. The proposed HRM reforms (Box 3.1) seek to address stability in the senior civil service by stabilising levels from Director General down. These proposals, however, would not apply to the Head of Office (the equivalent of administrative secretaries general/deputy ministers/permanent secretaries), who oversees many aspects of HRM within the individual ministries.

Human resources management reform in the Slovak Republic

The Slovak central government is in the midst of reforming many aspects of public employment and management, including devising a new Civil Service Act (CSA) to replace the 2009 legislation currently in force and developing an HRM Strategy to be implemented between 2015 and 2020. Both of these efforts were developed through inter-ministerial working groups, led by the Government Office. The reforms are based around core civil service principles or values such as political impartiality, legality, transparent recruitment, efficient management, impartiality, professionalism, transparent and equal remuneration, stability and fair treatment (Box 3.1).

Figure 3.13. **Use of separate human resources management practices for senior civil servants in central government**

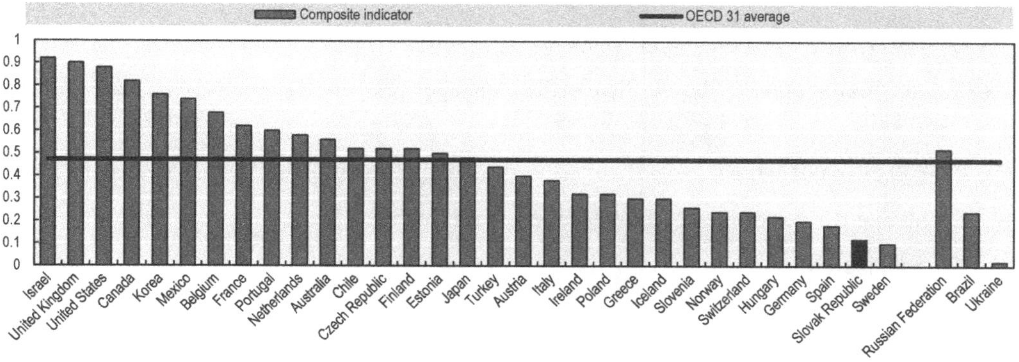

Notes: Denmark and New Zealand do not have a centralised HRM policy regarding senior civil servants and have therefore been removed from the index. The index is composed of the following variables: the existence of a separate group of senior civil servants; the existence of policies for the identification of potential senior civil servants early in their careers; the use of a centrally defined skills profile for senior civil service; and the use of separate recruitment, performance management and performance-related pay practices for the senior civil service. The index ranges between 0 (HRM practices are not differentiated for the senior civil service) and 1 (HRM practices are much differentiated for the senior civil service). Missing data for countries were estimated by mean replacement. For further details on the methodology and factors used in constructing this index, see OECD (2011b), *Government at a Glance 2011*, Annex E, available at: www.oecd.org/gov/indicators/govataglance; http://dx.doi.org/10.1787/gov_glance-2011-en.

Source: OECD (2010), "Survey on Strategic Human Resources Management in Central/Federal Governments of OECD Countries", OECD, Paris.

Box 3.1. **The civil service reform framework in the Slovak central government**

The Slovak central government is in the midst of reforming many aspects of its public employment and management. The reform actions proposed are centred around core civil service principles and include specific actions:

- **Political impartiality,** civil servants put the public interest above political interests.
  - Abolishing dismissal of superior employees without stating reasons.
  - Protecting civil servants at dismissal, particularly dismissal due to organisational changes.
  - Establishing the Civil Service Council as a politically independent authority.
- **Legality,** civil servants and the service offices act in accordance with the law and legal regulations.
  - Supervision of service offices by superior service offices and by the Government Office.
  - Establishing disciplinary procedures for violating civil servants' rights and obligations.
- **Transparent recruitment,** public access to information on vacancies, equal opportunities and unified conditions for admission based on merit.
  - Compulsory selection procedures into the temporary civil service.
  - Standard methods and procedures for selection.

Box 3.1. **The civil service reform framework in the Slovak central government** (*continued*)

- New modern methods of selection:
  - ❖ assessment centre
  - ❖ pooling system.
- Central registry for selection procedures.

- **Efficient management,** the service office manages the civil servants efficiently, effectively and economically.
  - Planning of civil service posts in the central registry in accordance with principles of planning.
  - Evaluating the performance of civil servants and linking it to:
    - ❖ remuneration
    - ❖ training
    - ❖ possibility to dismiss from the civil service.
- **Impartiality,** civil servant puts the public interest above personal interests.
  - Establishing rights and obligations of the civil servant.
  - Adopting a Code of Ethics.
  - Establishing a Civil Service Council.
- **Professionalism,** the principle of professionalism emphasises the need to develop the expertise of civil servants.
  - Establishing a mentor for newly recruited civil servants.
  - Establishing career growth institutions – compulsory selection procedures for higher post; internal competition.
- **Transparent and equal remuneration,** civil servants are remunerated based on predefined legal criteria. For equal work, equal pay is deserved.
  - Abolishing the first two salary scales.
  - Monitoring the classification of civil servants into salary scales based on the tasks performed via the central registry.
  - Linking performance evaluation and disciplinary procedure results to remuneration.
- **Stability and fair treatment,** the civil servant is protected from dismissal for other than legally stated reasons and the service office keeps performing civil servants in the civil service system.
  - Registration of surplus employees in the central registry.
  - Abolishing dismissals of superior employees without stating reasons.
  - Supporting career growth.
- **Fair treatment,** the service office proceeds, acts and takes decisions towards civil servants and candidates for the civil service impartially while respecting their privacy, constitutional rights and legal rights.

Box 3.1. **The civil service reform framework in the Slovak central government** *(continued)*

- Follow-up on the Anti-discrimination Law.
- Civil Service Council.

Source: Information provided by Slovak officials during the workshop "Scaling up HRM reforms to strengthen the capability of the public service" held in May 2015 in Bratislava.

Implementation of these reforms is proposed via the new Civil Service Act, secondary legislation supporting the act, the strategy for human resource management in the civil service, concrete institutions such as the proposed Civil Service Council and the central registry for the civil service, and ensuring the Government Office's role as a supervisory and specialised HRM body.

Assessment

Strengthening strategic workforce planning and management across the public sector

Improving data as a foundation for strategic workforce planning and management

Improving the quality of data on the public workforce will provide a solid foundation for workforce planning and management. The HRM Strategy to 2020 proposes a central register of establishments, civil service positions and civil servants on a single IT platform. This can facilitate control of public employment costs and provide more reliable data for decision makers to determine how best to manage the workforce to deliver public services. A more standardised approach to defining civil service positions across ministries, as proposed in the HRM Strategy to 2020, would facilitate the collection of workforce data. To the extent that staffing can be better planned and managed, there is likely to be scope to have fewer but better paid positions, thereby improving the ability to attract and retain good staff.

Recently, the Government Office conducted a survey regarding the skills structure of the civil service. This is a positive step in the planned establishment of a civil service personnel register. It would be advisable to keep the data collection relatively basic in the initial stage so as not to over-burden ministries: simply having an accurate record of the number of public servants in each ministry would be a step forward. Good co-ordination between the Government Office and the Ministry for Finance from the outset will be necessary so that the links between budgeting and workforce management can be established.

A number of ministries have their own human resource information systems (HRIS), which could likely complicate the establishment of a centralised workforce information system as data may not be in a standard format. Investing in ministry-specific HRIS does not represent the most effective use of resources and a more co-ordinated approach is desirable. ICT systems are not solutions in themselves, but can be effective platforms to enable data collection and analysis. The proposal in the HRM Strategy to 2020 of a common IT solution as a tool for HR is a positive step.

Once the basics have been solidly established, workforce data can go beyond counting the number of employees in a given organisation to support organisations to plan, support and develop workforce capacity. Including factors such as level of education, skills and competencies supports organisations in aligning particular capacities with the right priorities. It is also important to consider factors that impact cost, such as age and rank, and years of service. These factors also ensure that planning can aim to strike a balance between young and more experienced staff, and helps for succession and renewal planning. Ultimately, the collection and use of good workforce data has to come from senior management and requires a supportive organisational culture. However, overcoming the initial barriers and gaining the co-operation of ministries is likely to require sustained commitment at the political level.

The practices of several OECD countries which carry out whole-of-government assessment and analysis of the government workforce may be of interest to the Slovak government. As shown in the examples in Box 3.2, this enables governments to keep track of overall numbers of employees and to promote a strategic dialogue on HRM across levels of government.

Box 3.2. Workforce information management practices in selected countries

In 2004, **Belgium** implemented the SEPP Project as a standard methodology to count civil servants in each of the federal public services. It takes into account the paid workforce of a service, including management, statutory and contractual staff. The methodology includes strict time parameters for counting staff to avoid the problem of constant flux of the workforce due to flows in and out of employment. SEPP provides an estimation of an employee's cost based on the real latest paid salary, an estimation of the average cost of existing personnel and a standardised definition of the overhead costs. SEPP is used annually in the workforce planning process and monthly to track progress of the workforce plan. The government uses SEPP on a yearly basis to analyse the risk level for all services in their workforce planning process and to avoid bankruptcy (*ex ante* control), which is published in the personnel plan assessment; and every four months to analyse the evolution of the number of civil servants.

Canada has a "Public Service Management (PSM) Dashboard" which pulls together data from different systems, such as the central payroll system, department-specific data systems, recruitment systems, etc. The PSM Dashboard is an online suite of information and knowledge transfer tools developed to meet the performance monitoring and reporting needs of central agencies, as well as to inform decision making by deputy heads and departmental HR officials. It contains more than 250 performance measures accessible to over 1 700 users across the public service. The PSM Dashboard will eventually incorporate additional performance measures, toolkits, hyperlinks and functionalities to enable a high-performing public service.

The **United Kingdom** publishes the business plan quarterly data summaries (QDS) designed to provide a quarterly snapshot on how each department is spending its budget, the results it has achieved and how it is deploying its workforce. Their primary purpose is to make more of the management information currently held by government available to members of the public on a regular basis in an easy-to-read format. The UK government intends for an annual version of this information to be formally laid in parliament in an annual report and accounts. The QDS template is the same for all departments, though many of the individual indicators are unique to the department (especially input and impact indicators). In addition, there is monthly management information on staff numbers and pay bill costs in Cabinet Office and non-consolidated performance-related pay data for the Cabinet Office.

Brazil's Ministry of Planning Budgeting and Management publishes every month a Personnel Statistical Bulletin (*Boletim Estatístico de Pessoal*). It contains data on personnel expenditure, distribution of staff by organisation and entity of the federal administration, the number of public servants and the distribution based on the level of remuneration, as well as information on the profiles

Box 3.2. **Workforce information management practices in selected countries** (*continued*)

of jobs contained in the job structure.

The **Irish** civil service has an HR Management System which records all personnel details and information for all civil servants. This provides transparency to citizens about HR resources and assists with evidence-based HR policy decisions by providing evidence for consideration of policy options. A databank website (http://databank.per.gov.ie) provides comprehensive information on every aspect of government expenditure over the years, including public service numbers. Users can easily create tables and spreadsheets showing how spending on current, capital or pay has evolved since 1994, whether for the whole of government or for individual departments. The databanks provide the public with an unprecedented volume of historical and current data about how public money is spent, in what area and how the expenditure trends have evolved over the years.

Colombia has recently built an Information and Public Management System (SIGEP is the Spanish acronym) which intends to eventually integrate employment information of all public sector employees at the state, territorial and local levels. SIGEP brings together information that identifies and characterises civil servants and government contractors, as well as information on the organisational structures of state institutions. The system has been built and institutions are now populating it with data. The data are available through an online portal (www.sigep.gov.co/home) which is open to the public, increasing the transparency of public employment policy and the structure of public institutions.

Sources: Huerta Melchor, O. (2012), "The government workforce of the future: Innovation in strategic workforce planning in OECD countries", *OECD Working Papers on Public Governance*, No. 21, OECD Publishing, Paris, http://dx.doi.org/10.1787/5k487727gwvb-en; Information from the Civil Service HR Division, Department of Public Expenditure and Reform, Republic of Ireland; SIGEP website and presentations given on missions in 2014.

Linking workforce planning to other public service reforms

A number of OECD countries have established procedures to link workforce planning to the strategic planning, budgeting and performance management frameworks of organisations. This facilitates a whole-of-government approach to managing the size of the public service and increasing the efficiency of service delivery. Integrating workforce planning in this way with other public service reforms in the Slovak Republic over the medium term would put workforce planning on a firm foundation and should, in time, enable a transition from the current system of tight *ex ante* controls to a more flexible and strategic system of managing workforce numbers and costs within an overall management accountability framework. If a roadmap for this could be established, it could help to incentivise ministries to engage in the change process.

As the delivery of public services in the Slovak Republic is highly decentralised and most staff work in deconcentrated services of the central government, a targeted investment in establishing workforce planning at this level may be the best strategy, rather than trying to achieve a whole-of-government reform all at the same time. The Ministry of the Interior is already taking a more strategic approach to workforce management in the district offices and this can be built upon to bring early benefits in terms of improved service delivery, thereby providing a good practice example for other areas of the public service. Other key services such as health, education and those supporting industry and enterprise could also be prioritised. Getting strategic workforce planning and management established in such major sectors would be a significant step in scaling up HRM reforms.

Effective workforce planning will require better HRM tools to manage staff: mobility mechanisms, compensation, career management and training are all essential for more flexible and strategic management of the workforce. The Government Office could facilitate the development of these tools by establishing policy frameworks and encouraging pilot projects, as well as carrying forward the implementation of already planned HRM reforms. Measures to favour mobility could usefully be developed at the district office level in the first instance.

Another important contribution the Government Office could make would be to develop tools and frameworks and to organise training in workforce planning so as to enable the service offices of ministries to build their capacity. It would also be important to communicate, incentivise and demonstrate the benefits of strategic workforce planning and management to staff in the service offices. Pilot projects to highlight the benefits could be a useful starting point, particularly by demonstrating how this can enable capacity building in areas such as analysis and digital government. Co-ordination between ministries and the Government Office could also be considered when building the analytical capacities necessary for existing analytical units, or those currently being developed in some ministries.

Competency management and common job profiles to support strategic workforce planning and human capital development

Competency management and the use of common job profiles are tools which the Slovak government could benefit from to advance the strategic orientation and integration of key HRM areas including workforce planning, recruitment and selection, mobility, and training and development so as to build human capital in the public service.

Competency frameworks help organisations to identify competency gaps and strategies to fill them. The example of the United Kingdom's civil service competency framework (Box 3.3) gives a glimpse at how one country has structured and grouped its competencies. The Irish example gives a view of how various competencies apply to a particular position within the administration, in this case a service delivery supervisor.

Box 3.3. **OECD country examples of a competency framework**

The United Kingdom: Professional Skills for Government competency framework

The Professional Skills for Government (PSG) competency framework is used for jobs and careers in the British civil service. It sets out the skills that staff in the civil service need to do their job well, at all levels and no matter where they work. The PSG competency framework applies to all civil service jobs at all grades. The PSG framework can help civil servants identify: 1) the mix of skills and experience they should have in their current or prospective job; and 2) the skills they might need to gain to change roles or seek promotion. Civil servants are encouraged to think about the framework in line with their appraisal cycle, which provides an opportunity to look at the skills they have and the skills they need. This is a valuable tool for civil servants to plan their careers.

The PSG competency framework is divided into four separate, but supporting, areas:

1. Leadership: civil service leadership qualities sit at the centre of the framework to provide direction for the organisation, deliver results, build capacity for the organisation to address current and future challenges, and act with integrity.
2. Core skills: every civil servant needs certain core skills to perform effectively. For example, at Grade 7 the four core skills are people management, financial management, analysis and use of

Box 3.3. **OECD country examples of a competency framework** (*continued*)

evidence, and programme and project management.

3. Professional skills: job-specific professional skills are related to the work civil servants do. Everyone in the civil service requires some professional skills in, for example, policy development, operational delivery or providing expert advice (for example, scientists, economists and communicators). This area of the PSG is supported by heads of profession, who set standards for all professions in the civil service.
4. Broader experience: for senior civil service (SCS) members and those aspiring to the SCS, both depth and breadth of experience are important. Deep professional knowledge is valuable, but as civil servants progress in their careers, breadth of experience becomes increasingly important. Heads of profession lead the work to define broader experience in each professional context. This experience could be gained within the profession, within another part of the civil service or in other sectors.

Ireland: An example of a competency framework for service supervisors

Team work

- Leads by example, keeps an eye on performance and tries to get the best out of people.
- Shows respect for and builds good working relationships with colleagues and co-workers.
- Works to build team spirit and resolve difficulties between team members.

Initiative and problem solving

- Comes up with practical solutions to work problems.
- Makes sound decisions and can stand by them.
- Is flexible and regularly looks to see how work can be improved.

Delivery of results

- Takes responsibility for own work and the work of the team.
- Approaches and carries out all work in a thorough and organised manner, prioritising where necessary.
- Ensures work is completed to a high standard.

Customer service and communication skills

- Listens to customers and is respectful, courteous and professional.
- Tries to calm down difficult situations when dealing with people who are unhappy/angry.
- Communicates clearly and fluently with customers, the team and other managers.

Drive and commitment

- Takes pride in a job well done, even if work is routine or less pleasant.
- Is personally honest and trustworthy.
- Is interested in work and doing the job well.
- Is resilient and sticks with tasks, seeking to overcome obstacles or setbacks.

Specialist knowledge, expertise and self development

- Develops and maintains the skills and expertise required to perform in the role effectively.
- Understands the importance of health and safety in the workplace and follows safety guidelines.
- Provides others with advice and guidance on a range of areas/issues.

Source: UK Civil Service website, www.civilservice.gov.uk (accessed on 5 November 2012); Information provided by the Civil Service HR Division, Department of Public Expenditure and Reform, Republic of Ireland.

Together with competency management, job profiling reflects the changing nature of organisations and work. Traditional job descriptions, which tended to describe jobs in terms of a finite set of tasks to be done, have come to be regarded as a source of rigidity. Job profiling focuses instead on the outputs of results and on the profile of the person needed to do the job. Many organisations use competencies as part of the job profile as a way of defining and measuring the skills, abilities and behaviours considered necessary for the job. Box 3.4 shows an example of a standard job profile template and a menu of competencies from which employing organisations could select.

Adopting a competency management framework could help the Slovak central government secure the principle of merit in recruitment and selection arrangements, while also standardising the structure of job descriptions across ministries, thereby making it easier to promote mobility. The idea is not to replace hard credentials with behavioural competencies, but to use education and skills credentials to set minimum standards and then use competency testing to supplement this assessment for a more fine-tuned selection process. This requires the incorporation of new tools into the selection process, such as experience-based interviewing, behaviour simulations, assessment centres and the validation of transferable competencies that may be acquired through experience in other job settings.

A competency management framework could also ensure a more strategic approach to career and skills development in the Slovak government, contributing to the development of human capital along the lines already highlighted in the HRM Strategy to 2020. The examples in Box 3.5 highlight the use of competency management in recruitment and selection, career management and skills development in a number of OECD countries, which the Slovak central government could consider using to strengthen the capacity of its workforce.

Box 3.4. **Example of a job profile template**

Job title:

Employing organisation:

Job purpose:

Job level or grade:

Reporting relationship:

Accountabilities

(Major outputs for which the job holder is personally accountable)

Key result areas:

(How achievement of outputs is measured)

Competencies required for the job (to be selected from a standard list):

- Technical/specialised knowledge and skills (scaled according to level required)
- Interpersonal competencies (communication, team-working, relational skills, etc.) (scaled according to level required)
- Qualifications (relevant academic and/or professional qualifications)
- Experience (for entry-level positions no experience is required)
- Management and leadership competencies (if relevant)

As with all HRM reforms, the development and implementation of a new competency framework can be difficult unless senior and middle managers, as well as employees, are involved and committed. Benefits to employees in terms of improved career path, professional development and career flexibility should be clearly communicated to all parties involved. The roadmap in Box 3.6 presents one way to think through the process and may help the Slovak government to consider some of the necessary elements to advance towards competency management.

Building a professional, educated and stable workforce managed through fair, rules-based and transparent practices

Stability at management level and ensuring a certain level of tenure and employment guarantees for civil servants is essential for the overall effective functioning of government, and for the successful implementation of the PAR agenda, as recognised in the HRM Strategy to 2020. Moreover, as the labour market improves, the government is likely to find itself in competition with private sector employers for recruiting staff. This underlines the importance of creating an employment offering that will enable the public service to attract and retain the right staff.

Box 3.5. Competency-based recruitment and selection, career management and training and development in selected OECD countries

Korea. In the process of recruitment and selection, competency management is used at selection examinations. Testing for the selection of new civil servants consists of several stages, and each stage uses various selection tools for evaluating different competencies and knowledge. In a series of civil service entrance examinations for a Grade 5 position, the first exam (the Public Service Aptitude Test or PSAT) evaluates the basic traits and competencies necessary for civil servants; the second exam measures professional knowledge; and the third exam estimates competencies, attitude and values through interviews and group discussions. Recently emphasised is the application of the competency model throughout the selection process. For example, for competency-based interviews, at the third entrance examination for Grade 5, the government identifies specific competencies for each grade and job category by applying qualitative and quantitative approaches, then constructs competency maps and a competency encyclopaedia by mapping the identified competencies. In the interviews, competency assessment, applying Behavioural Event Interview (BEI) and Assessment Centre (AC) tactics, is implemented.

Netherlands. In 2004 and 2005, the career management programme "management learning lines" was prepared under the "modernising government" umbrella. The idea was that a prospective manager follows a partly structured path towards a top management position. The paths may vary but will, as a rule, consist of a variety of work experiences, training, coaching, intervision and other developmental activities (ABD, 2005; 2006). The actual offer of a variety of work experience opportunities increased because the ABD career programme expanded to include, amongst others, the ministries and the four largest municipalities (Amsterdam, Rotterdam, The Hague and Utrecht). The programme aims at providing learning lines, career possibilities and instruments for the development of prospective managers. One project consists of enhancing collaboration between the ministries' management development programmes. Another project is "portfolio management", a concept for exchanging information about the qualities, performance and potential of people on the basis of a personalised dossier with objectified information, such as a CV, an ambition document, an assessment and 360-degree feedback reports.

Australia. The Australian Public Service (APS) Commission has been working closely with agencies throughout the APS to address some of the strategic issues around building capability in the APS. In 2001, it decided to address the development challenges of one particular group of employees: those working in human resources management areas. The role of HR practitioners has broadened in the APS, as attempts to integrate HR planning, policies and practices increasingly link it with organisational change, workforce planning and achieving business outcomes. The HR Capability Model articulates the capabilities required of effective HR staff in the APS. To support agencies further, and in conjunction with 13 agencies that contributed to its funding and realisation, the APS Commission

Box 3.5. **Competency-based recruitment and selection, career management and training and development in selected OECD countries** (*continued*)

designed an HR Capability Development Programme to assist participants to develop their capabilities against the model (APSC, 2003). The HR Capability Development Programme is very practical in its approach and design. The programme's focus is on developing skills that will give HR staff greater ability to be effective in strategic HR roles. The programme does not explore HR theory in depth, nor does it focus on the theoretical or operational aspects of different HR practice areas. What the programme does do is help participants develop the capabilities necessary to understand key business issues in their agencies and how these issues need to drive HR services and initiatives (APSC, 2009a).

In 1999, a Career Development Assessment Centre (CDAC) was established to assess members of the Senior Executive Selection (SES) feeder group and to help identify their development needs for possible future promotion to the SES. It uses the Senior Executive Leadership Capabilities (SELC) framework as a basis in assessing participant performance through a series of formal scenario activities, and in supporting 360-degree feedback. Participants are measured against the SELC Framework and the Integrated Leadership System (ILS), the APS Commission's benchmarks for APS career advancement. At the end, programme participants are provided with detailed feedback to guide their future development (APSC, 2009b).

Belgium. According to the OECD (2007), certified training schemes have become one of the main competency management tools in the federal government. Every six or eight years, public servants from levels A through D can voluntarily take certified training organised by the OFO, the training institute of the federal government. Its goal: to update and to develop the qualifications and competencies of all civil servants. They are also the sole key to career development. Public servants are stimulated to participate in these trainings by a "competency allowance", which they receive when training objectives are met. The competency allowance is a bonus to the normal remuneration (Dupont, 2006; Hondeghem et al., 2005; Scheepers and Parys, 2005).

In 2009, the range of certified training programmes was extended, and new ground rules and quality requirements were fixed (Dispositions of 29 April 2009, Official Journal of 4 May 2009), which enhanced the transparency of the system. The certified trainings are delivered according to the position of the civil servant and the speciality he or she exercises. The trainings aim to develop generic competencies that are common to most of the functions, and are sanctioned by a test that examines the degree of compliance to the learning objectives. Some training is open to participants of different levels. In that case, there is a difference in the degree of difficulty of the test. When successful – one has to obtain 60% – according to the level, either a special competency allowance is given or access is granted to a higher salary scale (FOD P&O, 2009).

United Kingdom. The United Kingdom's SCS competency framework is used by senior managers as cues on how to do their work and to identify leadership potential. Some 100 individuals are invited each year for a series of challenging leadership workshops, which are complemented by psychometric assessments designed to give the selectors a better idea of the match between competencies and the individuals. The aim is to develop a leadership profile for each candidate so that individual-specific trajectories and development interventions can be made. To what extent this has resulted in a more competent SCS than in the past remains an open question (Hondeghem et al., 2005).

Source: OECD (2009), "OECD Survey on Competency Management in Government", OECD, Paris.

Demonstrating the benefits of a stable and professional civil service – in an aim to create buy-in and understanding – could be done by highlighting the successes of the Institute for Financial Policy (IFP) in this regard. The IFP serves as a centre of excellence, having sufficient personnel capacities with necessary skills. It was able to organise its staff with the aim to create better paying positions and attract and retain highly skilled employees. These reforms have widely been deemed as successful in stabilising the organisation's workforce. This home-grown practice of good workforce management could be replicated in other ministries.

Reasonable tenure arrangements should form part of the reform package. The current practice of giving ministries discretion to define breaches of discipline and decide on the dismissal of civil servants is highly unusual compared to the situation in most OECD countries, where such matters are typically defined in basic civil service legislation and are tightly controlled in order to protect civil servants from arbitrary dismissal. Civil servants could also be better supported in the context of reorganisations, through organisational review processes combined with retraining and redeployment measures, as is the case in most OECD countries (OECD, 2011a; 2012b). A necessary counterpoint to job security measures is to have good performance management processes, including effective measures to deal with poor performers, and incentives for good performance.

Box 3.6. Roadmap for implementing competency management

This roadmap has been created based on the experience of OECD member countries in introducing competency management. It is not a prescription, but a checklist or guidelines on how to engage in competency management.

Step 1: Deciding to introduce competency-based management. This is a strategic choice and a long-term commitment. Competency management should be regarded as means to achieve an objective. It is important to establish the objectives for the competency modelling project in advance. Formulating the objectives clearly can contribute to creating a shared perspective on competency management among the different stakeholders. The link to the organisational mission and vision should be made here. The decision to introduce competency management should not be taken lightly, as it is by no means an easy process. Nevertheless, competency management can leverage changing the organisational culture. The introduction of competency management can be an interesting opportunity to introduce organisational change during a period of broader government reforms.

Step 2: Organising, planning and communicating the shift to competency-based management. Three aspects should be considered: 1) determining the organisation of competency management, which refers to the HR governance structure that is applied; 2) planning the approach for the development of a competency management system, which involves defining concepts, determining the relevant parts of the organisation and selecting the development tools; 3) developing and implementing communication plans to obtain support from staff.

Step 3: Identifying competencies and developing competency models for the specified target groups. This diagnostic phase begins with specifying the target groups of competency management. Then, the competency model is specified and the competencies are identified. There is no ideal competency management system, but a good competency management system must always be aligned with the specific goals of an organisation. A government's competency model ideally includes a mix of competencies specific to public service, and competencies that appear in both public and private sector organisations. Competencies specific to the public service generally take the form of (public service) values, for example: commitment, service, integrity, transparency, accountability and equity. Other competencies with an emphasis specific to public service are public service professionalism and probity, affinity with public sector management, political awareness, political savvy and public service motivation.

Step 4: Integrating competencies into various HR processes. The integration of competencies into the various HR processes can happen gradually or suddenly. With gradual integration, it is possible to start with a pilot project in one department, with a group of employees or in one HR process (selection, remuneration, workforce planning, etc.). Competency management is more than simply using competencies in various HR processes; it requires organisation-wide dynamics. Therefore, the competency-based HR systems should be integrated so that they are aligned and mutually supportive.

Box 3.6. **Roadmap for implementing competency management** *(continued)*

The challenge is to develop competency management as an integrated, core part of HRM and to avoid the risk of it becoming an isolated tool or an end in itself.

Step 5: Revising and updating the competency management system on a regular basis. It is particularly important to grasp the dynamic nature of individual job-related competencies. Regular updates and revisions of the competency management system must be scheduled. Competency modelling is a continuous process, not a one-time project. To be useful, the list of competencies needs to be revised as business strategies and conditions change. In terms of timing, there are several options, such as periodic evaluation or a comprehensive review over several years.

Source: OECD (2011a), *Public Servants as Partners for Growth: Toward a Stronger, Leaner and More Equitable Workforce*, OECD Publishing, Paris, http://dx.doi.org/10.1787/9789264166707-en.

Professionalising the civil service through merit-based recruitment

The Slovak government's stated commitment to reinstating the principle of merit in recruitment and selection arrangements is to be welcomed. In addition to the planned civil service legislation, the proposed HRM reform framework gives commitment to transparent recruitment processes through adopting standard methods and procedures for selection, new modern methods of selection (such as assessment centres and a pooling system), a central registry for selection procedures, compulsory selection procedures into the temporary civil service and methodological support for service offices in the area of recruitment and selection. A more structured approach to graduate recruitment, combined with improved career structures, will also make an important contribution to building human capital. These elements constitute a step in the right direction and the Government Office is preparing concrete projects for their implementation, which will need to be carefully monitored and adequately resourced.

These mechanisms can be reinforced by having recruitment and promotion decisions adopted collectively through a collegial body, not entrusted to a person individually, regardless of his/her rank in the hierarchy. The Australian system may provide some inspiration to the Slovak authorities in this regard as it shows how a range of work-related qualities of candidates are taken into account in the recruitment system (Box 3.7).

As the HRM reforms and concrete projects proposed by the Government Office already support the development of an independent Civil Service Council to provide strategic oversight of recruitment and merit, the following examples of the role played by public service commissions in several OECD countries may be of use to the Slovak government (Box 3.8). The example of the UK Civil Service Commission could be of particular interest, as it developed recruitment principles while allowing departments and agencies to develop their own approaches to recruitment provided they are consistent with the principles.

Towards a merit-based and transparent compensation system

Pay setting in the public service is complex and requires a difficult balance between a number of dynamic economic factors. A good pay-setting process typically results in pay levels that reflect different levels of skills, competencies and performance expectations; it also needs to be competitive with other employers in order to attract people with the necessary competencies; and it needs to be economically sustainable.

The HRM reforms proposed to address the current challenges in the compensation system of the Slovak civil service are good first steps; however, efforts to improve base salaries and better link them to job content and competencies could be strengthened. The HRM Strategy to 2020 identifies a number of possible remuneration reforms to increase motivation and performance, including pay banding, minimising allowances, regular performance evaluation, market comparisons, horizontal equality in pay for the same activities and vertical salary decompression. The planned reintroduction of performance appraisals is crucial. In this context, the large amount of total compensation tied to performance appraisals should be reconsidered as – especially at the beginning – performance evaluation and management is difficult to get right and a sound system needs to be well implemented before the link with compensation can reliably be established.

Box 3.7. Merit-based recruitment in the Australian public service

Employment decisions in the Australian Public Service (APS) are based on merit, which is one of the APS' values.

At a minimum, all employment decisions should be based on an assessment of a person's work-related qualities and those required to do the job. For decisions that may result in the engagement or promotion of an APS employee, the assessment must be competitive. Under the Public Service Act 1999, a decision is based on merit if:

- it is taken of the relative suitability of the candidates for the duties, using a competitive selection process, and
- it is based on the relationship between the candidates' work-related qualities and the work-related qualities genuinely required for the duties, and
- it focuses on the relative capacity of the candidates to achieve outcomes related to the duties, and
- it is the primary consideration in taking the decision.

For the assessment to be competitive, it should also be open to all eligible members of the community. For ongoing jobs and non-ongoing jobs for more than 12 months, this is achieved by notifying the job in the APS Employment Gazette on the APS jobs website.

The work-related qualities that may be taken into account when making an assessment include:

- skills and abilities
- qualifications, training and competencies
- standard of work performance
- capacity to produce outcomes from effective performance at the level required
- relevant personal qualities
- demonstrated potential for further development
- ability to contribute to team performance.

Source: Information provided by the Australian Public Service Commission.

Institutional arrangements for human resources management

Finding the right balance between standardisation and delegated human resources management

Finding a way to balance delegation of HRM to ministries with the need for more consistent and standardised approaches to HRM and compliance with the Civil Service Act will be key to successfully implementing reforms and ensuring a more coherent approach to HRM.

Central frameworks are needed to guide strategic HRM and enable a whole-of-government approach to managing the workforce, while delegated HRM responsibilities for ministries need to be underpinned by oversight, reporting and performance management arrangements to ensure accountability. Ensuring institutional capacity and adequate resourcing at the centre of government to co-ordinate and oversee the implementation of the reforms envisaged is a key factor that will need to be balanced with the current model of strongly independent line ministries.

Box 3.8. **Examples of the role played by public service commissions in selected OECD member countries**

Australia: The Merit Protection Commissioner is an independent statutory office holder appointed by the Governor-General in Council on the advice of the Public Service Minister. The commissioner provides assurance, in certain key areas of the Australian Public Service (APS) employment framework, that the APS' values are being applied effectively by agencies, their agency heads and staff. These key areas are:

- merit-based employment decisions
- ethical standards
- a fair system of review of employment decisions and actions.

Ireland: The Commission for Public Service Appointments is an independent body which sets and safeguards standards for recruitment and bound by law to ensure that recruitment and selection are carried out by fair, open and merit-based means. Its primary statutory responsibility is to set standards for recruitment and selection, which it publishes as Codes of Practice. The commission safeguards these standards through regular monitoring and auditing of recruitment and selection activities and it also investigates alleged breaches of the codes of practice.

United Kingdom: The Civil Service Commission oversees the principle of fair and open competition and appointment on merit. It also helps promote the civil service values of honesty, integrity, objectivity and impartiality, and hears complaints under the Civil Service Code. The commission establishes recruitment principles. Departments and agencies are free to develop their own approaches to recruitment as long as they are consistent with the recruitment principles.

Sources: Australia: www.apsc.gov.au; Ireland: www.cpsa.ie/en/; United Kingdom: http://civilservicecommission.independent.gov.uk (accessed 5 November 2012).

Typical core responsibilities of the central HRM body in OECD member countries include:

- strategic workforce planning across the central government

- the design, promotion and enforcement of shared systems, such as job classification, competency management, career management and performance assessments
- the oversight and promotion of public service values and ethics
- whole-of-service training
- recruitment and retention strategies
- management of the senior public service.

The Slovak government could adopt an incremental approach to strengthening central HRM responsibilities as the Government Office builds its capacity to take on such functions. The way Canada and Finland, for example, have set broad HRM standards – with the central HRM authority taking on guidance, support and monitoring capacities – could be of interest to the Slovak government as it considers how to set up central co-ordinating functions for HRM in the Government Office (Box 3.9).

Box 3.9. **Functions of central HRM institutions in Canada and Finland**

Canada's Office of the Chief Human Resources Officer provides advice and support to departments and agencies in four main areas while also monitoring the implementation of core HRM policies:

- Compensation and Labour Relations (CLR): labour management relations and compensation operations: it conducts collective bargaining for the core public administration; oversees pay administration; develops and interprets government-wide administrative policies; and provides advice and support to departments and agencies on labour relations issues. The CLR also supports the Treasury Board in its role in ensuring fiscally responsible expenditure management by determining compensation for the core public administration (except for the executive group), the Canadian forces and the Royal Canadian Mounted Police. The branch also supports other federal public service employers in obtaining their negotiations mandates from the Treasury Board.
- Executive Policies and Talent Management: provides the tools and support deputy heads need to manage and develop members of the executive group. The sector has four areas of responsibility (executive management policies, leadership development, executive talent management and the Interchange Canada Program).
- Governance, Planning and Policy: broad policy frameworks and standards, monitoring and reporting on people management, improving policies and processes, oversight of departmental performance.
- Pensions and Benefits in the public service.

In **Finland,** prime responsibility for HRM and the implementation of common policy guidelines must be carried out by individual agencies, with the Personnel and Governance Policy Department (i.e. Office for the Government as Employer) in the Ministry of Finance acting to set common HRM policies.

Individual agencies have prime responsibility for the following HRM functions:

- operating units define their own strategies on the basis of common policy lines and their own operational needs
- operating units recruit and develop their own personnel

Box 3.9. **Functions of central HRM institutions in Canada and Finland** *(continued)*

- appointments of senior civil servants by the Council of State.

The Personnel and Governance Policy Department in the Ministry of Finance:

- is in charge of government general employer and personnel policy (e.g. drafts related to legislation and policy decisions)
- is responsible for general governance policy and public services
- is responsible for manager policy and general leadership development in the government administration
- negotiates wage and salary agreements on central level
- produces personnel data and research services (e.g. personnel costs in state budget).

Sources: Treasury Board of Canada Secretariat (n.d.), "Office of the Chief Human Resources Officer", www.tbs-sct.gc.ca/chro-dprh/index-eng.asp; Information provided by the Office for the Government as Employer, Ministry of Finance, Finland.

Enhancing performance management and accountability and building leadership capacity to steer strategic policy development and implementation

Government-wide performance management and accountability frameworks can drive organisational performance and management for results

The Slovak government could benefit from enhancing its performance orientation and developing a foundation for performance management by linking the management of people with organisational goals and strategies and, ultimately, with the government's programme and objectives. The reimplementation of performance measures at the individual level provides a good opportunity to start linking these to organisational objectives and strategies. Linking employee effort to organisational output requires that each organisation clearly articulate its strategic objectives, which each sub-unit clearly articulates in a way that contributes to the overall objectives of the organisation, and that each employee's work objectives contribute to the goals of his/her work unit. Many OECD countries are enabling this through a model of co-operative goal setting whereby managers and employees work together to set goals and then evaluate, at the end of the year, whether and how these goals were achieved. This is often supplemented by a mid-year review, which gives the manager and the employee an opportunity to discuss progress against goals, and how the organisational environment supports and/or hinders the employee's achievement of these goals.

Overall, human resources management needs to be understood as supporting organisational performance. While managers in the Slovak government enjoy a high degree of managerial flexibility, there is little accountability for management practices and results. In the absence of accountability frameworks, it appears ministries have little incentive to take HRM seriously and there seems to be little rationale linking HRM to producing the required results. This may warrant a reform strategy linked to using performance indicators and organisational performance management frameworks to drive and incentivise HRM. Finding the right balance between flexibility and control is particularly important in a public service which is still developing its core values and essential administrative foundations. The Slovak government could consider building monitoring mechanisms to determine where additional support may be needed. This should, however, be done in a way that is sensitive to the limited capacities of small HRM offices.

The Canadian Management Accountability Framework (MAF) defines the conditions that need to be in place to ensure that the government is well managed and to promote management excellence. The MAF makes annual assessments of most departments and agencies and public reports on the state of management, including HRM (Box 3.10). This is one highly developed tool that the Slovak government could consider as a best practice example, noting, however, that its development has been a long-term process.

Building senior civil servants' capabilities and ensuring an effective political-administrative interface

OECD countries are increasingly placing a high level of importance on the management of senior managers, recognising that the competencies required for effective leaders and managers are not the same as those for professionals. Senior civil servants are expected to play a leadership role and to embody and transmit core public service values such as integrity, impartiality, transparency and merit. They set the example in terms of performance and probity, and are essential players in the development of future planning and strategic capacity.

Box 3.10. **The Canadian Management Accountability Framework: People Management Component**

Canada's Management Accountability Framework (MAF) was implemented in 2003 to hold heads of departments and agencies accountable for management performance, and to continuously improve management performance.

The MAF aims to:

- clarify management expectations of deputy heads and support ongoing dialogue on management priorities with their executive team and the Treasury Board Secretariat
- provide a comprehensive perspective on the state of management practices and challenges in the federal government
- identify government-wide trends and general issues in order to help deputy heads set priorities and resolve issues.

Figure 3.14. **Canadian Management Accountability Framework**

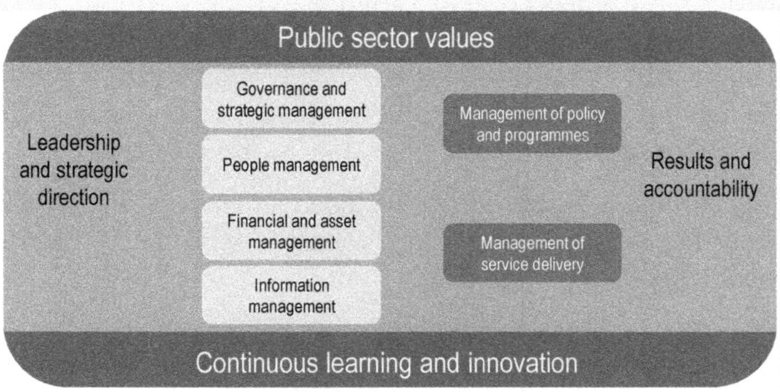

On an annual cycle, the Treasury Board Secretariat evaluates departmental performance on each of the ten aspects of the MAF framework, provides a score and identifies the priority areas for

Box 3.10. **The Canadian Management Accountability Framework: People Management Component** *(continued)*

management improvement, which must be measurably improved by the agency over the next 12 months. Departments electronically submit supporting evidence of their performance in 15 areas of management, and this evidence is evaluated by the Treasury Board Secretariat and a score is given on each element of the MAF. For areas of management that receive a low score, the department must prepare an improvement plan for implementation during the next year. MAF scores are posted on a public website by the Treasury Board Secretariat. A department head's performance on the MAF helps determine his or her performance pay for the year. Over the past ten years, since the MAF was introduced, departmental management scores have steadily improved, demonstrating the effectiveness of the MAF in improving public management.

The people management component of the MAF in 2012-13 included the following elements:

- employee engagement
- executive leadership
- diversity and employment
- employee learning
- performance and talent management
- workload and workforce planning effectiveness
- staffing
- official languages
- organisational context.

Sources: Treasury Board of Canada Secretariat (n.d.), www.tbs-sct.gc.ca; OECD (2014c), *Kazakhstan: Review of the Central Administration*, OECD Public Governance Reviews, OECD Publishing, Paris, http://dx.doi.org/10.1787/9789264224605-en.

There is an increased tendency among OECD countries to group senior civil servants separately and manage them under different HRM policies, with the aim to build collegiate leadership and to facilitate enhanced attention to recruitment, leadership development strategies, performance management and other key aspects of building leadership capacity. While a great deal of variation exists across OECD countries in their approach to senior management, there is a common concern to ensure the best possible capabilities and standards. Some countries have also introduced fixed-term appointments for senior public servants in order to support a greater performance orientation and to gain flexibility in filling senior positions.

The Finnish government has recently developed a common framework for leadership development, focusing on a number of key elements which may be of interest to the Slovak government (Box 3.11).

In addition, the political-administrative interface appears blurred in the Slovak Republic. This can affect the neutrality of policy advice and the professional nature of the group. Clarifying the political-administrative interface can generate continuity and leadership capacity at the senior levels of the civil service to carry forward reforms. To help build a clear distinction between political appointees and professional senior civil servants, the Slovak government could consider the example of the Chilean approach to managing senior directors (Box 3.12). A key lesson from the Chilean experience is that the reform was implemented gradually, with posts incorporated into the senior civil service system as they became vacant.

Over the longer term, the community of senior civil servants will increasingly need to act as an effective interface between the political leadership and the civil service, with a common public service value set based on providing effective, non-partisan, evidence-based advice to ministers and the head of government. This can help break down institutional siloes and optimise the implementation of whole-of-government strategy in pursuit of a common purpose beyond single organisational mandates.

Further increasing the number of women in senior management positions is also an element on which the Slovak government could focus. A first step could be to analyse why more women are not progressing through to senior ranks. Factors such as flexible working arrangements, which appear to be underdeveloped in the Slovak civil service, may be at play, among other things. The Slovak government could look at the extensive experience of OECD countries in increasing female representation at senior levels and improving the diversity of the senior civil service (OECD, 2011a).

Box 3.11. Common framework for leadership development in Finland

The Finnish Ministry of Finance is responsible for the joint leadership and management policy as well as some centralised management development activities. The target groups are mainly the senior civil service and to some extent other managers as well. The common framework for management development consists of four elements: offices and employment, recruitment, performance management and joint development.

Management of senior civil servants is more centralised than the management of other groups of managers. The senior civil service consists of approximately 130 managers in ministries and agencies. They are permanent secretaries of state (civil servants under ministers heading ministries), permanent under-secretaries of state and directors general in ministries and directors general/heads of government agencies.

According to the common development framework and recent legislation, all senior civil service appointments are made for a fixed period of five years. There is no limitation to the number of appointments for a certain position. The aim is to increase the mobility of senior civil servants. Secondly, there is also legislation regulating the selection criteria of senior civil servants. The requirements for these posts have been made more explicit, and all candidates are assessed using uniform selection principles. Greater emphasis is placed on leadership and executive management skills. The Ministry of Finance has also introduced a model for professional recruitment procedures and practices of managers and experts.

Thirdly, one aim of the central government management policy is to enhance performance-oriented management and the accountability of managers. When a person takes up a managerial position, his/her personal aims must be defined, taking into account the present state and future challenges of the operating unit in question. The Ministry of Finance has introduced a model for personnel management agreements and a bonus element based on a performance appraisal system for senior civil servants. The Ministry of Finance is responsible for the pay determination of senior civil servants. The management agreement procedure combines the development of managerial practices with performance management. The management agreement should be part of the operating unit's steering process and thus compatible with the performance agreement and the framework budget (spending limits) laid down for the unit.

Box 3.11. Common framework for leadership development in Finland *(continued)*

Fourthly, the Ministry of Finance organises some management development and training for the senior civil service and the potential group on the next level. One of the activities is the Forum for the Government Administration Management. The goal of the forum is to both strengthen the common goals of the central government and support senior civil servants in their leadership duties. The forum meets twice a year in one or half a day seminars and, furthermore, several times a year in one-hour informal meetings called "morning coffees". The purpose of the groups is to increase free and confidential interaction between senior managers and thus support their leadership duties and their personal development. The Ministry of Finance has also organised a special programme called Future Leaders, which is meant for potential future senior civil servants and those managers who have recently been assigned to senior civil service posts. The programme lasts three weeks and has five modules. The main themes of the programme are future anticipation and leadership. The participants are selected by the Ministry of Finance in co-operation with the ministries. Since 2008, more than 175 managers have participated in the course. According to the feedback, the main benefits for the participants are an increased understanding of the whole-of-government aspect and a possibility to create wider networks. The Ministry of Finance has set up a working group to evaluate the programme and to redesign joint management training organised by the ministry.

Source: Information provided by the Office for the Government as Employer, Ministry of Finance, Finland.

Box 3.12. Chile's senior management system

In 2003, the Chilean government, with the agreement of' all political actors (opposition political parties, non-governmental organisations, civil society), created the *Sistema de Alta Dirección Pública* (ADP), a central senior civil service system. The aim of the ADP was to establish a professional senior management. Following the reform, there are three distinct groups:

- The most senior positions which are filled by direct designation by the government (1 000 positions out of 2 000 000 in central government).
- The ADP, for which recruitment is based on public competition (1 000 positions in central government). There are two levels within the ADP: approximately 1% at the first hierarchical level (heads of service, directors general) and the remainder at the second hierarchical level (regional directors, heads of division).
- Middle management positions (2 000 positions in central government) at the third hierarchical level, which form part of the career civil service.

The ADP has been implemented gradually by recruiting by open competition whenever a post falls vacant and by expanding it over time to additional groups. For example, it has been expended to include 3 600 municipal education directors and 2 800 new senior management posts in municipalities.

Key features of the ADP are:

- competitive selection based on professional merit
- profile based on competencies which are evaluated by expert consultants
- three-year term of office, renewable for two subsequent terms
- right to severance pay
- assessment under management performance agreements
- possibility of removal by the President for poor performance or loss of confidence.

Box 3.12. **Chile's senior management system** *(continued)*

Most of the selection process for the ADP is contracted out to specialised recruitment agencies. The National Civil Service Directorate is responsible for management of the ADP. However, the Senior Public Management Council (Consejo de Alta Dirección Pública) is in charge of guaranteeing the transparency, confidentiality and absence of discrimination of the selection process. It is chaired by the Director of the National Civil Service Directorate and has four members proposed by the President of Chile and approved by the Senate. The selection process, which takes about four months, begins with the publication of the vacancy in the media. A specialised enterprise commissioned by the council analyses the curricula vitae of the different candidates and prepares a shortlist for the council or a selection committee (under the council's supervision). Professional competence, integrity and probity are some of the criteria used in the selection process. Subsequently, the council or the committee selects the best candidates for interview and prepares a final shortlist for the competent authority for the final appointment.

The ADP system was based on international experience. In particular, the experience of OECD countries such as Australia and New Zealand strongly influenced the Chilean model. The system is considered one of the main achievements of the modernisation of Chile's public management. One effect has been the decline in the number of political appointees in the central government; they currently represent only 0.5% of the total public workforce. It is also argued that the presence of women in senior positions has increased under the system; they occupy 32% of positions, compared to 15% in the Chilean private sector.

Source: Weber, A. (2012), "Alta dirección pública", presentation given at the seminar "Fortaleciendo la Capacidad del Empleo Público Colombiano", Bogota, 27 July 2012.

Strengthening the government's capacity to deliver on its human resources management reform agenda

The Slovak government is in the midst of proposing an ambitious set of reforms to its public employment and management, based partly on the self-critical analysis of the HRM Strategy to 2020 (see Box 3.1). The decision to centre HRM reforms around core public sector values, such as political impartiality, legality, transparent recruitment, efficient management, impartiality, professionalism, transparent and equal remuneration, stability and fair treatment, is positive. Reforms will have much more of a chance of succeeding if the core values embedded in new legislation and new HRM instruments are clear and well accepted by all stakeholders.

Institutional ownership for human resources management reforms will need to be strengthened if reforms are to be successful

The proposed HRM reform agenda will require strong leadership at the political and senior management levels if it is to be successful. It may be necessary to consider building shared responsibility or strategic partnerships for HRM reforms across centre-of-government (CoG) institutions, namely between the Government Office, the Ministry of Finance and the Ministry of the Interior – each operating in their appropriate domain, but fully co-ordinated to achieve the common purpose of designing, implementing and monitoring the performance of the HRM strategy. This mirrors the assessment in Chapter 1 on the need for greater co-ordination between the key components of the CoG to optimise links between strategic HRM, budget setting and strategy making and implementation to achieve strategic policy outcomes more effectively. The positive experience of collaboration in developing the HRM Strategy to 2020 and drafting the new Civil Service Act provides a solid foundation for building structured and ongoing collaboration.

Building capacity, knowledge and resources in the Government Office's human resources management section and in ministries' service offices

The implementation of HRM reforms requires building the capacity of the HRM function both at the centre and within ministries. The Government Office needs to have the resources, authority and capabilities to steer the HRM reform. HRM units within government organisations (i.e. service offices) also need to be properly equipped to take on new responsibilities. A positive step in this regard is the involvement of managers from service offices in working groups that are developing reform proposals. This undoubtedly helps to build ownership of reforms and could form the basis of a more permanent network of HR managers to encourage good practices across ministries. The Slovak government could consider creating a professional network across ministries' service offices to share best practices and experiences in implementing reforms, along the lines developed in some other OECD countries (Box 3.13).

Potential for shared human resources management services

There is potential for efficiency gains in organising personnel administration and other HRM administration activities as shared services, as recognised in the HRM Strategy to 2020. Payroll activities, personnel record keeping and administration of recruitment services are areas that could be considered in this regard. This could support the objective of reducing the number of staff employed in administration and support activities.

Box 3.13. **Personnel Officer's Network in Ireland**

The key function of the Personnel Officers Network (PON) is to provide a forum for personnel officers and HR managers in the civil service to discuss best practice human resources management procedures. The PON provides regular active networking opportunities which allows members to share their experience and address issues of mutual concern. In this way, the PON serves to identify and build upon administrative and policy initiatives, as well as develop and assist in the delivery of members' training needs, which improve HR management in the civil service.

The quarterly meetings of the PON comprise a mix of presentations and focused discussion regarding a variety of topics. They are structured in such a way that members have ample opportunity to network. The objectives of the meetings are:

- to discuss and develop best practice HR management in the civil service
- to agree cross-departmental approaches to the implementation of HR processes
- to provide the opportunity for personnel officers to present their experiences and learn from each other
- to invite speakers to inform on strategic issues relating to HR management
- to provide feedback and ideas on the development and implementation of HR policies to the Department of Public Expenditure and Reform.

An electronic workspace has been provided for the network and is used for discussions, sharing of ideas and initiatives. This workspace stores presentations and meeting agendas,

Box 3.13. **Personnel Officer's Network in Ireland** *(continued)*

records membership and contact details, provides opportunities to engage on work items, allows queries to be posted and contributed to, provides a facility for surveys and questionnaires, and ensures more productive formal meeting outputs and outcomes.

The Executive Committee is drawn from members of the network and must consist of at least eight members. Committee meetings are held prior to each network meeting and as required to discuss and agree the agenda and future work plans. A quorum of five attendees is required for an Executive Committee meeting.

Secretarial support to the network is provided by the Civil Service Human Resources Directorate to assist with administrative and logistical arrangements.

There are sub-committees of the Personnel Officers Network which meet and discuss topics as they arise. Such topics have included reform of sick leave, anti-bullying, and harassment and recruitment policies.

Source: Information provided from the Civil Service HR Division, Department of Public Expenditure and Reform, Republic of Ireland.

The vision in the HRM Strategy to 2020 is promising, but could be better communicated to ministries, employees and the public to build support among key stakeholders

One key lesson from OECD countries is that HRM reforms are more effective and stand a better chance of succeeding when they are based on an overall view of how government should function in order to meet emerging challenges. This means framing them in the context of a compelling vision of the future, based on an understanding of how the nature of public administration is changing and what kind of workforce the Slovak government needs to meet future challenges. It also means linking the design of HRM reforms to broader public administration reform initiatives and positioning HRM reforms as crucial elements of these broader initiatives.

Building support among key stakeholders is essential for managing change successfully. Public service employees and their union, managers, staff of personnel offices in ministries, politicians, public service users and relevant non-governmental organisations are all stakeholders with an interest in the reform. The vision for the civil service that is being developed in the HRM Strategy to 2020 constitutes a step in the right direction. This could be used to communicate broadly (both within the public sector and to citizens) the value for society of a professional, well-functioning civil service, to build support for public sector reforms and to launch a discussion on what type of public workforce will be needed to meet future challenges. Currently, there is little evidence that the reason for HRM reforms is well understood by stakeholders within or outside the public sector. As the reform takes shape, it will be essential to find ways to include key stakeholders and gain their support in order to manage the change successfully.

Recommendations

The Slovak government could consider the following recommendations aimed at strengthening the capability of the state civil service and reinforcing work that is already currently in progress under the leadership of the Government Office:

- Collect data on the public workforce to use as a foundation for strategic workforce planning and management. The Slovak government could consider prioritising the collection of quality data on the public workforce as a basis for strategic HR planning and management. A central database of workforce statistics would be a first essential step to improve workforce planning in order to better align the capacity of the public service with organisational and service demands. There are indications that a central registry of civil servants would be developed as part of the HRM reforms. This is a step in the right direction. Initially this will be beneficial to understand workforce numbers and costs and could, in time, be expanded to include factors such as education, skills and competencies.

- Start to develop strategic workforce planning and management. In parallel with building up the collection of workforce data, it is necessary to build skills and capacity in the ministries' service offices to use this data effectively for workforce planning. The necessary skills will need to be developed through targeted training programmes and it is likely that skilled HR personnel will also need to be recruited. Rather than trying to get all ministries up to the same level simultaneously, a more promising approach may be to start with pilot projects in the ministries that are better prepared to take this on. For example, pilot projects led by the Ministry of the Interior at selected district offices have the advantage of supporting the reorganisation of services at district level and could, in time, serve as demonstration projects for other ministries. The Ministry of Finance may also be well placed to act as an early adopter of workforce planning.

- Build on competency-based management and job profiling. The Slovak government could move towards more strategic human resource management by building tools such as competency management and job profiling. The roadmap for implementing competency management (see Box 3.6) would be a good starting point. Developing common job profiles for public service functions and incorporating a common competency framework – along the lines of the example presented in Box 3.5 – could be the first step. This would help improve recruitment and selection methods and support a merit-based recruitment process. A common competency framework could eventually be integrated into planning, career management and skills development practices.

- Professionalise the civil service through ensuring appropriate tenure arrangements. Reasonable tenure arrangements for civil servants are essential to stability, continuity and ensuring a professional civil service. The Slovak central government could consider stabilising the civil service by managing civil servants' careers through fair, rule-based and transparent practices, and by ensuring a reasonable degree of tenure and employment guarantees for them. The Slovak government could consider widely communicating the benefits of a stable and professional workforce. This could be done, for example, by highlighting the successful management practices of the Institute for Financial Policy in this regard.

- Reinstate the principle of merit in recruitment and selection arrangements by ensuring common standards and oversight. The proposed HRM reforms already give commitment to transparent recruitment processes through adopting standard methods and procedures for selection, new modern methods of selection (such as assessment centres and a pooling system), a central registry for selection procedures and compulsory selection procedures into the temporary civil service, all of which constitute positive first steps, provided they are implemented in a consistent and sustainable manner. These measures could be reinforced by allowing the proposed Civil Service Council to play a strategic oversight role, to monitor and ensure merit in the staffing of the public service (similar to a public service commission in many OECD countries). The council could focus on setting principles and guidelines, carrying out audits of recruitment and investigating suspected breaches of merit.

- Clarify the compensation system and ensure it is based on merit and transparency. The Slovak government could consider strengthening the merit principle by ensuring that employees' compensation is based on the nature of their work and the competencies they bring to it, and not so strongly on seniority or tenure factors. A well-structured and transparent compensation system with appropriate incentives will contribute to the ability of the civil service to attract, retain and motivate staff. The Slovak central government could consider:
  - simplifying the compensation system by incorporating the large levels of discretionary bonuses into clear and understandable base salaries, and better linking these to job content and competencies
  - linking performance-related pay to performance appraisals based on objective setting, ensuring, however, that performance pay constitutes a smaller portion of an employee's total compensation.
- Develop performance and accountability mechanisms to drive and ensure results. The Slovak government could consider developing an integrated performance management framework to drive public organisations to deliver on government-wide objectives. The government could consider developing performance appraisals based on objective setting, and tying individual objectives to organisational and whole-of-government priority goals. This requires a system of organisational and whole-of-government performance management which is not yet firmly established. Developing a system of organisational and whole-of-government objective setting, performance reporting and accountability would be essential to provide the organisational context for linking and assessing individual and team objectives. The Slovak government could develop management accountability structures to ensure delegation of HRM is met with capacity and accountability at the ministry level.
- Clarify the political-administrative interface and manage senior civil servants as a group serving a "single" government. The Slovak government could consider active approaches to clarifying the political-administrative interface, and to managing and developing the competencies of senior leaders in the civil service. Management of the administrative-political interface is a critical part of the development of a professional civil service. The government could make a clear distinction between political appointees and professional senior civil servants, and start managing and training senior managers in order to build competencies specific to this group along with a common value set that upholds its members' duty to serve a "single" government and pursue the "common purpose" of meeting the needs of citizens and businesses, regardless of which portfolio or ministry employs them. Over time, this could lead to more effective collaboration across institutional silos by the senior ranks of the civil service in pursuit of common, whole-of-government strategic objectives, notably those identified in

the Government Manifesto at the beginning of the government's mandate, and could thus contribute over time to breaking down barriers to cross-ministry collaboration at all levels of the civil service.

- Ensure adequate capacity, knowledge and resources in the Government Office to support ministries' service offices and make government-wide HRM reform happen. Adequate capacity, expertise and resources in the Government Office section responsible for HRM will be essential to support the proposed reform initiatives and help ministries' service offices implement new working methods. As the proposed HRM reform envisions that the Government Office will play a strategic and co-ordinating role, set frameworks and standards, and lead the implementation of reforms, the Slovak government should consider building adequate human and financial resources, and a solid knowledge base, to enable the Government Office execute these new competencies.
- Build professional networks across ministries' service offices and with the Government Office to share best practices and support new working methods. Ensuring two-way communication between the Government Office and service office staff – through information sharing and genuine consultation – will be important for the implementation of the proposed HRM reforms. It will also be important to develop a network of support among HRM professionals across the government, as a forum for ministries to discuss and share experience and best practice amongst themselves.
- Integrate change management strategies into the design of HRM reforms. Integrating change management strategies into the reform at an early stage will help to identify the concerns of key stakeholders and develop ways of addressing the issues and tensions that inevitably arise in the course of a reform. This includes communicating with and involving stakeholders, as well as anticipating possible difficulties and devising ways of building support for changes.

Bibliography

ABD (2006), *Jaarverslag 2005*, Den Haag: Bureau Algemene Bestuursdienst.

ABD (2005), *Jaarverslag 2004*, Den Haag: Bureau Algemene Bestuursdienst.

APSC (2009a), *Human Resource Capability Development Programme,* Australian Public Service Commission, available at: http://www.apsc.gov.au/HRCDP/index.html.

APSC (2009b), *Career Development Assessment Centre (CDAC),* Australian Public Service Commission, available at: http://www.apsc.gov.au/learn/cdac.htm.

APSC (2003), *The Australian Experience of Public Sector Reform*, Occasional Paper Two, Australian Public Service Commission, Canberra, Commonwealth of Australia.

Dupont, C. (2006), Algemene beleidsnota van de minister van Ambtenarenzaken, Maatschappelijke Integratie, Grootstedenbeleid en Gelijke Kansen belast met de

Interculturaliteit – Deel Ambtenarenzaken 2006-2007, Belgische Kamer van Volksvertegenwoordigers, 31 oktober.

FOD P&O (2009), *Major HRM Developments in Belgium (federal administration)*, Handout at the Annual Meeting of the Public Employment and Management Working Party, OECD Conference Centre, Paris, 15-16 December 2009.

Hondeghem et al. (2005), "Modèles de gestion des competences en Europe", *Revue française d'administration publique*, 16, pp. 561-576.

Huerta Melchor, O. (2012), "The government workforce of the future: Innovation in strategic workforce planning in OECD countries", *OECD Working Papers on Public Governance*, No. 21, OECD Publishing, Paris, http://dx.doi.org/10.1787/5k487727gwvb-en.

Government of the Slovak Republic (2014), "Joint Strategy for Human Resources in State Administration 2015-2020", draft document.

ILO (2014), ILOSTAT (database), www.ilo.org/ilostat.

OECD (2015), *Government at a Glance 2015*, OECD Publishing, Paris, http://dx.doi.org/10.1787/gov_glance-2015-en.

OECD (2014a), "Labour Force Statistics", *OECD Employment and Labour Market Statistics* (database), http://dx.doi.org/10.1787/lfs-lfs-data-en (accessed on 21 March 2015).

OECD (2014b), *OECD National Accounts Statistics* (database), http://dx.doi.org/10.1787/na-data-en (accessed on 21 March 2015).

OECD (2014c), *Kazakhstan: Review of the Central Administration*, OECD Public Governance Reviews, OECD Publishing, Paris, http://dx.doi.org/10.1787/9789264224605-en.

OECD (2012a), "Human resources management country profiles: Slovak Republic", OECD, Paris, available at: www.oecd.org/gov/pem/OECD%20HRM%20Profile%20-%20Slovak%20Republic.pdf.

OECD (2012b), *Public Sector Compensation in Times of Austerity*, OECD Publishing, Paris, http://dx.doi.org/10.1787/9789264177758-en.

OECD (2011a), *Public Servants as Partners for Growth: Toward a Stronger, Leaner and More Equitable Workforce*, OECD Publishing, Paris, http://dx.doi.org/10.1787/9789264166707-en.

OECD (2011b), *OECD Government at a Glance 2011*, OECD Publishing, Paris, available at: www.oecd.org/gov/indicators/govataglance; http://dx.doi.org/10.1787/gov_glance-2011-en.

OECD (2010), "Survey on Strategic Human Resources Management in Central/Federal Governments of OECD Countries", OECD, Paris.

OECD (2009), "Survey on Competency Management in Government", OECD, Paris.

OECD (2007), *OECD Reviews of Human Resource Management in Government: Belgium 2007: Brussels-Capital Region, Federal Government, Flemish Government, French Community, Walloon Region*, OECD Publishing, Paris, http://dx.doi.org/10.1787/9789264038202-en.

OECD (2005), *Performance-related Pay Policies for Government Employees*, OECD Publishing, Paris, http://dx.doi.org/10.1787/9789264007550-en.

Scheepers and Parys (2005), "De moeizame weg van personeelsadministratie naar modern HRM en competentiemanagement", in Hondeghem, A. & Depré, R. (Red.) (2005) *De Copernicushervorming in perspectief: veranderingsmanagement in de federale overheid*, Vanden Broele, Brugge.

Staroňová, K. (2013), "Innovative elements in civil service reform in Slovakia: Road to professionalization?", paper presented at the 21st NISPAcee Annual Conference on 16-18 May 2013 in Belgrade, Serbia, available at: www.nispa.org/conf_papers_list.php?s_wg_select=124&cid=21.

Treasury Board of Canada Secretariat (n.d.), "Office of the Chief Human Resources Officer", www.tbs-sct.gc.ca/chro-dprh/index-eng.asp.

Weber, A. (2012), "Alta dirección pública", presentation given at the seminar "Fortaleciendo la Capacidad del Empleo Público Colombiano", Bogota, 27 July 2012.

Chapter 4.

Scaling up digital government in the Slovak Republic

This chapter examines the process of digitisation in the Slovak administration over the past decade. Though there has been measurable progress in a number of areas, particularly with regards to Internet connectivity and usage, when it comes to the online delivery of public services and citizen engagement, the Slovak Republic has lagged behind peer countries both within the European Union and the OECD. There is, however, strong demand-side potential for digital services, evidenced by the relatively high uptake levels of Internet-based activities by the Slovakian population as a whole. With the embrace of some key improvements to its approach, many of the elements are in place for the Slovak Republic to rapidly become a regional leader in digital government.

The statistical data for Israel are supplied by and under the responsibility of the relevant Israeli authorities. The use of such data by the OECD is without prejudice to the status of the Golan Heights, East Jerusalem and Israeli settlements in the West Bank under the terms of international law.

Introduction

The use of ICT to improve services and enhance engagement with citizens, businesses and other stakeholders – commonly referred to as "digital government" – is increasingly becoming core to the modernisation and public sector reform agenda for countries across the OECD. According to the 2014 OECD *Recommendation of the Council on Digital Government Strategies*, digital government is defined as: "…the use of digital technologies, as an integrated part of governments' modernisation strategies, to create public value. It relies on a digital government ecosystem comprised of government actors, non-governmental organisations, businesses, citizens' associations and individuals which supports the production of and access to data, services and content through interactions with the government" (OECD, 2014b).

Box 4.1. **Recommendation of the Council on Digital Government Strategies**

Adopted on 15 July 2014, the OECD *Recommendation of the Council on Digital Government Strategies* is a structuring element for decision makers and stakeholders that need to navigate government objectives and resources in an increasingly complex policy-making environment. Digital technologies create both opportunities and challenges for successful government reforms in any policy domain, e.g. welfare, economic development, administrative services efficiency. A set of 12 principles, grouped under 3 pillars, guide decision makers:

1. Engage citizens and open up government to maintain public trust.

1. Ensure greater transparency, openness and inclusiveness of government processes and operations.
2. Encourage engagement and participation of public, private and civil society stakeholders in policy making and public service design and delivery.
3. Create a data-driven culture in the public sector.
4. Reflect a risk management approach to addressing digital security and privacy issues, and include the adoption of effective and appropriate security measures.

2. Adopt cohesive approaches to deliver public value throughout government.

5. Secure leadership and political commitment to the strategy.
6. Ensure coherent use of digital technologies across policy areas and levels of government.
7. Establish effective organisational and governance frameworks to co-ordinate the implementation of the digital strategy within and across levels of government.
8. Strengthen international co-operation with other governments.

3. Strengthen government capabilities to ensure returns on IT investments.

9. Develop clear business cases to sustain the funding and focused implementation of digital technologies projects.
10. Reinforce institutional capacities to manage and monitor projects' implementation.
11. Procure digital technologies based on assessment of existing assets.
12. Ensure that general and sector-specific legal and regulatory frameworks allow digital opportunities to be seized.

Source: OECD (2014b), *Recommendation of the Council on Digital Government Strategies*, OECD, Paris, available at: www.oecd.org/gov/public-innovation/Recommendation-digital-government-strategies.pdf.

Increasingly citizen's expectations with regards to services provided by government are rising as they compare the offerings of public services to those provided by the private sector, specifically with regards to digital services. If governments cannot provide digital services of the quality that citizens have come to expect from commercial or even non-profit providers, this can ultimately erode trust in the public sector. As digital technologies become increasingly embedded into daily life in both government and society at large, having well-run and high-performing digitalisation initiatives in the public sector is of increasing importance.

As the Slovak Republic starts its new EU programming period with the Operational Programme Integrated Infrastructure (2014-20), the timing is right to review how its digital government initiatives are being implemented. The Slovak Republic has had in place an active programme of digitisation over the past decade; however, in many respects it has not met expectations. Though there has been measurable progress in a number of areas, particularly with regards to Internet connectivity and usage, when it comes to the online delivery of public services and citizen engagement, the Slovak Republic has lagged behind peer countries both within the EU and OECD. This poor performance is despite the fact that during the 2007-13 EU programming period the Slovak Republic had access to approximately EUR 1 billion in EU funds earmarked for digitisation efforts and expanded broadband coverage.[1] The inability to effectively absorb all of this funding given the lack of tangible results raises concerns about the effectiveness of the current approach to digital government in the Slovak Republic.

While there are initial indications that some of the Slovak Republic's investments from the last EU programming period are beginning to reach fruition, it is clear that this progress is not happening as quickly or robustly as would be desired. A number of new online services have been or are about to be launched; however, they continue to lack a user-centric orientation. An overview of relevant European statistics on digital government show that the Slovak Republic continues to lag behind their peer countries on key indicators. In the 2015 rankings on the Digital Agenda for Europe as part of the European Commission's Europe 2020 initiative, overall the Slovak Republic ranked 20th out of 28 EU members on the digital agenda and was classified as being part of the cluster of "low performing countries".[2] The good news is that the Slovak Republic scores highly on the dimensions of human capital and use of Internet, meaning that there is a strong foundation in the country to build on. However, it significantly underperforms with regards to the provision of digital public services and still has considerable work to do on bridging connectivity gaps in the country.

The data from the European Commission is correlated by the United Nations e-government index which in 2014 ranked the Slovak Republic as 51st in the world, the 4th lowest score amongst OECD member countries and a steady decline in ranking over the past four UN e-government index reporting periods.[3] The Slovak Republic scores higher amongst the sub-index for e-participation, at 40th overall, and above average for Europe. This represents a steady and significant increase since 2010 when it ranked 117th.

This chapter will explore some of the major aspects of digital government initiatives within the Slovak Republic with the aim of providing tangible recommendations that can help advance progress in digitisation. Specifically, it will look at the themes of governance, national strategies, online service delivery, the digital divide, open government data, social media and a skilled ICT workforce, with an overview of the current state of play for the Slovak Republic in each of these areas and examples of international practices from across the OECD.

Key facts and findings

Governance

The governance of digitisation covers not only the introduction of technology but the allocation of tasks, the development of new skills, and the adoption of common arrangements and tools to reap efficiency savings government wide. There is a need to ensure value for money in the public sector through sector-level efficiency estimates, budgetary frameworks, funding arrangements, business-case frameworks, productivity measures and the concept of a value chain for public service delivery. Among the emerging developments across OECD countries are the changing role and relations with the services' users, the role of data, new ethical challenges and a shift from a "government-centred" or supply-driven approach to a "user-centred" or demand-driven approach. This includes the importance of actors' engagement in the development and implementation of digital innovation projects and the need to ensure that digital initiatives do not leave behind those on the other side of the digital divide (see OECD, 2014b: Principle 1). In addition, the importance of measurement and the use of existing public data are underlined as tools to create better dialogue among stakeholders and to address asymmetrical information challenges (see OECD, 2014b: Principles 2 and 3).

The Slovak Republic has a highly fragmented approach to its governance of digital initiatives. For central co-ordination of digital government initiatives, there are three key players within the national government:

- The Ministry of Finance plays the central role in co-ordinating digital government related policy and strategy, in part formalised by the Competence Act 575/2001, and is the intermediary body for Priority Axis 7 Information Society and related EU funding mechanisms. Digital government initiatives funded under the new Operational Programme Integrated Infrastructure (2014-20) are overseen and implemented by the Ministry of Finance, primarily through the Architectural Office of Public Administration (AOPS).
- The Government Office provided formal oversight on the implementation of the previous Operational Programme Information Society (2007-13). As of 2016 it will no longer have a formal oversight role on digitisation initiatives funded through the new operational programme, but plans to continue to be involved in the broader digitisation agenda in the Slovak Republic.
- The Ministry of the Interior is responsible for the management of most of the primary databases which are critical for online service delivery.[4] It also operates a number of online services and manages the e-ID card system that provides a digital signature for all online government services.

In addition to these central bodies, other key organisations that play a role in digitisation include:

- The National Agency for Network and Electronic Services (NASES), which is a semi-independent body of the Government Office that is responsible for managing the government-wide portals for both online services and open government data as well as providing the IT network for all government Ministries.

- The Ministry of Transportation, which is responsible for broadband and telecommunications policy and acts as the managing authority for the new Operational Programme Integrated Infrastructure (2014-20).
- The National Security Office, which provides centralised guidance to ministries with respect to cybersecurity threats and mitigation strategies. In addition, the Computer Security Incident Response Team Slovakia, which was established by the Ministry of Finance, provides operational support for cybersecurity activities for critical national infrastructure and state authorities.

While each line ministry has a director general responsible for ICT-related issues, there is no government-wide equivalent of a Chief Information Officer or any type of mechanism for all of those responsible for ICT and digitisation efforts to collaborate and co-ordinate on a regular basis. Formal co-ordination has tended to be *ad hoc* in nature and linked primarily to specific funding and accountability requirements. There is a Digital Champion for the Slovak Republic;[5] however, it is a political role mandated as an interlocutor by the EU and does not appear to have a significant institutional co-ordination role within the civil service itself.

The Slovak Republic stands as the only OECD country that does not have a Chief Information Officer (CIO) or equivalent (Figure 4.1). While governments across the OECD have taken different approaches to provide government-wide co-ordination on digital government initiatives, experience has shown having a central steering mechanism in place is a critical success factor in order to achieve results in the area of digital government.

Figure 4.1. **C-suite digital government positions in OECD countries**

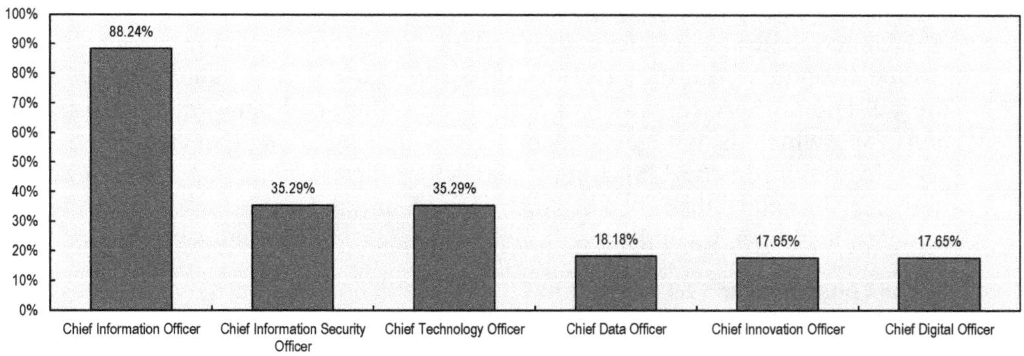

Source: OECD (2014a), "Digital Performance Survey", OECD, Paris; desk research.

The role of the CIO and other senior digital government officials can take different forms depending on the governance model being used in the country. Across the OECD, a large majority of CIOs have "soft" levers at their disposal to set strategy and co-ordinate national approaches. A smaller minority also have more coercive levers which allow them to control funding and mandate external reviews of ICT projects (Figure 4.2).

Figure 4.2. **Responsibilities of the Chief Information Officer in OECD countries**

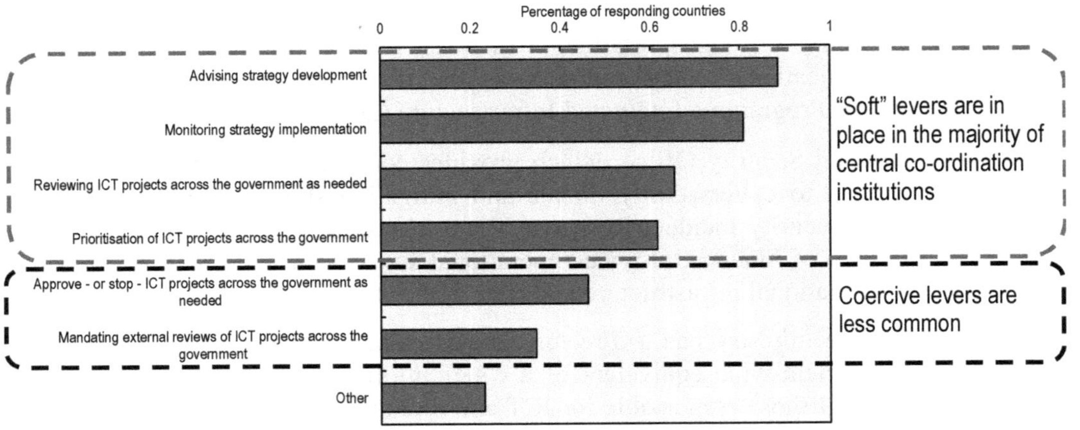

Source: OECD (2014a), "Digital Performance Survey", OECD, Paris.

There is no single preferred structure for the governance of digital government programmes, as any successful approach must take into account the context of the specific public administration. However, a few examples of current governance structures for digital initiatives across OECD countries help to illustrate the different approaches that can be taken:

- The United Kingdom has become a leader in digital service delivery in part through the creation of its centralised Government Digital Service, which provides oversight and guidance to all government departments in support of their digitisation initiatives and has focused on bringing top talent in the digital domain into government.
- The United States has in recent years adopted a somewhat similar approach to the United Kingdom with the creation of two in-house digital consultancy services, the US Digital Service, which is part of the Office of Management and Budget, and 18F, which is an independent agency managed by the General Services Administration. In the US example, however, these centralised services are less universal in nature than in the United Kingdom, and focus only on top priority projects, leaving a broad degree of independence to individual departments.
- Other countries such as Canada have a more blended digital governance system. A national Chief Information Officer has a central policy-setting role, and takes into account ministerial accountability imperatives by chairing a government-wide Chief Information Officer Council to assist in co-ordinating the work of departmental CIOs who are not directly responsible to the national CIO but to their respective departmental senior management. Canada also has centralised management of core ICT infrastructure through Shared Services Canada, which was created in 2011 with responsibility across all core government ministries for e-mail, data centres, network infrastructure and workplace technology devices (e.g. laptops, tablets, software).
- In contrast, Denmark, while it does not have a specific national CIO position, still has robust governance of digital initiatives through its Steering Committee for Joint Government Co-operation (*Styregruppen for Tværoffentlige Samarbejder*,

STS). The STS is a cross-government co-ordination body that brings together those leading ICT activities at the national, regional and local level in Denmark with the goal of creating joint ownership of modernisation efforts across the horizontal and vertical layers of the state administration. There is also an Agency for Digitisation which has a mandate to facilitate digitisation in the public sector and acts as a secretariat for, and implementation and co-ordination body of, the STS.

Proper governance becomes increasingly important when examining some of the significant challenges that exist in the effective implementation of digital government initiatives. Across the OECD there has been a long history of ICT project failures due to technical or organisational challenges including, in some cases, outdated and inflexible procurement processes. This can be a result of both the size and duration of ICT projects, which can involve complicated development and implementation processes exacerbated by the long timeframes for the completion of these projects. In a survey of OECD countries, it was found that more than half of countries responding have an average project duration length of more than three years for large ICT projects (Figure 4.3).

Figure 4.3. **Average length of central government ICT projects with a total project value greater than USD 10 million, 2014**

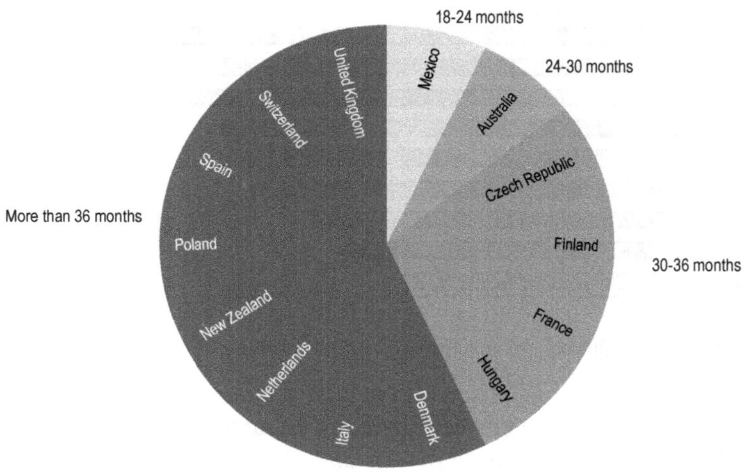

Source: OECD (2015c), *Government at a Glance 2015*, OECD Publishing, Paris, http://dx.doi.org/10.1787/gov_glance-2015-en.

For the purposes of comparison to Figure 4.3, the Slovak Republic has 39 ICT projects under the previous Operational Programme Information Society (2007-13) which are greater than USD 10 million. The average planned length of these projects was 24-30 months; however, based on information gathered from government officials, the actual implementation period is often in excess of 36 months.

Yet even against this backdrop of serious ICT project risks, many countries have not yet put in place strong governance structures for digital initiatives to mitigate these risks. Fully 86% of countries report lacking formal co-ordination between units on digital initiatives, 61% do not have mandatory business cases for ICT projects and 41% do not have a standardised model for ICT project management (OECD, 2014a). This speaks to the need to have a whole-of-government strategy for digital government activities, particularly as the introduction of digital technologies is increasingly touching upon all aspects of government business.

National strategies

Equally important to having the right governance structures in place, successful introduction of digital technologies into government require a whole-of-government approach that can provide consistent direction to the various actors involved in these initiatives. Given that digitisation initiatives are often cross-cutting in nature, both horizontally across different ministries and vertically to various levels of government and non-governmental and private sector organisations, the importance of a consistent national strategy becomes clear. National strategies can also help ensure that digitisation initiatives take a cross-sector approach across key policy areas. While all national strategies for digital government across the OECD cover issues of general public administration, 50-60% also cover a number of other key policy areas, such as education, economic affairs and health (Figure 4.4).

Figure 4.4. **Policy areas covered in the national digital strategies of OECD countries**

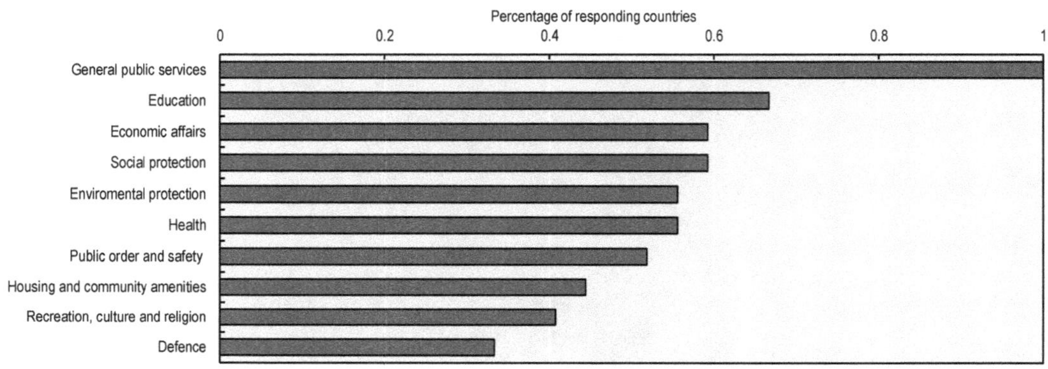

Source: OECD (2014a), "Digital Performance Survey", OECD, Paris.

Currently the key digital government strategy document for the Slovak government is the "Strategic Document for Digital Growth and Next Generation Access Infrastructure (2014-2020)" from the Ministry of Finance, which provides the basis upon which the next EU funding cycle, specifically the Operational Programme Integrated Infrastructure, will be implemented. It focuses specifically on the themes of services to citizens and businesses, effective public administration and broadband access. There is also a new National Conception of Public Administration Informatisation being developed by the Ministry of Finance which is expected to be approved in late 2015. In May 2014, a "proposal of centralisation and development of data centres in the state administration" was approved by the government of the Slovak Republic with the aim of consolidating all government data centres into two – one that will be managed by the Ministry of Finance and one by the Ministry of the Interior – which will provide cloud services.

These current strategic documents build upon a number of previous national strategies that have been put in place over the past ten years. For the previous EU programming period, to support the Operational Programme Information Society (2007-13) the key national strategy documents were:

- the eGovernment Strategy of the Slovak Republic (2008-13)

- the National Concept of eGovernment (2008-13)
- the National Strategy for Information Security of the Slovak Republic (2008-13)
- the Concept of Software Products Usage for Public Administration (2009-13).

A key finding from both survey data and in-person meetings with Slovak officials is that the Slovak Republic's national strategy setting and national priorities for digital government have, over the past decade, been almost entirely driven by the conditionality associated with obtaining external funding sources, namely EU funds. In most cases, EU funding is the primary source for digital government initiatives. The requirements around EU funding are also the main driver for most of the cost-benefit analysis being done by departments with regards to ICT investments.

The combination of high reliance on EU funding and the previously described fractured governance model for digital government initiatives means that a robust national vision for digital government that supersedes the requirements of individual funding sources does not exist. This has generated a situation where it is all but impossible for the Slovak government to set priorities for digitisation independently of the EU funding process or make trade-offs between potentially competing interests across ministries and levels of government.

Online service delivery

To be successful, the development of new online services by governments must be approached with a "digital by design" mind-set which uses the opportunities provided by digital platforms to innovate the entire service delivery process, not simply digitising existing processes. The launch of new online services represents a singular opportunity to build a sense of momentum in the government's digitisation agenda in the minds of citizens. At the same time, however, it raises the risk that if citizens' first online interactions are negative, and there is no active programme to improve these services with a user-centric focus, momentum could easily falter due to rising frustration and cynicism. Designing and delivering online services with a user-centric focus has become an increasing priority for many OECD countries and there is a growing body of knowledge on best practices in this domain. For example, the Government Digital Service in the United Kingdom has put in place an 18-point digital service standard that all new online services must adhere to before being launched in order to achieve their goal of "making services so good that people prefer to use them" (Box 4.2).

The provision of online services is the area where the Slovak Republic faces one of its greatest challenges, ranking 27th out of 28 amongst EU countries.[6] Historically the Slovak Republic has been slow compared to other European and OECD countries in providing online services for citizens. Moreover, when online services have been provided, they tend to be supply-side driven by internal priorities, often outsourced through fairly complex procurement arrangements that involved long timescales, thus providing little flexibility to respond to user demands and priorities or the participation of smaller suppliers. Where digital services do exist in the Slovak Republic, they tend to rank significantly below European averages (Figure 4.5).[7]

Box 4.2. UK government digital services 18-point digital service standard

The United Kingdom's Government Digital Service (GDS) has emerged as a world leader in ensuring high-quality, user-centric online government services. Part of this success has been due to a strong focus on putting in place centralised standards that ensure all digital services provided by government go through a similar evaluation process and meet the same level of quality. The Digital Service Standard provides 18 specific criteria that all new digital services must adhere to before they are allowed to go live on the central GOV.UK website:

1. Understand user needs. Research to develop a deep knowledge of who the service users are and what that means for digital and assisted digital service design.
2. Put a plan in place for ongoing user research and usability testing to continuously seek feedback from users to improve the service.
3. Put in place a sustainable multidisciplinary team that can design, build and operate the service, led by a suitably skilled and senior service manager with decision-making responsibility.
4. Build a service that can be iterated on a frequent basis and make sure that there are the capacity, resources and technical flexibility to do so.
5. Build the digital service using the agile, iterative and user-centred methods set out in the manual.
6. Evaluate what tools and systems will be used to build, host, operate and measure the digital service, and how to procure them.
7. Evaluate what user data and information the digital service will be providing or storing, and address the security level, legal responsibilities, privacy issues and risks associated with the service (consulting with experts where appropriate).
8. Make all new source code open and reusable, and publish it under appropriate licenses (or provide a convincing explanation as to why this cannot be done for specific sub-sets of the source code).
9. Use open standards and common government platforms where available.
10. Be able to test the end-to-end digital service in an environment identical to that of the live version on all common browsers and devices. Use dummy accounts and a representative sample of users.
11. Make a plan for the event of the digital service being taken temporarily offline.
12. Create a digital service that is simple and intuitive enough that users succeed the first time without assisted digital support.
13. Build a digital service consistent with the user experience of the rest of GOV.UK by using the design patterns and style guide.
14. Encourage all users to use the digital service, alongside an appropriate plan to phase out non-digital channels/services.
15. Use analytics tools that collect performance data, use this data to analyse the success of the service and to translate this into features and tasks for the next phase of development.
16. Establish performance benchmarks, in consultation with GDS, using the four key performance indicators: user satisfaction; completion rates; a plan to achieve low cost per transaction; and a plan to achieve high digital take-up and assisted digital support.
17. Report performance data on the Performance Platform.
18. Test the service from beginning to end with the minister responsible for it.

The United States Digital Service has recently launched a 13-point Digital Services Playbook (https://playbook.cio.gov) which is based in part on the successful practices implemented in the United Kingdom's Digital Service Standard.

Source: Based on information from GDS Standard, www.gov.uk/service-manual/digital-by-default.

Figure 4.5. **E-government performance across policy priorities**

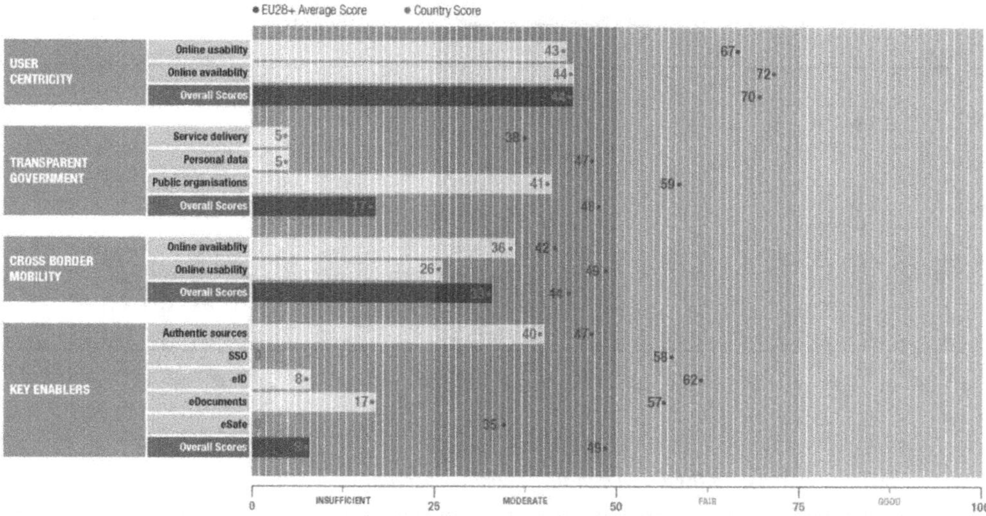

Source: European Commission (2013), "Slovakia: E-government state of play", available at: http://ec.europa.eu/information_society/newsroom/cf/dae/document.cfm?doc_id=5568.

The central website for accessing online services from the government is operated by NASES (slovensko.sk) and serves as a central hub for these efforts. While there are signs of increasing levels of online service delivery activities by ministries, it appears that this is happening in a somewhat haphazard manner, with some departments embracing these opportunities and others progressing at a much slower pace. As part of the conclusion of projects from the 2007-13 EU programming period, there are a number of key government services that are coming online in 2015. A few notable examples from the Ministry of the Interior include the new government-wide e-procurement system launched in February 2015, which has already had some impressive results in cost and time savings, as well as new online systems for both residential address changes and vehicle registration.

For the new programming period, objectives identified by Slovak officials include the development of mobile applications, developing services and process maps linked to life situations (e.g. births, deaths, marriage, etc.), improved website navigation, multi-channel access and client service centres, interoperability with EU services, ability for clients to access a central portfolio of their data held by government, and the creation of more open Application Programming Interface (APIs) and open data to allow third parties to build on existing services. However, as previously noted, unless some of the historical challenges with the design of online services in the Slovak Republic are addressed through a more user-centric approach, this increase in the quantity of online services may be hampered by low levels of quality (Figure 4.6).

Figure 4.6. **Problems with the use of e-government services, 2013**

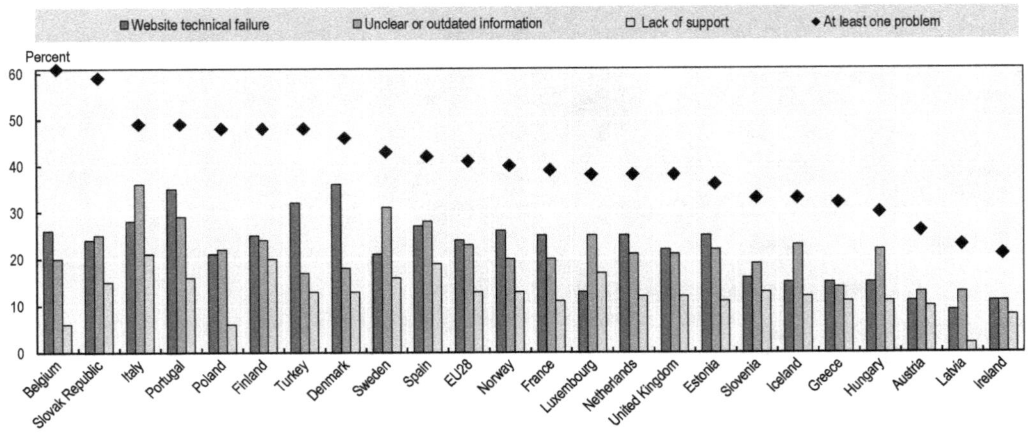

Source: OECD (2015a), *OECD Digital Economy Outlook 2015*, OECD Publishing, Paris, http://dx.doi.org/10.1787/9789264232440-en.

Another important part of the digital services eco-system in the Slovak Republic is the e-ID card system that was introduced in 2013 by the Ministry of the Interior. For the past two years citizens have been able to obtain e-ID cards that provide a secure electronic identification and signature for using online services by government. The use of the e-ID card for digital signature when accessing government services online will likely become more prevalent in the coming year as planned online services are launched by a number of ministries. However, to date, uptake and activation of e-ID cards by citizens has been relatively low. While 1 million cards have already been issued, only approximately 5% have had the digital signature activated, most of which are likely business clients as opposed to individual citizens. This may be in part due to lack of awareness and the absence of significant demand-side incentives to obtain a card given the relatively low number of full-service online systems available until recently.

Building robust back-end infrastructure to support digital service delivery is a critical enabling factor for developing high-quality online services. Given the privacy and security considerations related to many of the services that government typically provides, having a robust e-ID system is a critical enabling factor for greater uptake of digital services. Equally importantly, by building a secure infrastructure on the back-end, it also enables service providers in different ministries new opportunities to streamline services and enhance interoperability, thus easing the administrative burden for citizens and businesses. Estonia has had particular success in this area through the development of their X-Road infrastructure, which has provided a platform for all government agencies in the country to provide secure online services to their citizens and businesses (Box 4.3).

Digital divide

With regards to Internet connectivity and digital literacy in the Slovak Republic, there appears to be an evolving storyline. Data from five or ten years ago put the Slovak Republic in a relatively weak position compared to other European and OECD countries with regards to connectivity and digital skills. However, there are signs that the Slovak Republic's digital engagement has been increasing in recent years. The latest data from the European Commission show that the digital skills of the population are relatively high, with 76% being regular Internet users, approximately two-thirds of whom read news online and use social networks, and over 50% of whom use online banking and shop online.[8] Overall Internet connectivity in the Slovak Republic has risen significantly since the mid-2000s (Figure 4.8).

Box 4.3. **Building the infrastructure to support digital services: Estonia's X-Road**

The data exchange layer X-Road was launched in 2001 and has since become the standard platform for streamlining services between government agencies in Estonia. It is also used to create seamless workflows that involve non-government actors, e.g. to exchange information on income and assets from private companies to taxation and social security authorities.

Figure 4.7. **Estonia X-Road Data Exchange System**

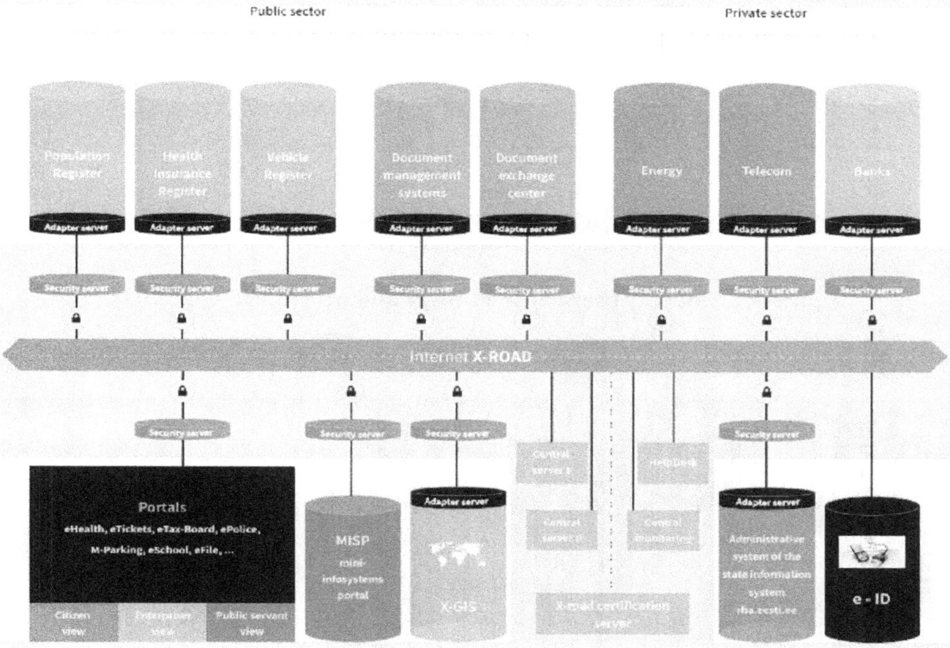

The use of the X-Road was initially made mandatory for any data exchange taking place between government ministries and agencies and has today become the quasi-standard for any data exchange. Government institutions have high incentives to use the platform because it provides fast and reliable access to the base registers and many other information systems that are relevant to more than one institution.

The Estonian X-Road has also proven to be an effective instrument to empower citizens *vis-à-vis* potential concerns about misuse of their personal information by civil servants and institutions as all access to their data via the X-Road is logged. It also allows citizens through the use of their secure e-ID card to be able to see what information the government holds on them at any given time from all databases in one central user portal.

Source: OECD (2015b), *OECD Public Governance Reviews: Estonia and Finland. Fostering Strategic Capacity Across Governments and Digital Services Across Borders*, OECD Publishing, Paris, http://dx.doi.org/10.1787/9789264229334-en.

However, there is evidence of a significant generational divide in Internet usage in the Slovak Republic. The percentage of young Slovaks 16-24 years old using the Internet is very high at 99.1%, higher than the OECD average of 95.6%. However, the use of the Internet of the older generation 65-74 years of age is only 35.7%, below the OECD average of 48.8% (Figure 4.9).

Figure 4.8. **Internet access in OECD countries**

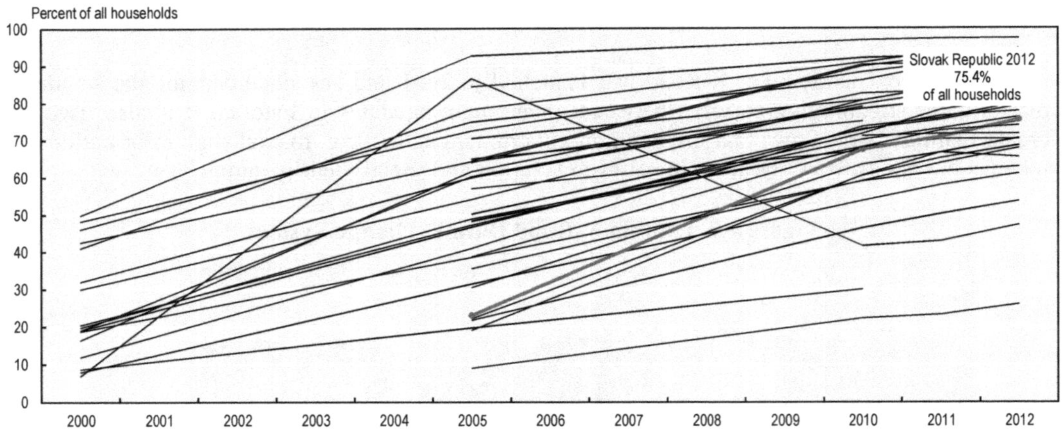

Source: OECD (2015d), Internet access (indicator), http://dx.doi.org/10.1787/69c2b997-en.

Figure 4.9. **Internet users by age, 16-24 and 65-74 year-olds, 2014**

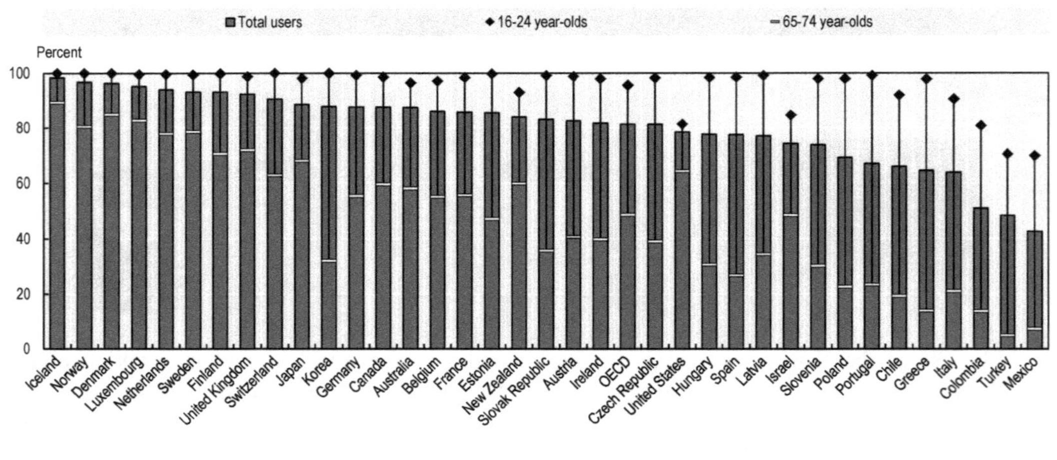

Source: OECD (2015), Internet users by age, 16-24 and 65-74 year-olds, 2014: As a percentage of population in each age group, in *OECD Digital Economy Outlook 2015*, OECD Publishing, Paris, http://dx.doi.org/10.1787/9789264232440-graph78-en.

The Slovak Republic has also significantly lagged in the provision of high-speed broadband connections across the country, particularly in rural areas. In part, this ongoing lack of broadband access stems from the inability to absorb funding ear-marked for broadband infrastructure projects under the 2007-13 EU Operational Programme Information Society. There are plans in place, backed by EU funds for the new programming period, to accelerate broadband Internet access across the Slovak Republic with the ambitious goal of having all households connected to broadband Internet (30Mbit/s or higher) by 2020. If these projects are successfully completed, it would appear that the digital divide in the Slovak Republic would be well on its way to being significantly reduced.

Figure 4.10. **Fixed (wired) broadband penetration by speed tiers, June 2014**

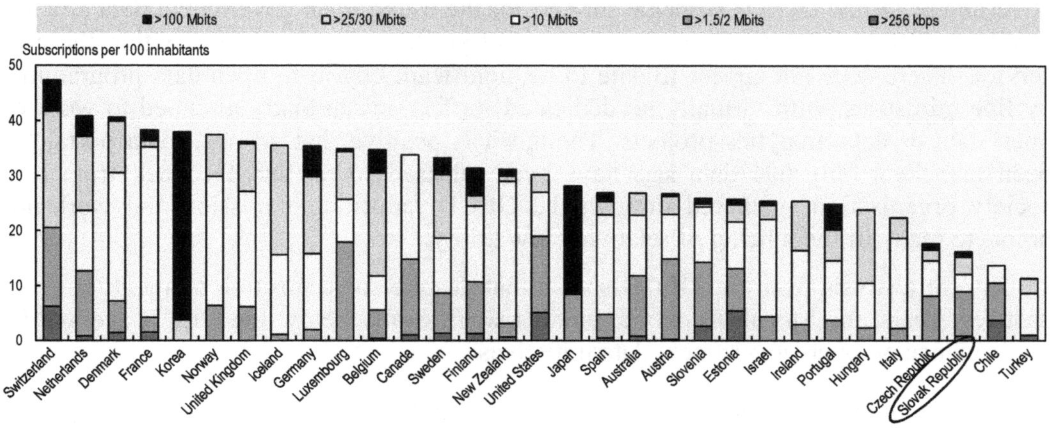

Source: OECD (2015a), *OECD Digital Economy Outlook 2015*, OECD Publishing, Paris, http://dx.doi.org/10.1787/9789264232440-en.

Open government data

Enhanced availability of open government data (OGD) and the public sector's ability to combine different datasets and analyse them can enable governments to map and understand trends in public service users' needs better, design programming aimed at prevention and early intervention in social policy fields, and unveil opportunities to strengthen the alignment of delivery goals with user expectations (Ubaldi, 2013).

- Open data can be utilised to spur public participation and social engagement with the purpose of better understanding and predicting user needs and levels of satisfaction with public service users.
- Stakeholder involvement can allow for a better understanding of the context of public demand (e.g. users' needs in terms of data, timeliness of updates, formats) and to craft appropriate strategies that support higher public service use given specific contexts (e.g. prioritise data based on the desired objective, adjust data supply to the needs). As a result, higher and more sustainable value creation can be generated.
- Capturing users' feedback enables new features, new lines of business, new markets, new competencies and new tools. But OGD can also facilitate collaboration with non-institutional users in designing responses to public needs (e.g. co-development and co-production of services through newly developed apps).
- Innovative service delivery is emerging from mashing up sets of data that originate from various sources, and by various parties, supporting early-intervention programming and predicting needs to design prevention programming in social policy areas.

The strategic use of data is an area where the Slovak Republic is poised to make rapid gains with the right focus. In recent years there has been some initial open data activity as a part of the Slovak Republic's commitments to the Open Government Partnership, including the launch of an open data portal (data.gov.sk) and an online registry of all grants, contributions and contracts. Similar to other digitisation initiatives in the Slovak Republic, open data would appear to be relatively fragmented across the government. While there is strategic support for the use of open government data as a key enabler of public sector reform, its use has not yet been mainstreamed within the civil service. There does not appear to date to be significant buy-in to open data programmes by line ministries, with virtually no dedicated staff in any ministry assigned to work on open data or data analytics projects. Though it is positive that an open data portal has been launched, only 604 data sets have been released so far and feedback from civil society organisations gathered through the OECD fact-finding mission and workshop points to many of them being of relatively low utility.

Recent analysis from the OECD shows that despite some positive momentum in the past few years, the Slovak Republic remains significantly below the OECD average for performance on open government data initiatives.

Figure 4.11. **OECD OURdata Index: "Open, Useful, Reusable" open government data**

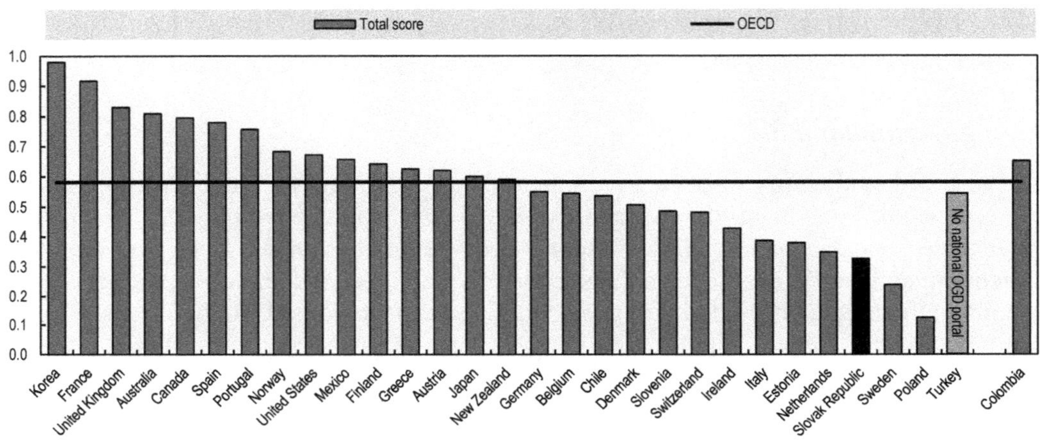

Source: OECD (2015c), *Government at a Glance 2015*, OECD Publishing, Paris, http://dx.doi.org/10.1787/gov_glance-2015-en.

A greater focus on interoperability and identifying areas of high value for the use of data both inside of government and with external partners could lead to significant advancement in this area and also support other key aspects of the public reform agenda, such as improved analytical and evaluation capacity. There has also been limited focus up to now on the potential opportunities for economic development and increased government efficiency and effectiveness by sharing high-value data sets and fostering an active open data community.

This is an area where potentially large gains could be made relatively quickly if there was sustained effort by the national government in partnership with regional/local government and civil society. In order to do so, a more concerted government approach to engaging with existing and potential data producers and reusers is needed. Communities, networks and events of different types can help the government achieve greater reach, take-up and eventually impact for OGD. This can include setting up more regular and intensive modes of engagement, including developing user groups and communities, in person or virtual meet-ups for open data producers and developers, contests, partnerships, etc. (OECD, 2015e).

Box 4.4. **Community-based approaches to open government data in OECD countries**

- The United Kingdom's Open Data User Group (ODUG) is a standing body composed of government representatives, civil society, academia and business stakeholders. It has been an influential actor in shaping OGD policies, exchanging practices and identifying opportunities for data reuse – for example, by establishing, managing and monitoring dataset requests to the national OGD portal (www.gov.uk/government/groups/129).
- In France, the Prime Minister's open government data unit Etalab holds monthly lunchtime events ("Bonjour Data") that are free for any interested parties to attend and discuss ideas and issues around OGD (www.etalab.gouv.fr/event/bonjour-data/all). In parallel to this unstructured, open-for-all set of meetings, the French government has been actively engaging government and non-government actors through its "DataConnexions" network.
- The German government held a public consultation in 2015 on the directions to take on open government data (www.open-data-aktionsplan.de). Germany has had a beta version of its open data portal in place for some time (www.govdata.de). The public online consultation represents an intensified commitment to OGD and allows the public to influence the national government's open data action plan for the near future. It is important to underline that this online consultation is only one step of a larger process that will now lead to workshops, drafting of an action plan and eventually resubmission of the draft action plan for public consultation before it becomes the German federal government's official action plan.

Source: OECD (2015e), *Open Government Data Review of Poland: Unlocking the Value of Government Data*, OECD Digital Government Studies, OECD Publishing, Paris, http://dx.doi.org/10.1787/9789264241787-en.

Use of social media

Across OECD countries the use of information and communication technologies, including social media, is emerging as a key tool for citizen engagement. As a rapidly increasing percentage of the population uses social media on a regular basis, this provides a key platform for government to be able to directly communicate with citizens and engage with them on issues of importance. It also has opportunities to be used in a passive manner to monitor conversations on key policy areas and feedback on government services. These can be important inputs into both planning and evaluation processes that allow non-traditional voices to be captured.

However, as governments increasingly use social media for such purposes it is important to recognise that there is no "one-size-fits-all" approach and country-specific considerations must be taken into account. Different social media platforms have greater levels of popularity and penetration in different regions, as well as along demographic, linguistic or socio-economic lines. For example, across Europe data indicate that in most countries, including the Slovak Republic, a significantly higher percentage of social media users are highly educated (Figure 4.12). This has clear implications for targeting the use of these platforms depending on the policy area or type of government service.

In the Slovak Republic some ministries, such as the Ministry of Foreign and European Affairs and the Ministry of the Interior, have a fairly active programme of social media use not only for broadcasting messages but also for engaging with citizens and stakeholders. The central government online portal also has an active Facebook campaign operating (http://facebook.com/slovensko.sk). However, most ministries are either not using social media at all or are doing so in a fairly limited manner, consisting primarily of pushing out one-directional information. In most cases, social media usage and interaction is centrally controlled by the communications and public affairs units. There is little to no guidance provided to rank-and-file civil servants on social media usage, either from the perspective of avoiding risks or the positive benefits of professional interactions. Given the relatively high usage of social media within the Slovakian population as a whole, this would appear to be a medium that is being under-utilised by the government.

Figure 4.12. **Social media uptake by level of educational attainment, 2013**

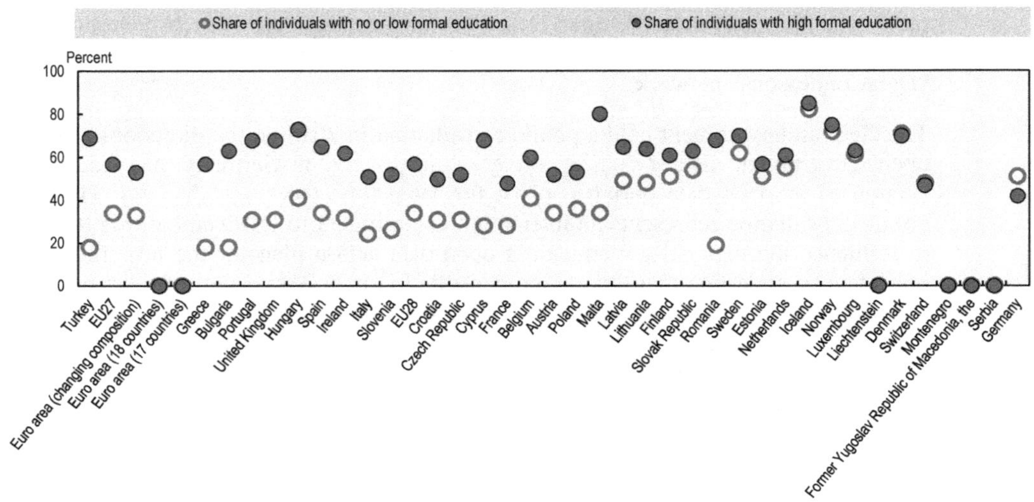

Source: Mickoleit, A. (2014), "Social media use by governments: A policy primer to discuss trends, identify policy opportunities and guide decision makers", *OECD Working Papers on Public Governance*, No. 26, OECD Publishing, Paris, http://dx.doi.org/10.1787/5jxrcmghmk0s-en.

Across the OECD the use of social media is still going through a phase of maturing as these platforms become more widely used. A 2013 survey of OECD countries found that only 50% of responding countries had a central government strategy or objectives for social media usage and only 19% use metrics or indicators to measure the impact of their social media usage (OECD, 2015c). As government agencies increasingly explore the use of social media tools as part of their communications and engagement with citizens, the need for central guidance on the use of social media becomes increasingly important, both for institutions and individual civil servants. Countries across the OECD have tackled this issue in different ways, though most of the countries that would be considered leading users of social media have some form of central guidance on its usage (Box 4.5).

Skilled ICT workforce

One of the challenges in the successful development of digital government that countries face is the recruitment and retention of civil servants with strong ICT skills for both technical development and project management. This is particularly an issue when it comes to the development of skills the public sector needs to operate in an increasingly data-rich environment with requirements to be able to conduct data analysis, develop systems for cross-linking data sources and effectively visualising data to inform decision making and policy. For example, among OECD countries, 58% report not having a strategy to increase open data literacy and 48% report not having a strategy to attract and retain ICT-skilled civil servants (OECD, 2014a). Creating these capacities is essential to drive better decisions, inform policies, support the development of both digital and data-driven processes and services, and deliver more innovative services.

Box 4.5. Institutional responsibilities for social media use in OECD countries

The following sub-set of countries indicates having a "rather" or "very centralised" approach to social media use in government. Responsibilities are typically shared between an institution at the centre of government and individual government ministries or departments.

Australia: The Australian Public Service Commission issues a code of conduct for all government officials (www.apsc.gov.au/publications-and-media/current-circulars-and-advices/2012/circular-20121). Beyond that, individual departments and agencies tailor social media policies to their specific functions and requirements.

Austria: Led by the Federal Chancellery, an inter-ministerial working group develops the strategy in co-operation with external social media experts. Each government institution remains autonomous as to the implementation of the strategy.

Canada: The Treasury Board of Canada is responsible for issuing policies and guidelines for official institutional or personal accounts. This includes a government-wide standard on social media account management (www.tbs-sct.gc.ca/pol/doc-eng.aspx?id=27033&section=text) and a YouTube video providing guidance about social media at work (www.youtube.com/watch?v=JRvY1SzWhl0).

Chile: Central guidelines are issued by the Ministry General Secretariat of the Presidency (www.guiadigital.gob.cl/plataformas-sociales). They include various documents, including a code of conduct and checklists to guide incorporation of social media into agencies' communication strategies.

Colombia: A "digital task force" at the Ministry of ICT is responsible for developing and overseeing the government's social media strategy and guidelines, which are available at: www.gobiernoenredes.co.

Estonia: The Government Office under the Prime Minister co-ordinates all social media policy and communication across the government, e.g. the code of conduct for government officials.

France: The Government Information Service (Service d'information du gouvernement) under the Prime Minister issues guidelines for social media use by central government institutions.

Korea: The Ministry of Security and Public Administration is responsible for the "Government 3.0 Action Plan", which also contains the strategy for social media use in the public sector (www.gov30.go.kr/gov30/index.do). Further to that, individual public agencies and local governments develop custom guidelines for social media use.

Netherlands: The Minister of General Affairs issues a general set of guidelines for social media use that is then adapted by individual ministries.

Norway: Government-wide guidelines are issued by the Norwegian Agency for Public Management and e-Governance under the Ministry of Government Administration, Reform and Church Affairs (www.difi.no/sosiale-medier/veileder-i-sosiale-medier).

Sweden: The eGovernment Delegation issues guidelines that can be further tailored by individual government agencies.

Source: Adapted from OECD (2013), "Survey on Government Use of Social Media", OECD, Paris.

One of the areas repeatedly highlighted in both survey data and in-person interviews was the lack of internal ICT capacity within the civil service of the Slovak Republic. While this is linked to some of the broader HRM issues in the Slovak civil service covered in Chapter 3, there is some specifically problematic context with regards to ICT. Salary differentials between the private sector and public sector are particularly stark in the Slovak Republic, with some officials indicating that employees with strong ICT management and programming skills could expect to make four to five times as much working in the private sector. This issue is exacerbated by the fact that the high reliance on private sector outsourcing for the large amount of ICT investments being funded by EU funds has meant that it has both driven the average salary for private ICT contractors working on government funding projects up, and provided an additional disincentive for talented ICT professionals to work inside government since all of the "interesting" work is being done externally.

The convergence of these factors has created a situation where in most ministries the amount of internal ICT capacity is very low and there is a risky level of reliance on outside experts for virtually all aspects of ICT services and digital delivery. Lacking this internal expertise can be a barrier to setting a government-wide vision for the strategic use of ICT and leaves ministries in a position of being less able to appropriately build two-way relationships with private sector partners delivering services on behalf of government or civil society organisations capable of providing technical advice, for example in the area of open data.

Assessment

While there are promising initial indications that some of the Slovak Republic's investments from the last EU programming period are beginning to pay off, such as the introduction of a national e-ID card and launch of a number of new online services such as the e-procurement system that is showing some initial signs of success, it is clear that this progress is not happening as quickly or robustly as it could. Information gathered through the survey data and fact-finding mission for this review points to key barriers that are preventing digitisation initiatives from reaching their full potential.

Robust government-wide co-ordination of the digital government agenda, framed by a strategic vision of the purpose and use of ICT in government, can go a long way in reducing barriers to progress in realising fully the benefits of implementing digital government that can accrue to the government itself, to citizens and to businesses. The current approach appears to be characterised by ministries operating with a focus almost exclusively on meeting accountability requirements for accessing EU funds as opposed to driving towards a shared whole-of-government vision on why and how digital government ought to be implemented. Having had almost all strategic activity in this area explicitly tied to funding sources has led to muddled priorities, where obtaining funding for digitisation has gone from being a means to an end to, in many cases, being the end itself. This short-term approach to digital government has led to challenges in being able to absorb these funds and neglect in building internal capacity in favour of outsourcing procurement to large private sector vendors. Lack of internal capacity has also manifested itself in a relatively weak focus on the data assets of the Slovakian government, both from the perspective of internal interoperability as well as the provision of open data as an economic and public asset to citizens, businesses and academia.

While there are undoubtedly challenges, the Slovak Republic is well positioned in a number of areas to be able to advance more rapidly in the area of digital government. There is strong demand-side potential for digital services, evidenced by the relatively high uptake levels of Internet-based activities by the Slovakian population as a whole. Moreover, while there have been challenges around connectivity, it appears that this is becoming less of a concern with increasing mobile penetration and the hopefully successful completion of major broadband projects in progress during the coming EU programming period.

The launch of a number of new online services by ministries during 2015-16, in part as a result of Act No. 305/2013 on e-government, which laid out a largely non-mandatory three-year time-period from 2013-16 for the digitisation of public services, means that many citizens will soon have tangible incentives to start interacting more regularly with government through online channels. This represents a singular opportunity to build a sense of momentum in the government's digitisation agenda.

The strategic use of data is another area where the Slovak Republic is poised to make rapid gains with the right focus. The investments from the previous EU programming period are now bearing fruit with the launch of the first set of robust online service offerings and the corresponding databases that power them. Initial efforts via the Open Government Partnership have led to some initial work moving forward in the realm of open government data. However, these have yet to be mainstreamed within the civil service and the use of data for other analytics or public release is still largely viewed as a side-project as opposed to a key enabler. A greater focus on interoperability and identifying areas of high value for use of data both inside of government and with external partners could lead to significant advancement in this area and also support other key areas of the public reform agenda, such as improved analytical and evaluation capacity.

As has also been highlighted, the use of social media by the government has not yet reached its full potential in the Slovak Republic. While some ministries have gone further in experimenting with its use, there remains a lack of central guidance or vision for how it could best be utilised as a part of the broader digital agenda for modernisation of the public administration in the Slovak Republic. When leveraged to its full potential, social media can provide a useful platform for not just communicating with citizens but also incorporating feedback into the design and delivery of policies and services. It also provides an important mechanism for improving government transparency and responsiveness.

Greater use of social media by the Slovak government is important to help promote new digital services and can serve as a cost-effective channel to gather feedback from citizens as digitisation initiatives are implemented. Use of social media can also provide an effective way to gather information on key policy issues and engage with citizens to build trust in government, particularly with the younger generation, which has a comparatively higher rate of social media usage. Building on the work done in other OECD countries, the Slovak Republic should put in place centralised guidance on both institutional use and civil servant use of social media which aims to promote its use as a way to inform and engage citizens, while mitigating any legitimate risks.

Perhaps most foundationally, there is a clear need to build on the current steering mechanism for digital government initiatives in the Slovak Republic located in the Ministry of Finance. At issue is not so much "who is in charge", but the need to provide mechanisms for those involved in the digital agenda, both at an operational level within line ministries and from a direction-setting level within the centre of government, to learn from each other's experiences and build a common sense of ownership based on a government-wide consensus on the strategic results that government stakeholders should be achieving as they pursue their digital government implementation agenda.

Mirroring some of the larger issues at play with public sector modernisation in the Slovak Republic, digital government initiatives are hampered by a lack of strong central co-ordination mechanisms in the government which has allowed for the creation of siloed approaches to ICT and digital service development by ministries. Human resource capacity is another major impediment, particularly the ability to recruit and retain civil service staff with strong ITC skills, resulting in a strong dependency on outsourcing to large private sector vendors. Finally, the heavy reliance on EU funds for digital government-related investments and activities present long-term sustainability risks for these initiatives.

These factors have combined to limit the capability of the Slovakian government to set and implement a robust whole-of-government vision for digital government. In its place has been a strategy that is driven by funding sources rather than by objectives, that is largely outsourced and treated with a low degree of ownership by the Slovakian civil service. It is clear from the experience of other OECD countries that not only is a strong vision and co-ordination across government required, but also a much greater partnership with a variety of private sector and civil society partners who can help deliver on that vision. While the relatively large amount of EU funds dedicated to digitisation have led to some important investments and to the development of basic digital government infrastructure, without serious and sustained reforms to how digital government is approached in the Slovak Republic, the country will not progress in its ranking against its European and international peers in this domain. However, with the embrace of some key improvements to its approach, many of the elements are in place for the Slovak Republic to rapidly become a regional leader in digital government.

Recommendations

Based on the review of the current state of digital government in the Slovak Republic and evidence pointing towards sub-optimal outcomes to date, the government of the Slovak Republic could consider the following recommendations, presented to illustrate key areas of focus to help improve the effectiveness of existing digitisation initiatives.

- Broaden and deepen the Slovak Republic's whole-of-government vision for digital government and communicate it widely across the public administration. A good starting point could be the government's new National Conception of Public Administration Systems, a document outlining a strategy for digital government that aims to bring a new systematic and co-ordinated approach to addressing e-government. The Ministry of Finance could use this concept document as the basis for engaging key digital government stakeholders from across the government in substantive dialogue on this vision, its desired outcomes, how to achieve them and how to measure success. Given the fragmented nature of the current digitisation initiatives underway in the Slovak government, there is a need to broaden and deepen the government's overarching vision for priorities in this area. As virtually all national strategies have been explicitly tied to funding sources, this has prevented a wider and more strategic discussion on the role that digital technology could and should play in helping to modernise and reform the

Slovak government in the long term and on what is needed to achieve those changes using digital government tools.

- Establish a Chief Information Officer (or equivalent) position and associated information-sharing mechanisms. This Review points to the need to have a strong central focal point that can act as co-ordinator and facilitator for implementing a vision for digital government and its various components government-wide. The position of CIO could build on the existing mandate and functions of the Director General of Information Society in the Ministry of Finance by strengthening it to cover all aspects of public sector digitisation. Given the current split of responsibilities, the CIO position, while located in the Ministry of Finance, could be structured to report jointly to the Government Office, the Ministry of Finance and the Ministry of the Interior. This would not necessarily require transferring any responsibilities from the existing ministries responsible for digital government activities; as is the case with the responsibilities of CIOs in other OECD countries, this "hub" role could focus on exercising levers related to leading and co-ordinating digital government strategy setting and implementation across the government, and information-sharing both within the Slovak administration and with international partners.
  - One of the most important roles that the new CIO could play is to help facilitate the sharing of lessons learnt and capacity building across the Slovak government. To that end, the government could act to strengthen the digital government co-ordination body's capacity.
- Strengthen the digital government co-ordination body's capacity to allow for regular exchange of information between officials responsible for digitisation initiatives and the management of ICT. The Ministry of Finance leads a committee through its Architectural Office of Public Administration that looks at ICT-enabled projects focused on funding and project oversight government-wide related *inter alia* to the Operational Programme Integrated Infrastructure. This co-ordination body could be led by the CIO and could more fully act as a forum to bring together those leading ICT-related work across the government on a regular basis to share lessons learnt both within the government and from other jurisdictions.
- Strengthen capacity in line ministry digital government/IT departments to drive enhanced performance in digital service design and delivery. Limited capacity and weak performance in IT departments of individual institutions in the Slovak public administration have been defined as a major challenge to the successful development and implementation of government-wide digital government strategies and to successfully delivering digital services to people and businesses. The structure and size of these units tend not to correspond to the requirements of rolling out state-of-the-art IT strategies and could put at risk the ability to reach government-wide performance targets in this area.
- Reinforce the application of mandatory standards for digital services across the public administration. Standards for online services are part of a set of standards for information systems of public administration, which are published by order of Ministry of Finance and are legally binding. Indeed the Ministry of Finance's Architectural Office manages customised open architecture standards – TOGAF® and ArchiMate®. That said, the Slovak Republic has consistently ranked poorly

in the quality of its digital services; this could be a key area of focus going forward. Building on the experience of countries such as Estonia, the United Kingdom and the United States in building user-centric digital services, the application of mandatory standards for all new online services could be reinforced, including through robust communications government-wide. Emphasis could be placed on interoperability and interconnectivity between new digital services so as to start breaking down the barriers between systems and databases that exist in various ministries. To ensure compliance, these standards could be linked to access to funding sources such as through the project evaluation process in the Operational Programme Effective Public Administration.

- Put in place performance measurement to ensure ongoing improvement of new digital services. While it is a positive development that a number of new online services are being launched in 2015, experience in other OECD countries has shown that it is important to put in place continual improvement processes to ensure ongoing enhancements and optimisation. This can include having active feedback mechanisms for those using the services as well as tracking and publishing metrics on the use of these services. For example, the Ministry of Finance currently conducts an annual survey on e-government user satisfaction. The government could expand this practice and use the survey results along with other input factors to inform decision making in the design and delivery of online services to citizens and businesses.
    - The four main key performance indicators used for the United Kingdom's digital services[9] – cost per transaction, user satisfaction, completion rate and digital take-up – would be a good starting point for consideration. It is also important that analytical capacity within the Slovak civil service is enhanced to be able to allow for this type of performance measurement to take place, as discussed in Chapter 2.
- Increase the uptake of the e-ID card. As a fundamental enabler of digital services, seeing a greater uptake of e-ID cards is an important priority. To date only 5% of the approximately 1 million e-ID cards issued have had their digital signature activated. There is a need to increase public awareness on the services that can be accessed through the use of an e-ID card, particularly as new services come online in 2015/16. Finally, being able to provide incentives to encourage the use of e-ID enabled services over traditional in-person or paper-based formats could be explored.
- Develop and apply social media guidelines across the public administration. Building on the work done in other OECD countries, the Slovak Republic could put in place centralised guidance on both institutional use and civil servant use of social media which aims to promote its use as a way to inform and engage citizens, while mitigating legitimate risks.
- Increase the number of datasets available on the open government data portal. The lack of high-value datasets on the open data portal is providing a barrier to the greater use of open data by government and non-governmental actors. Building on consultations that have been done through the Open Government Partnership and related initiatives, high-value datasets that have the greatest potential for reuse should be the primary focus. There is a need to also ensure uniform standards across similar datasets released from different ministries. As well, ensuring that

the licencing regime for any datasets released allows for unrestricted reuse is also important to fostering a more dynamic open data ecosystem in the Slovak Republic.

- Foster greater capacity for the use of open data inside government. The creation of a network of open data champions across all ministries could be an important first step towards greater institutionalising the creation and use of open data in the administration. Moreover, there may also be a need to develop greater centralised capacity and expertise on open government data – particularly with regards to the technical skills related to the creation, formatting and reuse of open government data – which can work with ministries and their open data champions as needed to enhance their open government data initiatives. This centralised capacity could take the form of a dedicated team of open data experts that can work with departments as well as a central data repository to ensure that all ministries can access data across the administration and the ability to put in place interoperability between various databases.
- Review procurement processes for ICT-enabled projects. While it is outside of the scope of this Review, throughout discussions with government and non-governmental experts, concerns were raised about the limitations of existing procurement rules. Specifically, allowing mechanisms for smaller companies to get involved in ICT procurements and making procurement processes more agile by breaking projects into smaller pieces would allow for more competition and reduce the risk of project failure, which has often been observed with high-value, long-duration contracts. The ability to use open source software should also be explored. Future reviews by the OECD or other organisations on the topic of government procurement should make ICT-enabled projects a priority for the review.

Notes

1. See: http://enrd.ec.europa.eu/enrd-static/fms/pdf/A185C492-B635-CD47-FE31-9EA2BE9E7A5D.pdf.
2. See: https://ec.europa.eu/digital-agenda/en/scoreboard/slovakia.
3. See: http://unpan3.un.org/egovkb/en-us/Data/Country-Information/id/155-Slovakia.
4. Databases operated by the Ministry of the Interior include: register of individuals; vehicle registration certificates; register of addresses; Ministry of the Interior (police) electronic services in the field of public order, security of persons and property; and electronic archive of the Ministry of the Interior.
5. See: https://ec.europa.eu/digital-agenda/en/digital-champion-slovakia.
6. See: https://ec.europa.eu/digital-agenda/en/scoreboard/slovakia.
7. See: http://ec.europa.eu/information_society/newsroom/cf/dae/document.cfm?doc_id=5568.

8. See: https://ec.europa.eu/digital-agenda/en/scoreboard/slovakia.
9. See: www.gov.uk/service-manual/measurement/other-kpis.html.

Bibliography

European Commission (2015), "Digital Agenda Scoreboard", https://ec.europa.eu/digital-agenda/en/scoreboard.

European Commission (2013), "Slovakia: E-government state of play", available at: http://ec.europa.eu/information_society/newsroom/cf/dae/document.cfm?doc_id=5568.

Mickoleit, A. (2014), "Social media use by governments: A policy primer to discuss trends, identify policy opportunities and guide decision makers", *OECD Working Papers on Public Governance*, No. 26, OECD Publishing, Paris, http://dx.doi.org/10.1787/5jxrcmghmk0s-en.

OECD (2015a), *OECD Digital Economy Outlook 2015*, OECD Publishing, Paris, http://dx.doi.org/10.1787/9789264232440-en.

OECD (2015b), *OECD Public Governance Reviews: Estonia and Finland. Fostering Strategic Capacity Across Governments and Digital Services Across Borders*, OECD Publishing, Paris, http://dx.doi.org/10.1787/9789264229334-en.

OECD (2015c), *Government at a Glance 2015*, OECD Publishing, Paris, http://dx.doi.org/10.1787/gov_glance-2015-en.

OECD (2015d), Internet access (indicator), http://dx.doi.org/10.1787/69c2b997-en.

OECD (2015e), *Open Government Data Review of Poland: Unlocking the Value of Government Data*, OECD Digital Government Studies, OECD Publishing, Paris, http://dx.doi.org/10.1787/9789264241787-en.

OECD (2014a), "Digital Performance Survey", OECD, Paris.

OECD (2014b), *Recommendation of the Council on Digital Government Strategies*, OECD, Paris, available at: www.oecd.org/gov/public-innovation/Recommendation-digital-government-strategies.pdf.

OECD (2013), "Government Use of Social Media Survey", OECD, Paris.

OECD (2010), *Denmark: Efficient E-Government for Smarter Public Service Delivery*, OECD Publishing, Paris, http://dx.doi.org/10.1787/9789264087118-en.

Ubaldi, B. (2013), "Open government data: Towards empirical analysis of open government data initiatives", *OECD Public Governance Working Papers*, No. 22, OECD Publishing, Paris, http://dx.doi.org/10.1787/5k46bj4f03s7-en.

United Nations (2014), "UN E-Government Survey 2014", http://unpan3.un.org/egovkb/Reports/UN-E-Government-Survey-2014.

Chapter 5.

Enhancing transparency and integrity in the Slovak Republic

This chapter reviews the existing integrity and transparency mechanisms in the Slovak public sector, especially in relation to codes of conduct, management of conflict of interest and ethics training. Examination of these three areas will give the opportunity to provide evidence-based guidance to help the Slovak Republic advance towards implementation of comprehensive integrity framework. This is important since the level of perceived corruption in the Slovak Republic still remains high, despite the government's efforts to enhance integrity across the public administration.

Introduction

Well-functioning democracies rely on the trust and confidence of citizens, which legitimises the decisions taken by government officials and creates the conditions for effective policy making and implementation. In turn, trust and confidence in government depend on transparency and integrity, to the extent that they set high standards of conduct in the public sector. In order to make more government more cost-effective, improve accountability and prevent corruption, enhancing the integrity and transparency of public governance is a key element in the Slovak Republic's political reform agenda.

The level of perceived corruption in the Slovak Republic still remains high. According to the 2013 Special Eurobarometer, 90% of Slovak respondents believe that corruption is widespread in their country, while the EU average stands at 76% (European Commission, 2014b). More than half of the respondents think that the abuse of positions for personal gain and giving or taking bribes are widespread in various public sectors. In addition, petty corruption appears to be widespread, with 40% of respondents claiming to have been affected by corruption in their daily lives, while the EU average stands at 26%. Transparency International's Global Corruption Barometer from 2013 noted that every fifth person having a contact with the Slovak institutions listed in the survey paid a bribe (Transparency International, 2013). These findings are similar to the results in the 2013 Special Eurobarometer.

The 2014 Eurobarometer shows that levels of trust in government and political parties in the Slovak Republic are lower than the average of 23 European OECD countries (Figure 5.1). Only 27% of Slovak respondents trust their national government, while the OECD average stands at 34%. In order to restore trust and confidence in the Slovak government, the public sector needs to be embedded within a comprehensive integrity framework.

Figure 5.1. **Trust in government and political parties in 23 European OECD countries, 2014**

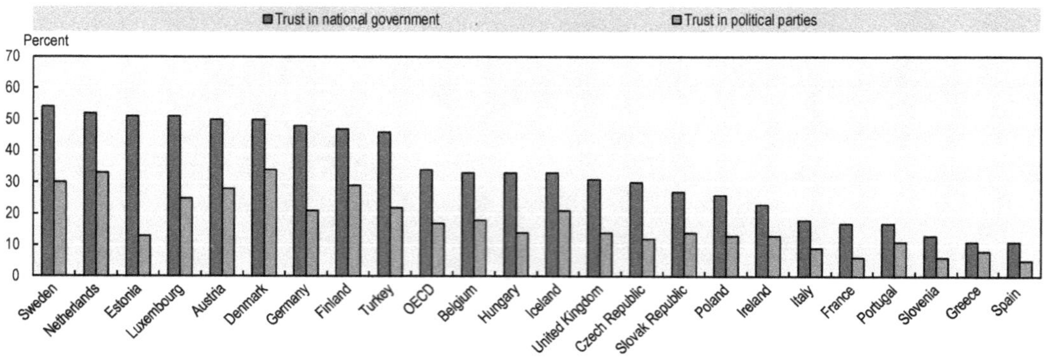

Notes: Trust in national government and political parties: percent of "tend to trust" answers to the question: How much trust do you have in certain institutions. For each of the following institutions, please tell me if you tend to trust it or tend not to trust it: national government and political parties.

Source: European Commission (2014c), "Standard Eurobarometer", http://ec.europa.eu/public_opinion/archives/eb_arch_en.htm.

To this end, the Slovak Republic has made efforts to enhance transparency and integrity across the public administration. Fighting corruption is featured in part 4 of the programme of the government of the Slovak Republic for the years 2012-16, entitled the "Role of state in the public sector: Internal regulations safety", which includes provisions for enhancing asset disclosure for public officials and the consistency of application of disciplinary measures to misconduct in the public sector. The government also approved the Strategic Plan for Fighting Corruption (Act No. 517/2011) in 2011, which included preventive measures such as the publication of state contracts, reform of the judiciary to increase the transparency of court decisions, competitive selection of judges and presidents of courts, as well as stricter rules for judicial governance and clear provisions for public procurement. The primary goal of the development of a national strategy was to "develop co-ordinated and conceptual preventive measures to reduce the level of corruption, especially in the public sector, while using the public funds and resources, and therewithal to increase transparency throughout the society".[1]

In addition to the approval of the Strategic Plan, the Slovak Republic has made further efforts to address the risks of corruption as part of the implementation of the OECD Convention on Combating Bribery of Foreign Public Officials in International Business Transactions. The National Criminal Agency of the Police Forces compiled a document entitled "Supplementation of tasks of the Strategic Plan of combating corruption in the Slovak Republic recommended by the stage 3 evaluations of the OECD Working Group for Bribery in International Business Transactions". This document has been approved by the government (Act No. 661/2014) and highlights a number of tasks and recommendations for both the public and private sectors, including the publication of internal anti-corruption programmes on the websites, providing education and training on prevention of corruption, strengthening transparency in international business transactions and incorporating the OECD Directive for Multinational Companies into anti-corruption programmes.

The most recent initiative by the government to enhance transparency and integrity in the Slovak Republic was to introduce whistleblower protection (Act No. 307/2014). The legislation drafted by the Ministry of the Interior in co-operation with other government agencies and Transparency International entered into force on 1 January 2015.

As a central co-ordination body to fulfil the tasks based on the Strategic Plan, an inter-ministerial working group of experts was established in August 2014. The working group is currently chaired by the National Anti-corruption Unit of the National Criminal Agency of the Police Force Presidium/Ministry of the Interior. The appointed representatives of the Government Office, the Ministry of the Interior, other central government bodies, the Prosecutor's General Office and the Association of Towns and Communities are members of the working group as well. Private sector representatives were also invited to the group. As observers, representatives of non-governmental organisations such as Transparency International and Fair Play Alliance also sit in the sessions of the working group. In order to contribute to the debate on updating the Civil Service Act by 2016 (see Chapter 3), the inter-ministerial working group is currently discussing a number of integrity reform plans to ensure the co-ordination, simultaneity and continuity of preventive measures and activities against corruption, as well as means of implementation, and the continuous evaluation of their effectiveness in the public sector.

Within the working group, there are two specialised sub-groups. The first sub-group is tasked to prepare legislative drafts for modifications of criminal laws regulating conditions and processes in the field of combating criminal act of corruption. The activity of the other sub-group focuses on the development of the National Anti-Corruption Project for the Operational Programme Effective Public Administration for the period 2014-20.

In order to contribute further to the anti-corruption debate and suggest ways to improve integrity measures and their enforcement in a more centrally co-ordinated manner, this chapter will review the existing integrity mechanisms in the Slovak public sector, especially in relation to: 1) codes of ethics; 2) management of conflict of interest; and 3) ethics training. Examination of these three areas will allow the opportunity to provide evidence-based guidance to help the Slovak Republic advance towards implementation of a comprehensive integrity framework.

Key facts and findings

Code of ethics

Embedding a culture of integrity in the public sector requires defining common values to which all public employees should adhere and drawing up concrete standards of conduct that they need to apply in their daily work. In other words, setting values and standards of conduct for public officials in a code of conduct is amongst the first steps towards safeguarding integrity and transparency in the public sector. This section will review key provisions of the code of conduct, monitoring of the implementation, enforcement and compliance in the public sector.

A code of conduct can improve organisational culture and prescribe a set of principles aimed to define conduct, culture and performance, constituting a key element of integrity framework. International conventions and instruments such as the OECD Principles for Managing Ethics in the Public Service and the United Nations Convention against Corruption (UNCAC) recognise the use of codes of conduct and ethics as effective tools for articulating the values of the public sector and the expected conduct of the public officials in an easily understandable and flexible manner. The majority of OECD member countries have drawn up codes of ethics in recent decades. Some countries such as Italy and New Zealand have adopted or are in the process of drafting second- or third-generation codes based on the lessons learnt from past experiences.

In the Slovak Republic, professional values, norms and requirements in the public sector are broadly governed by Act No. 400/2009 on the Civil Service and Amendments of Certain Acts. For example, §60 of the act includes basic rules of ethics governing civil servants' conduct *vis-à-vis* citizens and legal entities, superiors and other civil servants (Box 5.1).

At the same time, several ministries and government agencies also have specific codes of conduct applicable to their staff. For example, the professional values, standards and requirements for the staff of the Ministry of the Interior are also defined in the Codes of Ethics of employees performing work in the public interest in compliance with the Regulation of the Ministry of the Interior No. 180/2012. Similarly, there are other regulations, such as the Code of Ethics of the Police Force, and the Directive on the Code of Business Conduct of Customs Officers and Financial Administration's Employees Ethics.

There is no central body or mechanism in the Slovak Republic which ensures the coherence of basic principles embedded in different codes across ministries, oversees and monitors the implementation of the Civil Service Act for public officials. Such central co-ordination is useful to making the codes of conduct a valuable, efficient contribution to the improvement of overall integrity and transparency in the public sector while taking into consideration the specific risks associated with the administrative functions and sectors that are most exposed to corruption. For example, in Italy, this role is entrusted principally to the Department for Public Administration with the collaboration of the National Anti-Corruption Authority. The Anti-Corruption Law puts the heads of public entities in charge of overseeing implementation and requires the Department for Public Administration to carry out an annual review of how the codes have been implemented (OECD, 2013b). In the case of the United Kingdom, the Civil Service Commission was established to safeguard an impartial civil service. It is an executive non-departmental public body sponsored by the Cabinet Office (Box 5.2).

Box 5.1. Some elements of the Slovak Code of Ethics: §60 of the Civil Service and Amendments of Certain Acts

A civil servant is obliged to:

- comply with the Slovak Constitution, constitutional laws, laws, generally binding regulations and legally binding instruments of the European Communities and the European Union and the Service Regulations in performing civil service and to apply them to the best of his/her knowledge and belief, respect and protect human dignity and human rights
- perform civil service politically neutral and impartial and refrain in civil service anything that could jeopardise confidence in the impartiality and objectivity of the proceedings and decision making
- maintain the confidentiality of the facts brought to his/her knowledge in connection with the performance of civil services and in the interest of the service office that cannot be disclosed to other persons
- refrain from any action that could lead to a conflict of interest in the service office with personal interests, especially not to misuse information acquired in connection with the implementation of the civil service for their own benefit or the benefit of another
- perform service tasks duly and in a timely manner.

Source: ILO (n.d.), "Code of Ethics", www.ilo.org/dyn/natlex/docs/ELECTRONIC/84812/94622/F583540233/84812.pdf.

Box 5.2. The role of the Civil Service Commission in the United Kingdom

The Constitutional Reform and Governance Act 2010 established the Civil Service Commission on a statutory basis. The commission is independent of government and of the civil service. The UK Civil Service Commission is an executive non-departmental public body sponsored by the Cabinet Office.

The Civil Service Commission has two important roles in relation to the Civil Service Code, which defines the terms and conditions of UK civil servants. The commission hears complaints under the code from civil servants. It also works with departments to help them with their promotion of the code.

There are currently seven commissioners. They are recruited on merit following public advertisement and a fair and open selection competition. From their different careers and interests, commissioners bring experience of the public, private and voluntary sectors and a clear and independent perspective. This helps the Civil Service Commission to support a civil service that is effective, politically impartial and that builds upon its core values to meet the challenges.

Source: Civil Service Commission (n.d.), "About us", http://civilservicecommission.independent.gov.uk/about-us.

In many cases in the Slovak Republic, various codes of conduct are not strictly enforced in practice and public officials are not trained or educated on their content. While some sort of code of conduct training is often part of the induction programme for newly recruited staff, such training or periodic reminder is hardly provided to incumbent employees. In the event of misconduct, each public entity is generally responsible for taking appropriate action. With the absence of clearly defined guidelines or a mechanism of how to report misconduct and determine their severity, the risk of inconsistent application of sanctions remains high throughout the public sector. Diagnostic tools such as surveys and statistical data are not commonly adopted by the Slovak public sector to monitor and evaluate the effectiveness of the code of conduct. No government-wide monitoring is currently undertaken, and therefore, comparative data on the number of misconducts and sanctions applied is not available.

Acknowledging some of the challenges, new legislation on the civil service is expected to be discussed in detail by the parliament after the general elections in February 2016 (see Chapter 3). The new act aims to update the provisions of the Code of Ethics for civil servants and set up a new Council of Civil Service to monitor centrally the compliance of the code of conduct across the ministries.

Management of conflict of interest

Ensuring that the integrity of government decision making is not compromised by public officials' private interests has become a growing concern across OECD member countries. Different approaches to managing conflict of interest situations across countries often reflect their different historical, legal and public service traditions. In most countries, institutional measures such as external audit and verification and other internal supervisory approaches are widely observed while asset and private interest disclosure by senior public officials continues to be an essential tool for managing conflict of interest.

A modern conflict-of-interest policy should seek to strike a balance. If not adequately identified and managed, conflict of interest situations could lead to corruption. At the same time, an excessively strict approach can be costly and unworkable, and may deter experienced and competent potential candidates from entering the public service. The OECD Guidelines for Managing Conflict of Interest in the Public Service (OECD, 2003) provide policy makers with a set of tangible policy options based on promoting individual responsibility, supporting scrutiny and creating an appropriate organisational culture.

In the Slovak Republic, Act No. 357/2004 on Protection of Public Interest in Performance of Functions of Public Officials as amended by Act No. 545/2005 serves as a legal framework to manage conflict of interest in the public sector. Under Act No. 357/2004, the Committee of the National Council of the Slovak Republic on Conflicts of Interest keeps the list of functions of the public office holders who are covered by the committee, assesses the incompatibility of functions of public office holders with performing other duties, reviews their asset declarations and performs the tasks in detecting and imposing the penalties. This act is applicable to the President, the Prime Minister, ministers, other public office holders in the executive branch, judges and members of parliament amongst others, but not to most of the civil servants. In the case of violations of the conflict of interest policy, fines are imposed as a sanction, ranging from the equivalent of one month's salary to 12 months' salary. Since 2006, the committee has led the proceedings against a total of 668 public office holders and the penalties of the total value of EUR 664 884 were imposed on 424 cases.[2]

The implementation of this act in practice is often considered by the non-governmental organisations and the media to be inadequate due to the unwillingness of the committee to demand specific information regarding the assets of public office holders, to examine the submitted asset declarations thoroughly and to determine the consequences for violations of the rule on conflict of interest. For example, in 2012, of 650 public officials, 51 failed to submit their property reports to parliament by the 2 April deadline, the highest number since 2004, when the Law on Conflict of Interest was adopted.[3] While those who fail to submit their forms might end up being fined, current legislation does not have the power to force them to ever submit a declaration. Several amendments were proposed to overcome such shortcomings in the current legislation, but none of them has been adopted by the parliament so far since the necessary political consensus is yet to be formed.

Although not governed by Act No. 357/2004, all civil service employees must submit their asset declarations annually to their head of human resources department, but only the line manager reviews it and no other type of oversight is in place. Declaration forms do not need to include any supporting documents and are not audited after submission. There is no policy which provides clear definitions, a description or examples of what circumstances and relationships can lead to a conflict of interest situation. It is usually up to the manager to spot the violation of conflict of interest; however, there is no clear guideline on how managers should exercise judgement in individual cases to determine the most appropriate solution to resolve or manage the actual conflict situation. Civil service employees' asset declaration forms are not made public either.

There is no central function responsible for the development and maintenance of the conflict of interest policy and procedures in the Slovak public sector. According to the 2014 OECD Survey on Managing Conflict of Interest, 69% of respondent countries have such a central function and apply the same or almost same set of definitions of conflict of interest, guidelines for handling the situation and consequences for non-compliance to their ministries and agencies, ensuring the consistency of their preventive measures (Figure 5.2).

Figure 5.2. **Countries with central function (not necessarily an independent agency) responsible for the development and maintenance of conflict of interest policies**

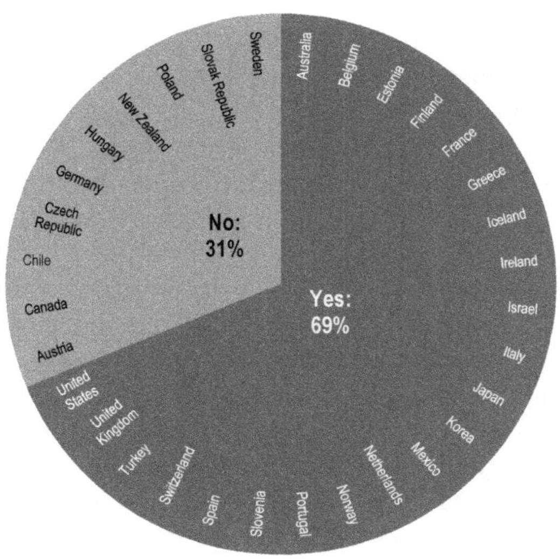

Source: OECD (2014b), "OECD Survey on Managing Conflict of Interest", OECD, Paris.

In many OECD member countries, an increasing concern relating to the management of conflict of interest is the practice of "revolving doors" – the movement of staff between related public and private sectors – and its negative effects on trust in governments (and the perception of increased policy capture by special interests having undue influence of former public office holders on relevant public policy as a result). It may heighten exposure to conflicts of interest and impropriety, such as the misuse of insider information, position and contacts. Concern over revolving doors has prompted countries such as Canada, Germany, Korea, Portugal and the United States to take measures to prevent and contain conflict of interest in pre- and post-public employment situations in order to ensure the integrity of present and former public officials. The Slovak Republic does not have any specific measures to address post-public employment such as a cooling-off period. There is no central function or body in the public sector responsible for monitoring and enforcing the post-public employment system (see Box 5.7 for more details).

Ethics training

Ethics training for public officials is one of the instruments for building integrity in the public sector and ensuring good quality public governance. The United Nations Convention against Corruption (UNCAC) requires that the state parties "promote education and training programmes to enable [public officials] to meet the requirements for the correct, honourable and proper performance of public functions and that provide them with specialised and appropriate training to enhance their awareness of the risks of corruption inherent in the performance of their functions".[4] For instance, in Estonia, the Ministry of Finance co-ordinates the horizontal "Central Training Programme" and is responsible for commissioning various training programmes, such as the induction programme and the general programmes on civil service and public service ethics.

Ethics training can deliver results only in the long term and in combination with other anti-corruption law enforcement and preventive measures. Ethics training therefore can be treated as a low priority investment in countries where governments seek quick results in a highly corrupt environment, and allocating budget to ethics training may not be popular. Therefore when designing and delivering ethics training, it is important to consider which programmes have the best design and produce the best results.

There are several ethics training opportunities in the Slovak public sector to provide civil servants with comprehensive information on the issue of corruption and fight against corruption, anti-corruption legislation in the Slovak Republic and international instruments related to corruption. The Division of the Control and Prevention of Corruption within the Government Office organises ethics trainings for civil servants approximately twice a year. The training usually lasts for 5 hours and each course accommodates 50-60 civil servants. The course is open to all civil servants across different ministries. Similarly, in 2013, the Ministry of Foreign and European Affairs, in co-operation with the Government Office, organised a seminar on "Increasing the Legal Awareness in Preventing Corruption and the Fight against Corruption" with the emphasis on the issue of corruption in international business deals, economic diplomacy and public procurement. The Special Prosecutor's Office periodically organises a training entitled "Corruption in the Central and Local Government Institutions" as well. These ethics trainings are usually organised in a seminar style, lectured by leading experts and academics. Other than the initiatives listed above, most ministries do not organise any ethics training or counselling for their employees to enhance their ability to identify and tackle corruption.

Taking these ethics trainings is voluntary and there is no standard programme, syllabus or manual to run such a training. The Government Office has a co-ordination role of organising inter-ministerial ethics training, but its Division of the Control and Prevention of Corruption is severely understaffed with a limited budget. The Government Office does not have a long-term strategy for ethics training in relation to needs assessment, selection of topics, participants and trainers, duration and content of the programme, training methods, training of trainers and follow-up methods. There seems to be a lack of political will and managerial leadership to improve the overall framework for the ethics training.

In addition to providing the necessary ethics training, it is equally important to evaluate the results of ethics training in order to ensure the use of public money is producing the desired effects, and to look for ways to improve and to modernise the training approaches to make them more effective. Currently, the Slovak Republic does not have a mechanism to monitor and evaluate the results of its ethics training. Neither the Government Office nor the other ministries have any comparative data regarding the number of public officials who attended such ethics training or systematic tools to assess the impact of such training. Information about the total number of civil servants who should be provided with ethics training and the number of those who actually received this training cannot therefore be identified.

Assessment

Code of ethics

With the new Civil Service Act currently in discussion, the Slovak Republic has the opportunity to update and adopt a new code of conduct with enough substance and powers of enforcement to address the existing shortcomings. Certain conditions need to be met to ensure the effective implementation of a code.

Build consensus on values and public employee's ownership of the code of ethics

An inclusive, consultative approach towards designing a code of ethics is essential to ensuring take-up and implementation. The experience of OECD countries demonstrates that consulting or actively involving stakeholders in drafting the code helps build a common understanding of public service values and the expected standards of public employee conduct. Stakeholder involvement would, in addition, improve the quality of the code so that it met both public employees' and citizens' expectations. The government would also be able to demonstrate commitment to greater transparency and accountability, thereby gaining public trust (OECD, 2001).

The inter-ministerial working group of experts could adopt such an approach in order to define: 1) the values of the public administration; 2) the standards of conduct expected of public officials; and 3) the scope of the code and to whom it shall apply. Similarly, surveys and other tools for collecting empirical data could help the Slovak Republic to identify the issues and concerns that are most relevant to its public service. It is essential that the content and issues covered by the code build on the Slovak Republic's existing sector-related codes of conduct so as to promote consistent values and standards of conduct throughout the public service.

Raise awareness of the code of ethics through guidance, manuals and training

A code of conduct ought to be part of a wider organisational strategy, with the institution in question committed to provide clear guidance and education on the behaviour expected of public officials in the workplace. At the moment, the Slovak Republic does not have a regular educational programme or government-wide manual on the code of conduct. In most OECD member countries, training modules are developed by a single central entity that also offers guidance on how public officials should apply their codes of conduct, particularly in sensitive situations. For example, the UK Civil Service Commission, working in conjunction with the Cabinet Office and a group of permanent secretaries, produced a best practice checklist of actions for departments to uphold and promote the code.[5] In the Netherlands, the government issued a brochure entitled "The Integrity Rules of the Game" that explains in clear, everyday terms the rules to which staff members must adhere. It considers real-life issues such as confidentiality, accepting gifts and invitations, investing in securities, holding additional positions or directorships, and dealing with operating assets.

The Slovak Republic could consider tasking a specialised organisation with designing a single code of conduct guidance to ensure that all public employees have the same understanding on the subject. Such an organisation could also offer guidance and counselling to public officials facing ethical dilemmas. Each public service body could then ensure that it takes into account the specific nature of its area of work.

Monitor the implementation of code of ethics

A code of ethics being a flexible instrument, monitoring its implementation can help determine whether it fits the bill of promoting high standards of conduct within the public service. If it does not, further guidelines may be drawn up to clarify the values and standards of conduct that the code lays down. To do so, the monitoring entity could assess:

- public employees' knowledge of standards of conduct (to determine, for example, if dissemination and training are sufficient)
- how public organisations provide guidance on the code
- whether there are mechanisms for reporting misconduct and if they are used
- how many disciplinary actions were taken.

Tools such as surveys of public employees or analysis of disciplinary procedures could support such monitoring and assessment (Box 5.3). It is important to stress that the positive results of such an assessment should not be considered a reason to refrain from conducting regular research in the future. It is only where such research is performed that there is an opportunity to ensure the actual functioning of ethical regulations and to adjust such regulations to a rapidly changing environment, including the rising expectations of the citizen.

A body which oversees and monitors the implementation of the code of conduct and compliance with standards of behaviour is also crucial. As currently discussed in the proposal of the new Civil Service Act, setting up an independent Council of Civil Service could ensure that that government-wide monitoring is undertaken to promote high standards of conduct throughout the public service. Effective institutional co-ordination between ministries involved in the implementation of the code remains essential as well.

Ensure enforcement and compliance

Institutional frameworks for code of ethics at managerial level in OECD countries generally include sanctions for non-compliance. Their severity varies:

- In Japan, non-compliant public officials may be formally reprimanded and urged to abide by the standards of conduct or they may be admonished and invited to resign from the chair of a committee (Box 5.4).
- In the United Kingdom, sanctions for violations of the public officials' code of conduct may include suspension.
- In the United States, violations of the executive branch code of conduct can result in disciplinary action that ranges from reprimand through dismissal.

Box 5.3. **Monitoring of the implementation of a code of ethics in Poland**

The survey, known as the monitoring of the functioning of "Ordinance No. 70 of the Prime Minister dated 6 October 2011 on the guidelines for compliance with the rules of the civil service and on the principles of the civil service code of ethics" was commissioned by the Head of the Civil Service in 2014. The Head of the Civil Service is the central government administration body in charge of civil service issues under the Chancellery of the Prime Minister.

The survey was carried out in three groups of respondents.

1. Members of the civil service corps

In this case the survey pertained to the degree of implementation of the ordinance in their respective offices and to their subjective assessment of the functioning and effectiveness of the ordinance – the members of the civil service corps were asked to complete a questionnaire containing 16 questions (most framed as closed questions, with a few allowing for supplementary information to be provided). The questions pertained, among the others, to the following issues:

- knowledge of the principles enumerated in the ordinance
- impact of the entry into force of the ordinance on changes in the civil service
- the need/advisability of expanding the list through the addition of new rules
- comprehensibility/clarity of the guidelines and principles laid down in the ordinance
- the usefulness of the ordinance for the purposes of solving professional dilemmas.

In addition, the correct understanding of the principle of "selflessness" and "dignified conduct" as well as the need to provide training in the field of compliance were also assessed. The questionnaires were available on the website of the Civil Service Department. Respondents were requested to fill it in and submit it electronically to a dedicated e-mail address.

2. Director generals, directors of treasury offices and directors of tax audit offices

In this case the survey was intended to verify the scope and manner of implementation of tasks which they were under a duty to perform according to the provisions of the ordinance, including, for example:

- the manner in which compliance with the rules in the given office is ensured
- information on whether the applicable principles were complied with when adopting decisions authorising members of the civil service corps to undertake additional employment or authorising every civil service employee occupying a higher position within the civil service to undertake income-generating activities
- the manner in which the principles in question are taken into account in the human resources management programmes which are being developed

Box 5.3. **Monitoring of the implementation of code of ethics in Poland** (*continued*)

- the manner in which the relevant principles were taken into account in the course of determination of the scope of preparatory service stage, etc.

3. Independent experts – public administration theorists and practitioners

In this case the survey was intended to obtain an additional, independent specialist evaluation of the functioning of ethical regulations within the civil service to obtain suggestions on the ethical principles applicable to the civil service and to identify the aspects of the management process which may need to be supplemented or updated, clarified or emphasised to a greater extent or even corrected or elaborated.

The response rate differed across three groups. The Head of the Civil Service received 1 291 questionnaires completed by members of the civil service corps (that constitutes approximately 1% of all civil service corps members), 107 questionnaires dedicated to the directors (100% of all directors generals, directors of treasury offices and directors of tax audit offices; 98 in total) and some more, additionally filled in (on a voluntary basis) by the head of the tax offices) and 7 replies from independent experts (approximately 13% of all experts invited to the study; 54). Keeping in mind that this survey was the first such exercise conducted at a large scale, information gathered could be used in further developing of the integrity policy in the Polish civil service system.

Source: Dudzik, K. (2015) "Creating whole-of-government vision and integrity values through code of ethics", presentation at the OECD workshop on Enhancing transparency and integrity in Bratislava on 8-9 June 2015.

Box 5.4. **Investigation and disciplinary action against ethical violations in Japan**

In Japan, the National Public Service Ethics Act was introduced in 1999 and specifies the duties of civil servants. The National Public Service Ethics Board was set up under the National Personnel Authority as an institution specialising in the maintenance of ethics pertaining to the duties of national public servants. The National Public Service Ethics Board has various authorities pertaining to the maintenance of ethics among national public service officials. Its responsibilities include:

- submission of opinions to the Cabinet regarding enactment, amendment and repeal of the National Public Service Officials Ethics Code
- preparation and revision of a standard of disciplinary actions applied to violations of the National Public Service Ethics Law
- research, study and planning regarding ethics issues of public officials
- comprehensive planning and co-ordination of training programmes on ethics for public officials
- guidance and advice regarding preparation in ministries and agencies for the system to observe the National Public Service Officials Ethics Code
- examination of reports on gifts, stock transactions and incomes
- if necessary to maintain the ethics of public officials, questioning any public official who is suspected of violating the National Public Service Ethics Law, conducting on-site investigations to clarify such suspected misconduct, summoning witnesses and requesting witnesses to submit a necessary report or any relevant materials

Box 5.4. **Investigation and disciplinary action against ethical violations in Japan** *(continued)*

- following the investigation, if necessary, requesting the head of each ministry or agency to take any measures necessary for supervising his/her officials
- following the investigation, if necessary, taking disciplinary action against any public official who has violated the National Public Service Ethics Law.

Any violations of the National Public Service Ethics Law and Ethics Regulation are subject to disciplinary measures whose criteria are defined in the Rules of the National Personnel Authority. Disciplinary measures are divided into dismissal, suspension, pay reduction and warning. From 2000 to 2013, 1 070 civil servants were subject to disciplinary measures.

The National Public Service Ethics Board and each ministry respectively have the authority to investigate a case of possible violation of the Ethics Act or the Ethics Code, and to execute the disciplinary procedure against the offenders. Each ministry has to report on investigation to the Ethics Board and ask for its approval for a disciplinary action. Furthermore, the Ethics Board guides each ministry to take appropriate measures for preventing future occurrences of similar kinds of violations.

Figure 5.3. **Investigation process of alleged ethical misconduct in Japan**

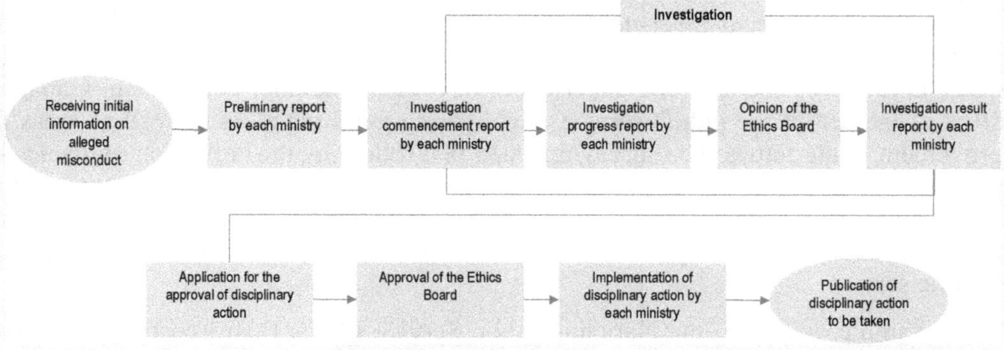

.

Source: The National Public Service Ethics Board (n.d.), www.jinji.go.jp/rinri/eng ; www.jinji.go.jp/rinri/cyousa/gaiyou.pdf.

It is essential that an efficient, consistent enforcement mechanism be designed in order to ensure compliance with the code in the Slovak Republic. The government needs to ensure that public entities adopt a consistent approach to sanctioning misconduct. In one study, Bruce (1996) showed that "a clearly worded code of ethics with sanctions" is the best way to curb corruption in government.

Management of conflict of interest

Establish clear definition of conflict of interest and procedures for its management

Management of conflict of interest is not strictly enforced in practice in the Slovak Republic. As regards the provisions of Act No. 357/2004 on Protection of Public Interest in Performance of Functions of Public Officials as amended by Act

No. 545/2005, insufficient attention is paid to the details of disclosure and auditing of the asset disclosure forms. Adequate enforcement of the rules on asset disclosure and conflict of interest requires strengthening the mandate of the Committee of the National Council of the Slovak Republic on Conflicts of Interest. Group of States against Corruption (GRECO) report in 2014 also pointed out that regulation of contacts with lobbyists and others with partial interests and of the acceptance of gifts and other advantages warrant strong attention in the Slovak Republic.[6]

Establishing clear procedures for identifying, managing and resolving conflict of interest situations is crucial. For example, the Australian Public Service Commission publishes detailed information regarding the management of conflict of interest on its website.[7] Information includes guidance on who is required to make a declaration, how to declare interests, what should be covered in the declaration, and procedures to resolve conflict of interest. The Slovak Republic should develop a policy which provides clear definitions, description and examples of what circumstances and relationships can lead to a conflict of interest situation in the public service. In particular, the government should provide a clear guideline on how managers should exercise judgement in individual cases to determine the most appropriate solution to resolve or manage the actual conflict situation.

Accuracy matters: Verify and audit asset discloser forms

Civil servants' annual asset declarations are not subject to internal audit and staff members are not educated on the content of conflict of interest policy. In 2012 and 2014, the OECD reviewed the data and experiences of over 30 member countries in managing conflict of interest in the public service, highlighting good practices as well as areas for improvement in the future. The survey revealed that following the collection of disclosure forms, 63% of respondents verify receipt of the forms and only 32% carry out audit or review the accuracy of the information (Table 5.1). The Slovak Republic should consider introducing a system to verify, audit and review the accuracy of the disclosure forms in the public service.

For example, in Japan, the National Public Service Ethics Board centrally examines all the disclosure forms with a view to assessing whether an inappropriate acceptance of gifts or an inappropriate exchange of stocks, for example, which could distort the fair execution of the national public service, has taken place and whether the report has been properly submitted (Box 5.5).

Provide online management of asset disclosure

Some countries also operate their disclosure system electronically (Table 5.2). For example, in Estonia, Korea, Mexico and the United Kingdom, most elements of the private interest disclosure system (completion and submission of the form, review and audit of the information, and access to the publically disclosed information) are managed electronically. The Slovak Republic could certainly consider introducing the online disclosure system in order to reduce the administrative burden and increase transparency in the public service.

Raise awareness on a regular basis

The Slovak Republic could also consider designing and providing central national programmes to raise awareness for managing conflict of interest in the public sector. While most OECD countries adopt various awareness-raising policies such as initial dissemination of rules/guidelines to public officials upon taking office and providing training, there is no systematic initiative to promote understanding of conflict of interest in the Slovak Republic (Table 5.3). In order to ensure co-ordination across the government, the Government Office or the Ministry of the Interior needs to ensure that training, education and guidance on management of conflict of interest are available to all public officials. From this perspective, the government could develop a national awareness programme which the heads of public entities could then apply and tailor to the organisational level.

Table 5.1. **Actions taken after collecting the private information for public officials in the executive branch**

	Verifying receipt of the submitted disclosure form	Verifying that all required information was included in the submitted disclosure form	Auditing or reviewing the accuracy of the information submitted in the disclosure form
Australia	●	●	●
Austria	○	○	○
Belgium	●	○	○
Canada	●	●	●
Chile	●	○	○
Czech Republic	○	○	○
Estonia	○	●	▲
Finland	●	●	○
France	●	●	●
Germany	●	●	▲
Greece	●	●	▲
Hungary	●	●	●
Iceland	●	●	●
Ireland	●	○	○
Israel	●	●	○
Italy	○	○	○
Japan	●	●	●
Korea	●	●	●
Mexico	▲	▲	▲
Netherlands	..	..	..
New Zealand	●	●	●
Norway	○	○	○
Poland	●	●	▲
Portugal	○	○	○
Slovak Republic	○	○	○
Slovenia	○	○	○
Spain	○	○	○
Sweden	●	●	●
Switzerland	●	●	●
Turkey	●	○	○
United Kingdom	●	●	●
United States	●	●	○

● For all those required to disclose private interest
▲ For some of those required to disclose private interest
○ Action is not taken

Source: OECD (2014b), "OECD Survey on Managing Conflict of Interest", OECD, Paris.

Box 5.5. Reviews of asset disclosure forms in Japan

The Ethics Act of Japan stipulates three types of mandatory reporting systems (see below) in order to promote a transparent relationship between national public employees and other stakeholders. The National Public Service Ethics Board examines copies of the reports sent from each ministry.

Types of reports

1. Mandatory reports on the receipt of gifts (to be submitted by the officials at the rank of assistant director and above at the headquarters; when then accept gifts, food and drink, remuneration for a lecture and other activities, and any other benefits from business counterparts which exceeds JPY 5 000, approximately EUR 36).
2. Mandatory reports on the exchange of stocks (to be submitted by the officials at the rank of deputy director general or above at the headquarters).
3. Mandatory reports on income (to be submitted by the officials at the rank of deputy director general or above at the headquarters).

Report procedure

Figure 5.4. **Asset disclosure mechanism in Japan**

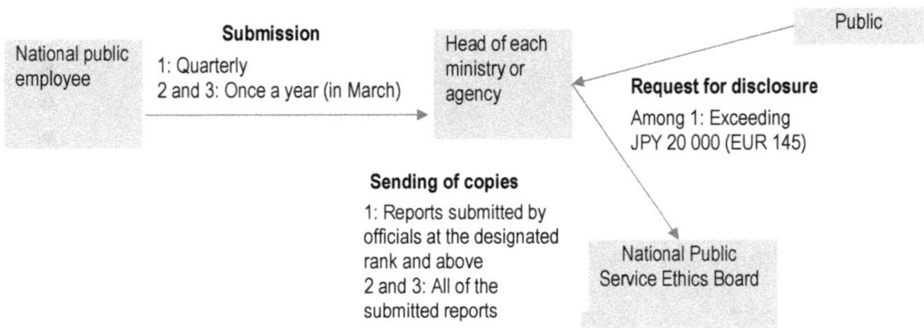

Source: The National Public Service Ethics Board (n.d.), www.jinji.go.jp/rinri/eng/index.htm.

Monitor the effectiveness of the conflict of interest policies

An emerging issue for many countries is to monitor and assess the effectiveness of the exiting conflict of interest policies. Once the Slovak Republic develops a more comprehensive strategy to manage conflict of interest in the public sector, the government also needs to adopt diagnostic tools in assessing the implementation of conflict of interest policies. The OECD survey clearly highlights that the number of countries with such diagnostic tools more than doubled between 2012 and 2014 (Figure 5.5).

Countries such as Australia, Canada, Estonia, Korea, New Zealand, Portugal and the United States use employee feedback mechanisms and other specific tools for assessing their policy implementation on a regular basis (Box 5.6).

Table 5.2. **Online management of information disclosure system**

	Completion of the form	Submission of the form	Review of the information submitted	Audit of the information submitted	Access to the publically disclosed information	No elements of the system are managed electronically
Australia	x	x	x	x.	x	x
Austria	●	●	●	O	●	O
Belgium	●	●	O	O	●	O
Canada	O	O	O	O	O	O
Chile	O	O	O	O	●	O
Denmark	O	O	O	O	O	●
Estonia	●	●	●	●	●	O
Finland	●	O	O	O	O	O
France	●	●	O	O	O	O
Germany	O	O	O	O	O	●
Hungary	O	O	O	O	●	O
Iceland	O	O	O	O	O	●
Ireland	O	O	O	O	O	●
Italy	O	O	O	O	O	●
Japan	O	O	O	O	O	●
Korea	●	●	●	●	●	O
Luxembourg	x	x	x	x	x	x
Mexico	●	●	●	●	●	O
Netherlands	O	O	O	O	●	O
New Zealand	●	●	O	●	●	O
Norway	x	x	x	x	x	x
Poland	O	O	O	O	●	O
Portugal	O	O	O	O	O	O
Slovak Republic	O	O	O	O	O	●
Slovenia	●	O	O	O	O	O
Spain	●	O	O	O	O	O
Sweden	O	O	O	O	O	●
Switzerland	O	O	O	O	O	●
Turkey	O	O	O	O	O	●
United Kingdom	●	●	●	●	●	O
United States	x	x	x	x	x	x

● Yes
O No

Source: OECD (2012b), "OECD Survey on Managing Conflict of Interest", OECD, Paris.

Box 5.6. **Monitoring of the conflict of interest programme in the United States**

The Unites States Office of Government Ethics comprehensively monitors implementation of the executive branch conflict of interest programme. The Office of Government Ethics employs several mechanisms including surveys, diagnostic tools, training and outreach to prevent and resolve conflict of interest. Over 130 executive branch agencies are required to submit an annual survey report to Office of Government Ethics concerning conflict of interest and other aspects of their ethics programmes. Responses are mandatory and provide the Office of Government Ethics with compliance metrics to assess the effectiveness of each agency's conflict of interest programme. The Office of Government Ethics also surveys ethics officials annually to assess the effectiveness of its guidance, training and support concerning conflict of interest.

Source: OECD (2012b), "OECD Survey on Managing Conflict of Interest", OECD, Paris.

Table 5.3. **Awareness-raising activities for managing conflict interest**

	Initial dissemination of rules/ guidelines to public officials upon taking office	Proactive updates regarding changes to conflict of interest rules/guidelines	Publish the conflict of interest policy online or on the Intranet of the organisation	Give regular reminders of what a conflict of interest is, and the responsibility of public officials to resolve these	Provide training	Provide regular guidance and assistance	Advice line or help desk where officials can receive guidance on filing requirements or conflict of interest identification or management
Australia	●	●	●	●	●	●	●
Austria	●	●	○	●	●	●	○
Belgium	●	○	●	●	●	●	●
Canada	●	●	●	●	●	●	●
Chile	●	○	●	○	●	●	○
Czech Republic	○	○	○	○	○	○	○
Estonia	○	●	●	○	●	●	●
Finland	●	○	●	○	●	○	○
France	○	○	○	●	●	○	●
Germany	●	●	●	●	●	●	●
Greece	●	●	●	○	○	○	○
Hungary	●	●	○	○	○	○	●
Iceland	●	●	●	●	●	●	●
Ireland	●	●	●	○	○	○	●
Israel	●	○	○	○	○	●	○
Italy	○	○	●	●	○	●	○
Japan	●	●	●	○	●	○	○
Korea	●	○	●	●	●	●	●
Mexico	●	●	○	○	○	○	○
Netherlands	●	●	●	●	●	●	●
New Zealand	●	●	●	●	●	●	●
Norway	●	●	●	○	●	●	●
Poland	●	○	●	○	○	●	○
Portugal	●	○	○	●	●	○	○
Slovak Republic	○	○	○	○	○	○	○
Slovenia	●	○	○	○	●	●	●
Spain	●	●	●	●	●	●	●
Sweden	●	●	●	●	●	○	○
Switzerland	●	●	●	●	●	●	●
Turkey	●	○	○	○	●	○	○
United Kingdom	●	●	●	●	●	●	●
United States	●	●	●	●	●	●	●
Yes ●	26	18	21	16	22	19	17
No ○	5	13	10	15	9	12	14

Source: OECD (2014b), "OECD Survey on Managing Conflict of Interest", OECD, Paris.

Address an emerging area of concern: Post-public employment and revolving doors

An emerging cause for concern over integrity in management of conflict of interest is the practice of the revolving doors. In the 2013 OECD Survey on Lobbying, one-quarter of lobbyists questioned had previously held positions in the public sector. Most said they had worked in senior managerial or advisory capacities in ministries or advisers to prime ministers. Revolving door practices pose a risk to fairness and impartiality in decision making. Setting a cooling-off period, during which public officials are not to lobby their former government departments, can be one way of dealing with the problem. Currently countries such as Australia, Canada, Chile, Norway and Slovenia have introduced a cooling off period (Box 5.7) and the Slovak Republic could also consider adopting a similar measure to strengthen the management of conflict of interest.

Figure 5.5. **Countries with diagnostic tools to monitor conflict of interest policies**

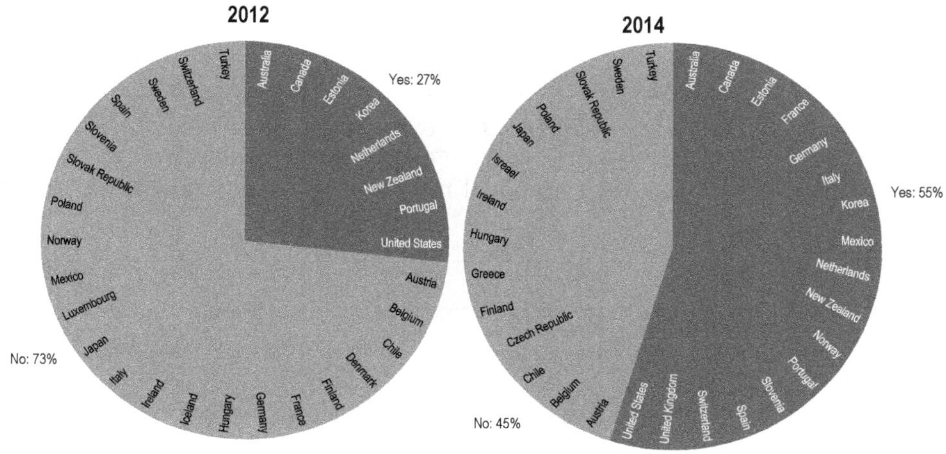

Sources: OECD (2014b), "OECD Survey on Managing Conflict of Interest", OECD, Paris; OECD (2012b), "OECD Survey on Managing Conflict of Interest", OECD, Paris.

Ethics training

Provide ethics training as part of a comprehensive anti-corruption and integrity policy

Ethics training in the Slovak public sector remains formalistic and has limited practical impact on the behaviour of public officials. More efforts are needed to update and improve the overall framework for ethics training in the public sector. Designing and delivering ethics training is a long-term investment; it can be expensive especially when it targets thousands of civils servants. Therefore, it is important to know which programmes have the best design and produce best results.

Provide political support and "leadership from above"

Political support for ethics training should also be demonstrated not only through declarations but also through the practical actions of the leadership, such as by setting an example of ethical behaviour and by allocating funds and staff for the implementation in ethics training and towards their positive impact on the behaviour of civil servants. Ethics training should be a part of a broader and comprehensive anti-corruption strategy. It is important to have a legislative or other official requirement to deliver and receive ethics training for public officials established in, for example, a Civil Service Act, code of conduct and other appropriate regulations. Without active political support to make ethics training a valuable tool to combat corruption in the public sector, any ethics training will end up with formalistic results, where public officials take the training to "tick the box" or when new public officials take ethics training as a part of their induction training but do not pay sufficient attention to it.

Mandate a lead agency and co-ordinate ethics training

It is important that there is at least one public agency responsible for the overall framework for ethics training, for central planning, co-ordination and evaluation of results. For example, in Turkey, the Council of Ethics for Public Officials is the leading institution in the provision of ethics training. In the Slovak Republic, the Division of the Control and Prevention of Corruption within the Government Office can play this role. Clear formulation of responsibilities of such central body should be complemented with proper co-ordination with other ministries and government agencies that provide ethics training as well. It is crucial to ensure a collaborative management between all the bodies involved to avoid inefficiency, organisational rivalry or self-promotion in the search for public money.

Box 5.7. **Restrictions on post-public employment**

Canada

For a period of five years after they cease to be public office holders, Article 10.11(1) of the Lobbying Act prohibits public officials from:

- communicating with a public office holder in respect of:
  - the development of any legislative proposal by the government of Canada or by a member of the Senate or the House of Commons
  - the introduction of any bill or resolution in either house of parliament or the passage, defeat or amendment of any bill or resolution that is before either house of parliament
  - the making or amendment of any regulation as defined in subsection 2(1) of the Statutory Instruments Act
  - the development or amendment of any policy or programme of the government of Canada
  - the awarding of any grant, contribution or other financial benefit by or on behalf of Her Majesty in right of Canada or
  - the awarding of any contract by or on behalf of Her Majesty in right of Canada.
- arranging meetings between a public office holder and any other person.

The activities listed above are prohibited if they are performed for remuneration and apply to consultant lobbyists. A similar ban applies to former designated public office holders who are employed as in-house lobbyists.

Chile

For a period of six months after they leave office, Chile prohibits officials from the executive branch of government from working in or for companies that were under the supervision and control of the public body in which they were previously employed.

Slovenia

Article 56 of Slovenia's Integrity and Prevention of Corruption Act stipulates that officials may not lobby until two years have elapsed since they left office. Similarly, Article 36 states that an official may not act as the representative of a commercial entity that has established or is about to establish business contacts with the body in which he/she held office until two years have passed since his/her employment terminated.

Source: The Lobbying Act (R.S.C., 1985, C. 44 (4th Supp.), Canada.

Organise effective ethics training

As the needs for ethics training vary significantly between countries, it is important to understand these needs before embarking on a long-term investment in training programmes. A needs assessment can help prioritise and focus training efforts and improve cost effectiveness. Surveys or studies that analyse the level of integrity in the public administration could help diagnose problems and evaluate the training needs. When such surveys are carried out on a regular basis, they can also provide a tool for assessing trends, and provide insight into the effectiveness of training programmes. For example, in Estonia, the Ministry of Finance, which is responsible for the public administration and public service development, carries out several regular surveys on ethics in view of identifying the specific concerns that need to be addressed by the ethics training (Box 5.8).

Box 5.8. **Needs assessment for ethics training in Estonia**

The Ministry of Finance carries out regular surveys about ethics and trust in the public sector, including the survey "Roles and Values in Civil Service" among civil servants and "Survey on Competence and Trust of Civil Servants" among citizens. Furthermore, the Ministry of Justice, which is responsible for general anti-corruption policy in Estonia, carries out a regular "Survey of Corruption among Three target Groups" among public officials, citizens and entrepreneurs.

The results of such surveys provide useful information on ethics training needs. For instance, the answers to the survey question on attitudes towards ethically questionable practices help to identify the integrity issues on which training may be required.

Similarly, answers to the survey question on the approaches to ethics training help to identify the best training methods adapted to the needs of the audience. The majority of participants in the survey tend to reject theoretical and legalistic approaches. Some are in favour of discussing practical issues and case studies, and the majority would prefer a combination of theoretical and practical approaches in ethics training programmes. It is important to also note that more than 25% of interviewed officials thought that they did not need ethics training, especially in the ministries. This is another aspect that should be analysed in all the surveys, as it represents an obstacle for the successful delivery of integrity training.

Source: Government Office (2009), "Role and Attitudes in Public Service", survey, Estonia.

Target training for specific groups of public officials

When there is a limited budget for training programmes, it is crucial to prioritise the target groups. Targeting also helps to make the training more focused on the practical needs of a specific group of public officials, thus increasing their motivation for participation. Several groups could be targeted for ethics training: all new public officials should be provided with ethics training; senior public officials in management positions and public officials in areas of risk should also be trained on ethics. Compulsory programmes for these target groups are advisable. It is also important to develop ethics training programmes for political/elected public officials. Finally, HR officers in each ministry could also be trained for their important role in dissemination of the integrity policy in the organisation.

Select proper trainers

The selection of trainers is also an important issue for ensuring high-quality ethics training. Ethics trainings are not only about delivering knowledge, but also about shaping attitudes and teaching skills for resolving ethical dilemmas. It is important to ensure the personal credibility of ethics trainers. On the one hand, trainers should possess in-depth knowledge about good governance, ethics norms and rules, preventing corruption and building a national integrity system. On the other hand, trainers should have experience working in the public service to avoid the situation of teaching theory without linkage to real life situations and in order to find a common language with trainees. Besides, since ethics training programmes are most effective when interactive methods are used, trainers should also have skills in modern training methods. It is important to build a pool of ethics trainers that can be invited to develop and deliver training programmes. It may be possible to train the trainers inside various public and academic institutions, for instance by using foreign expertise provided by various international organisations and donor-funded programmes.

It is useful to develop a pool of ethics trainers that can be based in public institutions, academic establishments or in private consultants. It is important to promote exchange of experience between them to ensure good quality standards. For this purpose, trainers could meet from time to time to discuss the problems they face, to exchange training case studies and agree on common approaches to ethical dilemmas. Trainers could also be encouraged to participate in each other's training. It is useful if the public agency responsible for ethics training for public officials takes on a duty for the development and maintenance of such a pool of trainers, as has been demonstrated by the Flemish government (Box 5.9).

Box 5.9. **Train the trainer programme in the Flemish government (Belgium)**

The HR agency of the Flemish government authorities offers train the trainer courses for facilitators-to-be of dilemma trainings. Participants are mostly integrity contact persons, HR officers and trusted intermediaries. The participants are trained to facilitate both standard dilemma training and made-to-measure dilemma trainings. The made-to-measure trainings answer the specific needs of an organisation, target group or topic in regard to integrity. After taking the course, the trainees become part of a pool of trainers who facilitate trainings in their own or in other organisations. As part of the pool, they will be offered feedback on their performance as a trainer, can take part in follow-up courses and other related sessions to broaden their training skills.

To enhance the skills of facilitators, the HR Agency also offers a specific course for internal trainers. It aims to help trainers to transfer their knowledge in an instructive and interactive manner and bring it to the next level. The training teaches the internal trainers to prepare and give trainings that effectively enhance learning and that meet the expectations of the participants and the client. They will be trained to translate the expectations of the client to clear learning objectives in a programme that develops the appropriate competences. In addition participants learn to give constructive feedback which stimulates further learning. The tips and tricks that are given during the course also stimulate personal growth of the internal trainers.

Source: Verbraeken, K. (2015) "Better use of ethics training to promote public sector integrity", presentation at the OECD workshop on Enhancing transparency and integrity, Bratislava, 8-9 June.

Make ethics training practical

To make the training less formalistic and more practice-oriented, and to use the limited time allocated for ethics training to its best, it is important to apply modern training methods. This can include a combination of theoretical lectures and practical tailor-made case studies and workshops. Ethics skills tend to include the following components:

- the ability to identify and formulate moral problems
- the ability to reason about moral issues

- the ability to clarify one's own moral aspirations.

To achieve these goals, two training approaches could be used. One is the theoretical-normative approach. Its aim is to give knowledge about ethical theories, principles and norms and to teach participants to apply those norms. Another approach puts the emphasis on influencing behaviour through teaching participants to think logically and critically about ethical issues by resolving ethics dilemmas. A combination of these approaches could be used in ethics training programmes according to the needs of the training group. Dilemmas and case studies are the most effective training methods for development of practical ethical decision-making skills. Dilemmas can be developed by trainers, in consultation with the institution for which the training is provided using needs-assessment questionnaires (Box 5.10).

Box 5.10. **Examples of dilemma exercise**

Dilemma 1: Your team starts a public procurement procedure for big printing jobs. The team is behind schedule and does not have a lot of time to get the first printing job done and distributed. Two companies, with whom you have never worked before, send in an offer. Two days after the ultimate deadline for tendering, you receive an offer from a printer who you have often worked with and who has always delivered excellent service. How would you solve the situation based on an ethical decision-making model?

Dilemma 2: One task of an official of a ministry is to prepare subscription orders for newspapers and magazines of the ministry. A publisher of a certain newspaper organises a lot of promotional events for the subscribers of this newspaper. In one of the promotional events, a prize is offered, which includes a seven-day spa package in a recently opened spa hotel. The official responsible for the ministry's subscriptions is offered the prize. How would you solve the situation based on an ethical decision-making model?

Dilemma 3: By chance you see your superior damaging another car while driving away from a car park. It is clear he has spotted you. After quickly assessing the damage, he looks around and just drives off. Next week your candidature for promotion will be decided on. How would you solve the situation based on an ethical decision-making model?

Dilemma 4: An official of the ministry who regularly attends European Commission working groups and often travels to Brussels and other European destinations, receives an invitation from the travel agency to celebrate the opening of a new flying route to Vienna. According to the invitation, the celebration is targeted to the most loyal customers of the travel agency. The programme of the celebration includes business class return tickets to Vienna, full catering, accommodation at a five-star hotel and a reception at the concert hall in Vienna. All expenses of the programme are covered by the travel agency. The official has used the services of the travel agency for official as well as personal travelling. How would you solve the situation based on ethical decision-making model?

The ethical decision-making model consists of six steps:

1. Identify the relevant facts.
2. Identify the relevant public sector ethics principles.
3. Identify other relevant ethics standards.
4. Decide what is important.
5. Reconsider any remaining conflicts.
6. Test your assessment widely.

Sources: OECD (2013a), "Ethics training for public officials", OECD, Paris, available at: www.oecd.org/corruption/acn/library/EthicsTrainingforPublicOfficialsBrochureEN.pdf; Verbraeken, K. (2015) "Better use of ethics training to promote public sector integrity", presentation at the OECD workshop on Enhancing transparency and integrity, Bratislava, 8-9 June.

Evaluate and follow up

It is also recommended to use evaluation methods to assess both the knowledge received by the participants of the training and to identify ways to further improve the training. Evaluation has two main objectives:

- evaluation of a specific training course in order to identify recommendations for its improvement, and
- evaluation of the impact of the training course or programme on integrity in the public administration.

Evaluation forms filled out by participants, the trainer's report and tests for participants are most commonly adopted measures of evaluation. In order to make the most of evaluation to improve the ethics training, evaluation forms to be filled in by the participants could include detailed and practical questions; reports by trainers could invite them to propose recommendations for improvements; and these could be shared with the relevant ministries and government agencies. The results of the evaluations could be made public as well.

Follow-up measures are useful to support the application of the newly acquired knowledge by the participants in the training courses in their work. The measurement of such follow-up may include individual action plans for participants and coaching at the workplace. It may also be possible to include ethics as an element of civil servants' performance appraisal. Catalonia provides a useful example, where participants in training are invited to develop their own individual ethics plan, which they start developing during the training course and continue implementing when they return to their workplace (Box 5.11).

Box 5.11. **Follow-up of ethics training in Catalonia**

Ethics training provided by the Anti-Fraud Office of Catalonia is based on a training itinerary rather than on a one-off training course approach. Follow-up to a training course is an important part of the itinerary. During the training course, each participant develops his or her own integrity action plan. In this plan each participant identifies integrity risks and challenges in their individual workplace. During the follow-up trainings, participants discuss the implementation of their personal plan. They discuss barriers that have been identified in implementing the actions proposed in their individual action plan, and provide each other support and share ideas about solutions.

Source: OECD (2013a), "Ethics training for public officials", OECD, Paris, available at: www.oecd.org/corruption/acn/library/EthicsTrainingforPublicOfficialsBrochureEN.pdf.

The Slovak Republic could also consider developing follow-up measures such as individual ethics action plans for participants in the training programmes and additional coaching in the workplace to support the implementation of such plans. Ultimately, the best way to evaluate the impact of an ethics training course on the participants' conduct is to study their performance in terms of integrity in their workplace. Discussing integrity issues in regular work meetings and as part of the annual performance appraisal interviews can also provide additional intermediary measures.

Recommendations

Integrity in the public administration is an important condition for the effective functioning of the state, for ensuring public trust in the government, and for creating conditions for sustainable social and economic development.

Based on a thorough evaluation of existing regulations and implementation concerning a code of conduct, conflict of interest and ethics training, this chapter highlighted key aspects for reform and offers recommendations to help the Slovak Republic advance towards the adoption of a more comprehensive integrity framework. The overarching theme is the importance of institutional arrangements in co-ordinating integrity policies across government and monitoring their effectiveness over time in lowering corruption in the public sector.

The government of the Slovak Republic could consider the advice in the following areas:

Code of ethics

Setting values and standards of conduct for public officials in a code of ethics is amongst the first steps towards safeguarding integrity and ensuring transparency in the public sector. This could be achieved by pursuing the following:

- Define clear, easily understandable values and standards of conduct in a consultative and participative manner. The New Civil Service Act currently in discussion will provide an opportunity to update and adopt a new code of ethics which has enough substance and powers of enforcement.
- Establish a government-wide co-ordinated system for ensuring consistency throughout the public sector in understanding the values and standards of conduct promoted by the code. This could be tasked to an independent Council of Civil Service currently under discussion.
- Ensure that all public officials have the same understanding on the code of ethics through guidance and training on how to apply the code in daily work. In particular, guidance and training on how public officials should apply their codes of ethics in sensitive situations must be provided.
- Monitor and assess the implementation of the code of ethics and its impact on promoting integrity in the public sector. Surveys could provide useful information to help determine whether the code serves its purpose.
- Incorporate ethical dimensions into management frameworks to achieve compliance with the values of the public service. The Slovak Republic should establish a clear mechanism to ensure compliance with the code of ethics.
- Promote the consistent application of sanctions for ethical misconduct by public officials while ensuring that sanctions are both proportionate and dissuasive.

Management of conflict of interest

Ensuring the integrity of government policy making is not compromised by public officials' private interests is a crucial anti-corruption measure. Modernising the management of conflict of interest by public officials can enhance transparency and accountability to the public. This could be pursued by acting on the following:

- Establish a central function within the public administration responsible for the development and maintenance of the conflict of interest polices. Such a function could be assigned to either the Government Office or the Ministry of the Interior.
- Develop clear procedures for identifying, managing and resolving conflict of interest situations.
- Introduce a proper oversight mechanism to ensure the accuracy of asset disclosure forms. Online management of the asset disclosure system could also reduce the administrative burden and increase transparency.
- Enhance communication on management of conflict of interest across the public administration. Measures such as online publication of guidance and setting up an advice line/help desk for employees could increase awareness among the public administration.
- Consider the development of a government-wide monitoring and evaluation system. The Slovak Republic could conduct surveys or design an employee feedback mechanism on a regular basis to assess the implementation of conflict of interest policies.
- Strengthen the policy measures to address the practice of revolving doors. For example, the Slovak Republic could consider introducing a cooling off period to manage the post-public employment.

Ethics training

Ethics training for public officials is one of the most effective instruments for building integrity in the public sector and ensuring good-quality public governance. This could be enabled by pursuing the following:

- Ensure top-level buy-in for ethics training government wide. Political support for ethics training should be demonstrated not only through declarations but also through practical actions, such as allocation of sufficient funds and staff to the ethics training programmes.
- Establish a leading department/agency for central co-ordination of planning, delivery and evaluation of ethics trainings. The Government Office or Ministry of the Interior could play an important role in this process.
- Organise trainings based on needs assessment, targeting for specific groups of public officials. At minimum, ethics training should be provided to all new public officials, senior public officials and those in areas of risk.
- Make ethics training practical and interactive with appropriately trained trainers. It is recommended to apply a combination of theoretical lectures and practical case studies into training. Dilemma exercise is one of the most effective training methods to develop practical ethical decision-making skills. A train the trainer programme is also an effective measure to maintain and improve the quality of the trainers for ethics training.
- Conduct evaluation and follow up of the results of ethics training in order to ensure the use of public money is producing the desired effects as well as to look for ways to improve the training approaches to make them more effective.

Notes

1. www.bojprotikorupcii.vlada.gov.sk/data/files/2240_8518.pdf.
2. Answer provided by the Ministry of the Interior to the OECD questionnaire.
3. http://spectator.sme.sk/c/20046719/moves-to-tighten-rules-for-officials.html.
4. UNCAC, Article 7(d).
5. http://civilservicecommission.independent.gov.uk/wp-content/uploads/2012/03/Best%20Practice%20Checklist.pdf.
6. www.coe.int/t/dghl/monitoring/greco/news/News(20141106)Eval4Slovakia_en.asp.
7. www.apsc.gov.au/publications-and-media/current-publications/aps-values-and-code-of-conduct-in-practice/conflict-of-interest.

Bibliography

Bruce, W. (1996), "Codes of ethics and codes of conduct: Perceived contribution to the practice of ethics in local government", *Public Integrity Annual*, Council of State Governments (CSG) and the American Society for Public Administration (ASPA).

Civil Service Commission (n.d.), "About us", http://civilservicecommission.independent.gov.uk/about-us.

Dudzik, K. (2015) "Creating whole-of-government vision and integrity values through code of ethics", presentation at the OECD workshop on Enhancing transparency and integrity in Bratislava on 8-9 June 2015.

European Commission (2014a), "Annex: Slovakia", *EU Anti-corruption Report*, COM(2014)38 final, European Union, Brussels, available at: http://ec.europa.eu/dgs/home-affairs/what-we-do/policies/organized-crime-and-human-trafficking/corruption/anti-corruption-report/.

European Commission (2014b), "Special Eurobarometer 397: Corruption", available at: http://ec.europa.eu/public_opinion/archives/ebs/ebs_397_en.pdf.

European Commission (2014c), "Standard Eurobarometer", http://ec.europa.eu/public_opinion/archives/eb_arch_en.htm.

Gilman, S. (2005), "Ethics codes and codes of conduct as tools for promoting an ethical and professional public service: Comparative success and lessons", available at: www.oecd.org/mena/governance/35521418.pdf.

Government Office (2009), "Role and Attitudes in Public Service", survey, Estonia.

ILO (n.d.), "Code of Ethics", www.ilo.org/dyn/natlex/docs/ELECTRONIC/84812/94622/F583540233/84812.pdf.

OECD (2015) *Government at a Glance 2015*, OECD Publishing, Paris, http://dx.doi.org/10.1787/gov_glance-2015-en.

OECD (2014a), *Lobbyists, Governments and Public Trust Volume 3: Implementing the OECD Principles for Transparency and Integrity*, OECD Publishing, Paris, http://dx.doi.org/10.1787/9789264214224-en.

OECD (2014b), "OECD Survey on Managing Conflict of Interest", OECD, Paris.

OECD (2013a), "Ethics training for public officials", OECD, Paris, available at: www.oecd.org/corruption/acn/library/EthicsTrainingforPublicOfficialsBrochureEN.pdf.

OECD (2013b), *OECD Integrity Review of Italy: Reinforcing Public Sector Integrity, Restoring Trust for Sustainable Growth*, OECD Public Governance Reviews, OECD Publishing, Paris, http://dx.doi.org/10.1787/9789264193819-en.

OECD (2012a), *Integrity Review of Brazil: Managing Risks for a Cleaner Public Service*, OECD Public Governance Reviews, OECD Publishing, Paris, http://dx.doi.org/10.1787/9789264119321-en.

OECD (2012b), "OECD Survey on Managing Conflict of Interest", OECD, Paris.

OECD (2003), *Managing Conflict of Interest in the Public Service: OECD Guidelines and Overview*, OECD Publishing, Paris, http://dx.doi.org/10.1787/9789264104938-en.

OECD (2001), *Citizens as Partners: Information, Consultation and Public Participation in Policy-Making*, OECD Publishing, Paris, http://dx.doi.org/10.1787/9789264195561-en.

The National Public Service Ethics Board (n.d.), www.jinji.go.jp/rinri/eng ; http://www.jinji.go.jp/rinri/cyousa/gaiyou.pdf.

Transparency International (2013), *Global Corruption Barometer 2013: Report*, Transparency International, available at: www.transparency.org/gcb2013/report.

Transparency International (2012), *National Integrity System Assessment: Slovak Republic*, Transparency International Slovakia, available at: http://issuu.com/transparencyinternational/docs/2011_nis_slovakexecsummary_en?e=2496456/3187179.

UN General Assembly (1996), *The International Code of Conduct for Public Officials*, Annex to General Assembly Resolution 51/59 on Action Against Corruption of 12 December.

Verbraeken, K. (2015) "Better use of ethics training to promote public sector integrity", presentation at the OECD workshop on Enhancing transparency and integrity, Bratislava, 8-9 June.

ORGANISATION FOR ECONOMIC CO-OPERATION AND DEVELOPMENT

The OECD is a unique forum where governments work together to address the economic, social and environmental challenges of globalisation. The OECD is also at the forefront of efforts to understand and to help governments respond to new developments and concerns, such as corporate governance, the information economy and the challenges of an ageing population. The Organisation provides a setting where governments can compare policy experiences, seek answers to common problems, identify good practice and work to co-ordinate domestic and international policies.

The OECD member countries are: Australia, Austria, Belgium, Canada, Chile, the Czech Republic, Denmark, Estonia, Finland, France, Germany, Greece, Hungary, Iceland, Ireland, Israel, Italy, Japan, Korea, Luxembourg, Mexico, the Netherlands, New Zealand, Norway, Poland, Portugal, the Slovak Republic, Slovenia, Spain, Sweden, Switzerland, Turkey, the United Kingdom and the United States. The European Union takes part in the work of the OECD.

OECD Publishing disseminates widely the results of the Organisation's statistics gathering and research on economic, social and environmental issues, as well as the conventions, guidelines and standards agreed by its members.

OECD PUBLISHING, 2, rue André-Pascal, 75775 PARIS CEDEX 16
(42 2015 21 1 P) ISBN 978-92-64-24762-8 – 2015

www.ingramcontent.com/pod-product-compliance
Lightning Source LLC
Chambersburg PA
CBHW061211240926
51846CB00006B/1184
* 9 7 8 9 2 6 4 2 4 7 6 2 8 *